12·12·'78

PRO FOOTBALL'S
GAMEBREAKERS

It happens on Sundays. Every week for 16 weeks leading up to the Super Bowl, heroes are created. With one play they can determine the outcome of a game. In a sense, they are the gamebreakers. And down through the years they have continually turned defeat into victory or greatly influenced the result of the contest.

Pro Football's Gamebreakers focuses on these heroes. Each has his own story. Some became stars overnight while a great many others worked years to reach the top, overcoming uncertainties, adversity, and criticism. This book tells the stories of quarterbacks such as Fran Tarkenton, Ken Stabler, and Bob Griese, running backs like O. J. Simpson, Walter Payton, and Delvin Williams, wide receivers and tight ends like Cliff Branch, Isaac Curtis, and Rich Caster, and many others. Each individual's story is illustrated by both color and black-and-white photographs and includes a special feature—the favorite play of each star as diagrammed by his coach.

PRO FOOTBALL'S
GAMEBREAKERS

Lou Sahadi
Foreword by
Pete Rozelle

cbi **Contemporary Books, Inc.**
Chicago

Library of Congress Cataloging in Publication Data

Sahadi, Lou.
    Pro football's gamebreakers.

    1. Football players—Biography.   2. National Foot-
ball league.   I. Title.
GV939.A1S25   1977   796.33'2'0922 [B]   77-75847
ISBN 0-8092-7753-0

Credits

Color Photography: Mickey Palmer
Cover Photo: Mickey Palmer

Published by Contemporary Books, Inc.
180 North Michigan Avenue, Chicago, Illinois 60601
Manufactured in the United States of America

Library of Congress Catalog Card Number: 77-75847
International Standard Book Number: 0-8092-7753-0

Published simultaneously in Canada by
Beaverbooks
953 Dillingham Road
Pickering, Ontario L1W 1Z7

To Maryann, first and always,
and to Joseph, Helen, David, Elizabeth, and John
. . . gamebreakers all.

Contents

The Receivers

Foreword

Professional football has enjoyed immense popularity over the past three decades, and as Commissioner of the National Football League since 1960, I have been associated with literally thousands of individuals who have contributed to this interest and growth of the sport. Among them are players, coaches, and administrators within our franchise organizations, plus members of the television, radio, and print establishments who view our game from the outside.

Pro Football's Gamebreakers concentrates on that segment of players who are the headliners, the big-play performers called quarterbacks, running backs, and receivers. But Gamebreakers does not dwell on the statistics that already have stamped O. J. Simpson and Fran Tarkenton as future Hall of Famers. The author, Lou Sahadi, has been a member of the pro football literary community for many years and has acquired an insight not only into the technical aspects of the game but also into the character and lifestyles of the players. In Gamebreakers, Sahadi reaches beyond the playing field to reveal some of the thoughts and personal feelings of his subjects. He has prepared well and his presentation makes this book a welcome addition to the expanding library of professional football lore.

Pete Rozelle
Commissioner,
National Football League

Acknowledgments

The author wishes to express special thanks to Joe Brown, Jim Heffernan, and Jim Rooney of the National Football League, and to the following: Marge Blatt, Baltimore Colts; Budd Thalman, Buffalo Bills; Ted Haracz, Chicago Bears; Al Heim, Cincinnati Bengals; Nate Wallack, Cleveland Browns; Doug Todd, Dallas Cowboys; Bob Peck, Denver Broncos; Lyall Smith, Detroit Lions; Jack Cherry, Houston Oilers; Jerry Wilcox, Los Angeles Rams; Bob Kearny, Miami Dolphins; Merrill Swanson, Minnesota Vikings; Pat Horne, New England Patriots; Ed Croke, New York Giants; Frank Ramos, New York Jets; Al LoCasale, Oakland Raiders; Joe Gordon, Pittsburgh Steelers; Nancy Johnson St. Louis Cardinals; Rick Smith, San Diego Chargers; George McFadden, San Francisco 49ers; and Mike Menchel, Washington Redskins.

Introduction

No sport has singularly captured the imagination of the American public more than professional football. It is a prodigious spectacle that has reached its zenith through the advent of television. Indeed, football is a perfect vehicle for television. Programmed as it is with high intensity and drama, the sport has cultivated millions of television fans practically overnight. The introduction of the instant replay has made the fan into perhaps the most knowledgeable one in sports. Expert analysis by commentators has even further enhanced the fans' education. Professional football has become an intellectually satisfying game in which the fan actually plays the role of an armchair quarterback.

No other sport presents the suspense, excitement, precision, and violence that professional football does. The sport's drama lies not only in the game as a whole, but in its individual players as well. The multicolored warriors are trumpeted as war gods. The stars have become status symbols for the teams on which they play. It happens every Sunday; every week for 16 weeks leading up to the Super Bowl, heroes are created. With one play, they can determine the outcome of a game. In a sense, they are the gamebreakers. And down through the years, they have continually turned victory into defeat or have greatly influenced the result of the contest.

Pro Football's Gamebreakers focuses on these heroes, presenting an in-depth look at each of the men. Each has his own story. Some were heralded early in their careers, while a great many others worked hard for their stardom, overcoming uncertainty, adversity, and criticism. From their stories, from the dramatic black-and-white and color photographs, and from their favorite plays as diagrammed by their coaches, you will know what truly makes these men professional football's gamebreakers . . .

Otis Armstrong

The memories are there. They'll never go away. The poverty. The ghetto. The crime. He grew up with it all. He knew all about street fights, disease, dope. It's certainly not a pleasant memory. One had to learn to survive. And, if you're a lot smaller than some of the other kids, it's all that much tougher. There was trouble practically every night. That's the way it is on Chicago's tough West Side. It's known as The Jungle. And the tough Black ghetto claimed many victims.

Otis Armstrong escaped. He did so by running. He ran from the police. He ran from store owners. He ran not to get caught. Not that he was involved in any serious crime, just mischief mostly. But when you're part of a gang and the leader says let's do this and let's do that, everybody has to take part. Armstrong didn't like it. Often he would run the other way. He'd run straight home. It was safe there. A lot safer than the streets. That's what Armstrong remembers.

"It was a terrible neighborhood," recalls Armstrong. "There were a lot of gangs, a lot of violence and crime. You almost became part of it. Your mother tells you to come home at night, but whether you do is another matter. When it started getting scary out there, shooting and that, I came home.

"I always was a little scared. I didn't like the trouble or the gangs. Like the guy would say, 'You gotta steal a bike today, because everyone else stole one. It's your turn.' I'd go steal a bike, but then I'd ride it so fast they'd never see me. Next day they'd say, 'Where were you yesterday?'"

He also remembers his older brother taking him to Franklin Park on Saturday mornings. That was the big day of the week. That's when they played the big football games. And Armstrong used to sit and watch, and then he began to play. Saturdays were something to look forward to. It was a beginning. It was better than the streets.

"We were all so poor," recalls Armstrong vividly. "We used to put on as many pairs of pants and as many shirts as we could to cushion the blows. There weren't any helmets. I was one of the youngest and smallest. So I always had to try and block and somebody else would run.

"I didn't have much ability then. I didn't know football. I couldn't run then, had no moves. I picked them up later. I progressed, improved, and matured every year. So I must have had some natural ability. But I was pretty small in those days, too."

Although he was small, he was good enough to play football at Farragut High School. He became so good by the time that he was a senior that college recruiters began making their way to Farragut. Several dozen, in fact. Armstrong remembers that, too.

"I remember Notre Dame was one of the first I heard from, although they never really came after me," said Armstrong. "I was really excited because the letter I got from them was one of the first. I carried it around and showed it to a few people.

"Purdue finally wrote in December, right before Christmas. That's when I really got excited, because they had Leroy Keyes, and he was always sort of a hero. It was his last year, and then I went up and visited and got a chance to meet him. When I got a chance to go to Purdue, that sold it."

He replaced Keyes. Keyes had worn number 23 and Armstrong was assigned number 24. He was warmly called Leroy Keyes Plus One for awhile. But not for long. By the time Armstrong finished playing, he stood alone. He set every school rushing record and a good many of the Big Ten ones, too. Armstrong accounted for 3,315 total yards. He became the first conference player since 1945 to capture the total offense crown without throwing a single pass. And he didn't catch many, either. He was certain to be a high draft choice.

Before the 1973 draft took place, the Denver Broncos, like every other NFL club, evaluated their personnel in relation to the available college talent. Coach John Ralston contended that the Broncos primarily needed an outstanding defensive lineman—a blue chipper. And there were a number of them around, namely Dave Butz of Purdue, John Matuszak of Tampa, and Wally Chambers of Eastern Kentucky. The Broncos felt that they had an excellent chance to secure one of them.

First Matuszak was taken. Then Butz. The Chicago Bears got ready to select. The Broncos next. Denver figured that the Bears would go for Armstrong, a hometown boy. Instead, the Bears picked

Chambers. The Broncos' coaching staff groaned. They felt they had lost the opportunity to fill a definite need with a blue-chip lineman. Ralston didn't appear upset. Or at least he didn't show it. He looked up on the big board that listed the running backs in order of their rating and, without hesitation, picked Armstrong.

"He's just super," explained Ralston, who already had a super back in Floyd Little. "Armstrong is an all-around player like Little. He runs like a deer. Just blazing speed. He might just be the best back in the country. Heck, he's the fastest. He runs like Floyd, too, in that he has the same lateral quickness. He's one of those runners that comes along once every five or six years, like a Little or an O.J. Simpson, that you can't pass up."

The entire week before the draft, Armstrong was extremely nervous. So much so that he didn't sleep well or even eat properly. He couldn't concentrate on his studies. The last two days he didn't even attend classes. His wife told him how much he tossed and turned in his sleep, that his moaning actually awakened their one-year-old daughter.

"When I awoke it wasn't any better," claimed Armstrong. "You think about signing a contract for a couple hundred thousand dollars, and it makes you kind of goose-pimply. It was the most exciting thing that ever happened to me. Our family never had a whole lot of money or anything."

Unquestionably, as soon as Armstrong reported to the Broncos that summer, comparisons between him and Little began. Since Little had joined the Broncos back in 1967, he had been the franchise. It was a team that never had a winning season. Never ever. All anybody ever knew about Denver was Floyd Little. Nothing else.

Armstrong was told that he would be the one to replace Little in the next year or two at the most. That meant he wouldn't play much. He was being looked upon as Little's backup. It was a strange role for Armstrong. He was used to being number one. He had started every game in high school and college. Now he had to adjust to being a reserve back. And in a strange position, too. Throughout his college days, Armstrong ran as a halfback. How he was placed in the fullback position.

So, Armstrong played very little his rookie season. He was used primarily as a kick return runner—which at least got him into every game. But he carried the ball only 26 times from scrimmage and gained only 90 yards. It wasn't enough to excite anybody, certainly not somebody who was a number one draft selection. Armstrong was a little confused by it all.

"I had to wonder why they drafted me number one," said Armstrong. "It didn't add up. I know that they wanted you to learn, but I'd never been near the bench before. I also felt that I could beat Little out if they would give me the chance. I had that much confidence."

It was just a matter of time—like one year. In 1974, Armstrong got his chance. In the second game of the season, he exploded. Against the powerful Pittsburgh Steelers, Armstrong carried the ball 19 times and gained 131 yards. Hardly anybody does that against the Steelers' defense. He also did more damage. He caught five passes for 86 yards and scored two touchdowns.

Ralston began using Armstrong at fullback and Little at halfback. They worked together well. In fact, they developed a close friendship. Little would spend extra time working with Armstrong, grooming him for the day when he would replace him. The unselfish gesture immeasurably aided Armstrong's development. And he finished the season with a flourish.

In the tenth game of the season, Little was sidelined with bruised ribs. Armstrong was shifted to halfback, and Jon Keyworth went in at fullback. Even though Armstrong was the team's leading rusher at the time, he was happy with the switch. He felt that he could do more at halfback, that being a fullback limited him, especially since it involved blocking assignments.

A week before the season ended, Armstrong really broke loose. He ran for a team record 183 yards against the defensively strong Houston Oilers. And nobody had done that before, either. He did it against a defense that was geared to stop him. Houston's thinking was to have linebacker Greg Bingham key on Armstrong. Ironically, Armstrong and Bingham were rivals in high school and teammates at Purdue. Bingham was a mobile linebacker who roamed all over the field. More important, he had a reputation for hitting hard.

Armstrong began to get his yardage, and he was paying for it, too. Near the end of the half, he felt tired. So much so that, when he came over to the sidelines, he asked Little to replace him. But Little refused. Instead, he explained to Armstrong that it was important for him to learn to catch his breath. Not only that, but to experience getting the tough yards even when he was tired.

"Floyd helped me more when he wasn't playing," remarked Armstrong. "He used to tell me to rest when I came off the field. I think he was looking after me, because I was just beginning to understand what it was to be number one and go through a lot of punishment. I'd tell him, 'Man, those guys are really hitting out there,' and he'd say, 'Go over there and sit down and rest. Take care of yourself.'

"I played hurt all year. It was the blocking. I didn't feel comfortable. But when Floyd got hurt and Keyworth went to fullback, it took the pressure off. I knew that things were going to be easier for me then, because they had to have a number one back."

Armstrong wound up the 1974 season number one in the entire league. He rushed for 1,407 yards, averaging 5.3 yards a carry. He also caught 38 passes for an additional 405 yards and finished with 12 touchdowns.

However, in 1975, the joy turned to frustration. He bruised his ribs in the second game of the season, one in which he was averaging 9.0 yards a carry. Two weeks later, he pulled a hamstring muscle so severely that he was finished for the entire year, one in which he only carried the ball 31 times for 155 yards.

Armstrong worked hard in the off-season to overcome his injury. He worked out every day except Saturday and Sunday. And when the regular season was over, Armstrong had gained 1,008 yards, tenth best in the NFL. He also pulled down 39 passes for another 457 yards. Armstrong was number one again. Still, he finds time to go back to Chicago and talk to the kids in Franklin Park.

He knows how much it means. He's been there . . .

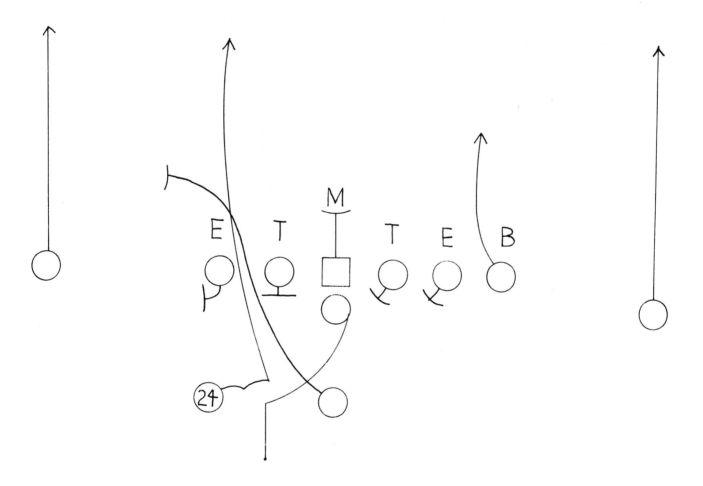

Diagrammed by Coach Red Miller

Larry Csonka

He sat on the ground holding his leg. The pain was there. He wasn't a stranger to pain. It had been his companion throughout his career. But this time it was different. He could tell by the way his leg felt that something was seriously wrong. A couple of his teammates bent over him. They could tell by the anguish on his face that he was hurt badly. They had never seen him take so long to get up after a tackle. Finally, with some assistance he got up on his feet. His face grimaced as he tried to walk to the sidelines. He hobbled badly. For the first time in his life, Larry Csonka had a serious injury. He had ripped the ligaments in his right knee and was finished for the rest of the season.

It was a sad ending to a new beginning. Just six months before, Csonka had signed a multimillion-dollar contract with the New York Giants. In 1975, the powerful fullback had toiled in relative obscurity in the doomed World Football League. After leading the Miami Dolphins to two consecutive Super Bowl wins, Csonka played out his option and signed with the struggling new league. He played most of the season for the Memphis Grizzlies. Csonka was wanted so desperately by the identity-seeking WFL that he received a guaranteed million-dollar contract. But when the league folded after its second season, Csonka was a free agent.

Many thought that Csonka would return to Miami, the scene of his past glories. The Dolphins were still a contending team, and Csonka could once again make them a winner. Besides, he had a great rapport with Coach Don Shula. He respected Shula and liked playing for him. Shula had keyed his offense around Csonka.

And that's the way the Giants were thinking when they outbid several other clubs for Csonka. They had been a losing team for years, and they felt Csonka could lead them out of the wilderness. Giant coach Bill Arnsparger, who had guided the Dolphins' defense in their days of glory, knew what the presence of a Csonka meant. So did management. Csonka was the first superstar they had had for so long that no one could remember. He would be a box-office smash.

"We do not expect to win because we have Csonka," cautioned Arnsparger. "But we do expect to be stronger with him; and by being stronger, we think we can win more easily. He gives us certain things we haven't had before. He has great power, especially straight ahead.

"We also feel we can make the passing game stronger with Csonka in the backfield. When a play-action pass is set up, most defensive players will have to show more respect if Csonka takes the fake handoff. I mean, what if he does have the ball, and they ignore him and leave the middle open? He intimidates defenses by just being on the field. The danger is to count too heavily on Larry. He is just one player. We must still get better in every other area of the team or we won't be able to take proper advantage of what he can do for us . . . or what he can do to others."

Arnsparger was saying something. He was saying a lot. What he was saying in reality was that the 1976 Giants were not a very good team. Csonka would help to make them a better one. But there would be no miracles or instant championships. Arnsparger was just putting everything in perspective and not letting emotions run all the way to the Super Bowl. That's the way Csonka saw it, too.

"There is one man carrying a football," illustrated Csonka. "That's me. There are other men trying to stop him. That's the defense. It all comes down to strength and desire and a man-to-man confrontation. I like that. I am a fullback. I make the tough yardage. I am not fast or elusive or tricky. I am straight ahead. I run with power. But I am not a savior and I am not a one-man offense. But I try."

If he is not a one-man offense, he is very close to being one. Like Franco Harris of the Pittsburgh Steelers, Csonka can control an offense with his punishing runs. He can get the big first down yardage or the key third down ones. That means an awful lot to the quarterback. He can pass off the run, which makes his aerial game much more effective. Shula often referred to Csonka as the constant of the offense. He kept it going.

Like in the 1974 Super Bowl game against the Minnesota Vikings. Csonka was such a devastating force that the Dolphins yawned their way to a 24–7 victory. They did so simply with Csonka's methodical

running. He was so effective that quarterback Bob Griese threw only seven passes the entire game. And, by passing off the run, Griese completed six of them.

Nobody had any idea that Csonka would be so awesome against the Vikings. For one thing, Minnesota was considered a strong defensive team, especially against the run. Being big and physical, many felt that the Vikings could handle Csonka's straight-ahead power. But they were wrong. Oh, how they were wrong! Csonka not only scored two touchdowns but also bulled his way for a record 145 yards on 33 carries.

On the Dolphins' first touchdown, Csonka accounted for 36 of the 62 yards, finally going over from the five-yard line. On the second touchdown, Csonka was responsible for 28 of 56 yards as the Dolphins took control. When the first period ended, Miami led 14–0, and the Vikings had had the ball for only seven plays!

When the half ended, the Dolphins had a comfortable 17–0 lead, and it was obvious the Vikings were doomed. Csonka had 78 yards by then, and the Vikings were frustrated. Their frustration grew on the opening series of the third period when Csonka went over from two yards out to give the Dolphins an insurmountable 24–0 lead. Csonka's presence was evident, even at the end. When the Dolphins got the ball with 6:24 left, Csonka controlled the ball until time ran out. In the 12 plays Miami ran, Csonka carried the ball on eight of them. He was the difference.

Even the Vikings knew it. Csonka drew praise from Minnesota's Fran Tarkenton, who had a quarterback's view of Csonka from the sidelines. He realized only too well what Csonka had accomplished.

"I don't think I ever saw a fullback play any better than Csonka," said Tarkenton. "He comes at you so hard. He has to be the strongest fullback I've ever seen."

Perhaps Tarkenton doesn't know it, but Csonka is also one of the quickest thinking. The Dolphins' final touchdown was a result of Csonka's alertness. With the ball on the Vikings' two-yard line, Griese called a running play. As he approached his center, Griese turned around with a puzzled look on his face. He cupped his mouth and asked Csonka something, and the big fullback whispered back immediately. Griese took the snap, spun around, and gave the ball to Csonka, who crashed through for the touchdown. Later, Csonka revealed what had actually happened.

"Oh, it wasn't anything," shrugged Csonka. "Griese forgot the count, that's all. I had to remind him or it would have been a broken play."

Csonka captivated everyone with his performance. He was compared with other great runners, modern day and old timers. One all-time great he was compared to was the legendary Bronko Nagurski, who was a bone-jarring fullback when he played. Yet Nagurski himself considered Csonka the better player.

"I really didn't think anyone could run like that against the Vikings," exclaimed Nagurski. "I've been watching Csonka for the last few years, and I'd rate him above Jim Brown, Jim Taylor, or any other fullback. I guess I was a pretty good runner, but, to be honest, Csonka is better than I ever was."

But Csonka actually shuns publicity or comparisons. He is a private person who has a great deal of compassion and awareness of what life is really about. It goes far beyond the football field.

"The biggest feeling of accomplishment is knowing you've played the game well," related Csonka. "I feel tremendously rewarded just walking on the football field. The publicity part is nice, but it's not reality. What you did on the field will remain with the people who were there with you. When you're on the field, all the adjectives and adverbs don't mean a damn. When you walk through that tunnel, you walk into reality."

The reality was that Csonka had finished the 1973 season with his third straight 1,000-yard campaign. He had averaged carrying the ball over 200 times a season, and in all three years, the Dolphins had made it to the Super Bowl. They had become the second team in NFL history to win two Super Bowl games in a row.

In his final year with the Dolphins in 1974, Csonka wanted so desperately to win another Super Bowl. Those are the goals he reaches for. Although he was bothered by nagging injuries most of the season, he still managed to gain 749 yards, and the Dolphins reached the playoffs. It took a last-second miracle touchdown by the Oakland Raiders to defeat them, 28–26.

Csonka has paid the price for his success as a runner. He is a target. He gets hit and hit hard. He has broken his nose about a dozen times. He has suffered concussions, a broken eardrum, and a ruptured blood vessel in one of his eyes. He has had surgery on an elbow and has suffered so many sprains and strains to his ribs, knees, and wrists that he doesn't even bother to count them all. That is all part of the reality that Csonka talks about.

"I like the contact the game offers," admitted Csonka. "Maybe that's because I have a temper, and the contact gives me a release from it. That's a good thing. It's too bad that business executives can't organize teams and go out there and pound the stuffing out of each other. They'd feel better.

"I'll admit I do have a high threshold for pain, and I will not take drugs or a painkiller. If you are needed in the pros, then you play. You owe it to the team when the money is on the line. Besides, you're not fighting for your alma mater, you're fighting for your livelihood. Somebody might come along and take your job away."

At Syracuse University, Csonka played one year as a linebacker. He was switched to fullback his last two seasons and broke the rushing records of such Syracuse greats as Jim Brown, Ernie Davis, Jim Nance, and Floyd Little. It was no wonder the Dolphins made him their number one draft pick in 1968, even though some sneered that, at 6'2", 237 pounds, Csonka wasn't fast enough for pro ball.

The Dolphins felt not only that Csonka was fast enough but also that he was an excellent blocker and durable. They realized he could take a pounding. And Csonka derives a great amount of satisfaction in delivering an important block. That's going one-on-one, too.

"It hurts when people are hitting you," admits Csonka. "And when you run with the ball, you have to be able to accept a great amount of pain. So, I try to forget the banging around until after the game. That's when I moan and walk around complaining about all the aches. But during a game, I try to be unaware of how I hurt at the moment.

"You can get old quickly in this game. All it takes is one injury, one play. But you have to put all that out of your mind."

Until it happens. Near the end of the 1976 season, when he underwent major surgery for the first time, Csonka awoke to the reality he always knew was there . . .

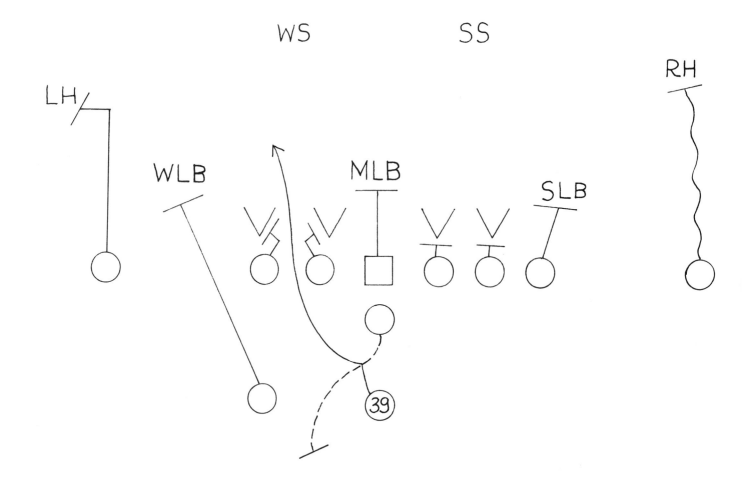

Diagrammed by Coach John McVay

Chuck Foreman

The look of frustration was there. Sadly, it's been there before. Like in 1974. And again in 1975. And now for a third time, in 1977. It's enough to get a guy down. Possibly do some soul-searching. Because having played in three Super Bowls and having lost each one can make a person bitter. Losing can do that. It can cause doubt and despair. And in the fleeting moments after a Super Bowl game, it's only natural to hit the depths of depression. That's the way it is when you lose. It is the only feeling Chuck Foreman has known after three such Super Bowls.

The questions are painfully the same. And as much as you try, the answers aren't any different. There is no way to explain a defeat when your team has been convincingly beaten. It would be easy if it were just one play that did it. That would be easy to describe. But when you lose so completely, the way the Minnesota Vikings did to the Oakland Raiders, 32–14, in Super Bowl XI, then you are really clutching for straws in the wind. That's one thing that Foreman never does. He's too much of a football player to do that. He just takes the blows.

"It really hurts me," remarked Foreman in the subdued Viking dressing room, just minutes after the 1977 Super Bowl game had mercifully ended. "It's going to take me a while to get over this one. But I'll come back from it. It's just a matter of putting things in perspective.

"I'm not going to explain it to anybody. We lost. Everybody

knows we lost. That's it. I'll have to deal with it and I'm sure that I can."

The disappointing loss mirrored Foreman's season. Unhappy with the money he was being paid, Foreman wanted the Vikings to renegotiate his contract. They refused. Their contention was that Foreman had two years remaining on his contract. Besides, it was strictly against Viking policy to renegotiate any existing contract. They have never violated this principle for anyone—not for Fran Tarkenton, Alan Page, or any other player in the club's history. Their position was clear and firm.

But Foreman was also unyielding. He was strongly adamant, to the point of not reporting to training camp for the 1976 season. He felt he was grossly underpaid and wanted equal compensation with other backs around the league. The stalemate revolved totally around principle, that's all. The Vikings felt that Foreman had a commitment and that he should live up to it. On the other hand, Foreman acknowledged the obligation but felt that he should be rewarded for the outstanding season he had in 1975.

What Foreman accomplished that season was something no other back had ever done. He led the league in pass receptions with 73; scored 22 touchdowns, more than anyone else, gained 1,070 yards; and was named to the Pro Bowl for the third straight year. He also established club records for most rushing attempts, 280; most yards rushing, 1,070; most pass receptions, 73; most touchdowns, 22; and most 100-yard games, five. Those figures are hard to come by.

"I don't think I have reached my peak as an NFL running back," reflected Foreman on his 1975 performance. "I was totally satisfied with my accomplishments, but I think I can do even better. Every back wants to achieve a 1,000-yard season. And I also was pleased with my receiving. I take pride in my receiving ability."

Minnesota coach Bud Grant isn't one for many words. Conservative by nature, he reflects this in his personality by being tight-lipped both on and off the field. However, Foreman's play brought some response.

"Foreman had a super year, both running and catching," remarked Grant. He handled the ball on 353 offensive plays. That shows the confidence we have in his ability. One of the primary reasons he was so successful was that he had the durability to play consistently. And Foreman is versatile, which fits into our system of moving backs around, flopping them, putting them at wing back, flanker, or fullback. We try to move Chuck around so he can go at the weakness of the defense. It is fair to say that things are pretty much set up to utilize his talents."

Which shows just how valuable Foreman is. Not many backs can be used in different positions, fullback, halfback, or flanker. Foreman is more effective running from fullback, however.

"Our best plays are for the fullback position," pointed out Fore-

man. "This is because our linemen are the best around at straight-ahead blocking, which is what is done for many of the fullback's plays, such as the off-tackle runs. And I can hit the holes faster from the fullback spot because I line up right behind the quarterback."

It's hard to believe that the Vikings wouldn't compensate Foreman above the $35,000 they were paying him. In an era of compromise, the Vikings refused to budge. They were resigned to upholding club policy. No exceptions. But Foreman was perhaps an exception. Other backs of his caliber were in the $100,000-a-year bracket. Foreman wasn't close to that. He wasn't even close to the Vikings' training camp in Mankato that summer. Foreman remained in Miami alone, working out by himself to keep in shape. At least he had that much going for him.

While his attorney handled the delicate negotiations with the Vikings, Foreman kept running as much as he could under the hot Miami sun. When he could run no more, he decided to report to the Vikings and give it all he had, the way he always played the game. The Vikings had already played two pre-season games. Although the contract negotiations did not progress, Foreman decided to bury his pride and help his teammates.

Without Foreman, the Minnesota offense wasn't exactly potent.

They had dropped two of the three games they played, scoring a total of only 23 points. Even with their renowned defense, 23 points won't win many football games. The offense welcomed him back.

"I'm really happy to be back in camp," exclaimed Foreman. "I worked out every day in Miami, and I thought about the guys and the season all the time. I sure as hell didn't want to stay out. All I can say now is that I am glad it's over.

"I think I'm worth more than I've been getting. But I'll let my attorney and management worry about that. My primary concern right now is to concentrate on playing football."

And play football Foreman did. Despite the unsettled contract situation, Foreman had another great year. He performed admirably, even though the Vikings did not renegotiate his contract. Foreman led the National Conference in touchdowns with 14, was second in pass receptions with 55, and finished fourth among the runners with 1,155 yards.

Even before the 1977 Super Bowl game, Foreman was hoping that the Vikings would give him a new contract. But it never came about. That, too, added to his disappointment. There wasn't much he could do about it.

Yet, there aren't many things that Foreman can't do. He is

considered perhaps the most versatile back in the long history of the National Football League. As is expected of him, he can run either inside or outside. He has excellent peripheral vision, which helps him immensely in making his moves. But he is also a complete back, in that he can catch passes and block. And he does it all willingly. That's how much of a team player he is.

The amazing thing about Foreman is that he fit right into the Minnesota system as a rookie. That isn't easy to do. In all the years he has been coaching, Vikings' coach Bud Grant had only started one rookie, Alan Page, a defensive tackle. Everybody knows about Page. He's been an All-Pro performer practically every season. But not everyone knew about Foreman. In the 1973 draft, the Vikings were in desperate need for a running back. They had their sights set on a couple of good ones, Sam Cunningham of USC and Otis Armstrong of Purdue. They also had high regard for Foreman, who played at the University of Miami. By the time the Vikings picked on the first round of the draft, Cunningham and Armstrong were already taken. So, naturally, they took Foreman.

It is hard to believe, but the Vikings contended that they wanted Foreman all along. It is hard to believe because Minnesota was definitely in the market for a better known back from a bigger school. Both Cunningham and Armstrong had bigger reputations than Foreman. That was a known fact. Not that Foreman was, by any stretch of the imagination, a total unknown. He had credentials, too. But Cunningham and Armstrong were more often in the national limelight.

It was just that Foreman was a nondescript player. He performed as a wide receiver and defensive back as well as a running back in his three years in college. All that time he never played on a winning team. Being on a loser doesn't bring much recognition.

One thing that made Foreman noticeable was his white shoes. He was attached to them. He brought them with him when he reported to the Vikings for the first time. However, he was quickly told that nobody wears white shoes on the Vikings. And one other thing. No one wears white socks high above the traditional team stockings.

"It wasn't a big thing," said Foreman. "The color of your shoes won't make you a better player."

Foreman did everything the Vikings wanted. He ran, caught passes, and blocked when he was asked to do so. He had a fine rookie season, running for 801 yards and catching 37 passes for another 362 yards. He hasn't stopped since, getting better every year and making the Vikings better, too. Which quarterback Fran Tarkenton fully appreciates.

"Chuck is strong to the inside and fast to the outside," says Tarkenton. "And, with all due respect to O. J. Simpson, Foreman is the best all-around back in the league. He can do whatever is asked of him. He runs with power. I've seen him break tackles many times. He runs with speed, too. I've seen him outrun cornerbacks and safeties, even when they've had the angle on him. And I don't know a better pass-receiving back. He has sure hands, runs his patterns well, and has a 'feel' for adjusting that I can anticipate.

"On third and ten, you're not afraid to give him the ball to get the first down. It's nice to have that threat. If the other team goes into a prevent defense with him in the game, they're taking a gamble. Because he can shake it, man. He can go get it."

One such time occurred in the 1976 NFC championship game against the Los Angeles Rams. With just 2:09 left in the game, the Vikings were in front, 17–13. They were faced with a third and four on their own 21. They needed to keep a drive going, to prevent the Rams from getting the ball back.

Tarkenton felt it was the right time to go to Foreman. He delivered a short pass over the middle to his favorite back. Foreman broke a couple of tackles and ran 57 yards to the Rams' 12-yard line before he was stopped. The play positioned the final Viking touchdown that broke the game open, 24–13. Foreman finished the day with 118 yards rushing on only 15 carries and five pass receptions for 81 more.

Now if Foreman can only get more money from the Vikings. There's no question he's worth it . . .

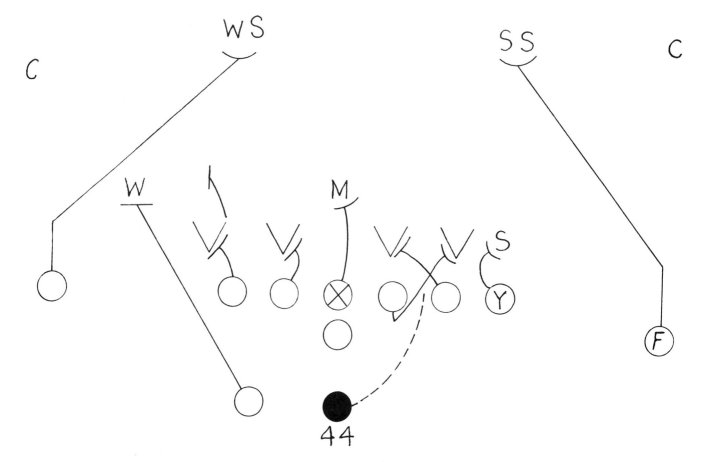

Diagrammed by Coach Bud Grant

Franco Harris

The pain was there. It shot through him like a knife. Every time he took a deep breath or twisted his body. His ribs were heavily taped. But they were tender. Even pain pills couldn't help. All he could do was stand there on the sidelines. It was a helpless feeling. The Pittsburgh Steelers were playing the Oakland Raiders for the 1976 American Football Conference championship. They were hoping to be able to try for a third straight Super Bowl win, something no team in the history of pro football has ever accomplished. And all Franco Harris could do was to stand and watch from the sidelines.

It was a strange feeling. Harris doesn't miss many games. The durable Steeler fullback has been the key to the Pittsburgh running game. He is the reason why the Steelers can control the offensive flow of a given game. Why they had won two successive world championships. Why they were picked to win an unprecedented third. But Harris was not a deterrent force this time. Not when he stood and watched the Oakland Raiders defeat the Steelers, 24–7, for the 1976 AFC title.

The week before, Harris was a devastating force. In the opening playoff game, he had shredded the Baltimore Colts' defense in a playful 40–14 romp. Harris had run for 132 yards before he was injured and left the game early in the fourth quarter. By then, the eventual outcome of the game was known. But what nobody knew at the time was how seriously Harris was injured. He had taken what appeared to be a late hit after he had picked up some yards. A Colt

defender had landed on Harris with his knee as he lay on the ground. Harris got up, clutched his ribs, and never returned to the game.

Harris had been an important part of the Steeler offense ever since he was drafted from Penn State on the first round of the 1972 college draft. Not that he was a unanimous selection. There were those among the Pittsburgh hierarchy who disagreed. Chuck Noll, the coach, for one. He opted for Robert Newhouse of the University of Houston as his selection. He reasoned that, although Newhouse was smaller than Harris, he was a more versatile back. He was dissuaded by Pittsburgh's Director of Personnel, Art Rooney, Jr.

What Rooney liked about Harris was his size, 6'3", 230 pounds. He also liked his speed. Unknown to many pro scouts, Harris ran the 40 in 4.5. For a big back, that's excellent speed. He also felt that little backs could never put two great years back to back. The big ones not only are capable of that, but they have longer and more consistent careers. Noll was sold. When the Steelers picked Harris ahead of his teammate at Penn State, Lydell Mitchell, who was named to the All-American team, a lot of people were surprised. It looked like a gamble.

The skeptics sneered after Harris got off to a slow start. They pointed to the fact that the Steelers had always made bad choices on the running backs they selected on the first round. Even Harris didn't brim with confidence at the beginning of his rookie season.

"I wasn't sure of my chances at first," confided Harris. "In my case, people wondered if I could do it. I felt I had the right mental attitude and that I was right physically. I didn't want anything to hold me back. I felt that it would hurt me if I played in the wrong frame of mind. I simply decided to be very positive in my approach.

"There's a big difference between pro and college ball, a big difference in mental attitude. When you're in high school or college, you don't always work hard. In the pros, you have to go all out every time. You can't relax. This mental maturity and toughness is what separates the players.

"I had thought that I was doing all right, but I heard that the coaches didn't think so. They didn't think I was hungry enough to make the team. They thought I should go all out more than I showed. It's that I just couldn't get excited in practice."

In his first pro game, against the Oakland Raiders, Harris carried the ball ten times and gained 28 yards. It was nothing to write home about. He didn't do much better against the Cincinnati Bengals the following week. He was given the ball 13 times, and all he could gain was 35 yards. The inefficiency bothered Harris. So much so that he had a private talk with Noll.

Harris felt that he was letting the team down. He also felt that the team had lost faith in him. He was really down. He had reached such a low point that he wanted to quit. But Noll convinced him

that he was only a rookie and that he had a lot to learn. He would need patience, and then everything would work out.

Noll decided to take the pressure off Harris. He didn't play him at all against the St. Louis Cardinals. He used him sparingly the following week against the Dallas Cowboys. Harris carried the ball only three times and picked up 16 yards. After four games, Harris had run with the ball 26 times, had gained only 79 yards, and hadn't scored a touchdown. He looked anything but a first-round draft choice.

However, without warning, Harris broke loose. Did he ever. Against the Houston Oilers, Harris didn't play the first half. He saw action the second half and ran for 115 yards on only 13 carries. It was all he needed. By the time the season ended, Harris was making headlines. He finished with 1,055 yards, only the fifth player in NFL history to gain 1,000 yards in his rookie season. Behind Harris's strong running, the Steelers finished with an 11–3 record and gained the playoffs for the first time in their 40-year history. Suddenly, Pittsburgh was a great place to live.

Harris wasn't finished yet. His rookie year had a storybook ending. And it occurred in the opening playoff game against the tough Oakland Raiders. It was a fiercely contested game, one in which both teams' defenses excelled. Only 1:13 remained in the game, one in which the Steelers were leading, 6–0, on a pair of field goals.

Oakland had the ball on the Steelers' 30-yard line. Raiders' quarterback Ken Stabler dropped back to pass, in an effort to get a game-winning touchdown. Finding no one open, he took off down the sidelines and went all the way for a touchdown. The extra point put the Raiders on top, 7–6. Pittsburgh's hopes sank.

They dropped even lower when quarterback Terry Bradshaw couldn't get the offense moving. All he needed was to get the Steelers in range for a game-winning field goal. With time a factor, all he could do was pass. He tried three passes from his 40-yard line, and each one was incomplete. Steeler fans were about to give up hope.

On fourth down, with 22 seconds remaining to play, Bradshaw

had no choice but to try another pass. Oakland was in a prevent defense, employing a three-man line and dropping eight defenders back to protect against the pass. Pittsburgh's chances were one in a million.

Bradshaw faded back for one more pass. He looked and waited for someone to get open. He had time, but all his receivers were covered. Finally, in desperation, he threw the ball toward running back Frenchy Fuqua, who was trying to get loose on Oakland's 37-yard line. But defensive back Jack Tatum knocked the ball away as the partisan crowd in Pittsburgh collectively groaned.

However, Harris grabbed the ball before it hit the ground. He made a remarkable catch just inches off the ground, kept his balance, and sped down the sidelines for the winning touchdown. Pittsburgh was bedlam. It was the most dramatic touchdown in the Steelers' history, one that provided them with an unbelievable 13–7 triumph. The catch by Harris was glorified as the "Immaculate Reception."

"I ran downfield to block for the receiver," explained Harris in the crowded Steeler dressing room. "Then when the play got messed up, I was running toward Fuqua, hoping that he would catch the ball and that I could block for him.

"Then I saw the ball bounce off Tatum and it came right toward me at shoe-top level. I grabbed it instinctively and took off for the end zone. The coaches ran out on the field, and all the officials were talking, and the referee went over to check the television replay. Oakland had felt that the ball had hit the ground before I caught it. But I knew it didn't. Still, at that moment, there was always the fear that they would call the play back.

"Fate put me in the right spot at the right time. But I was mentally ready and it paid off. Sure, it was a lucky play, but all that mattered was that we won. It taught me one important thing: Don't ever give up. Always give a little bit more, a little extra. I know from now on that is the only way I'm going to play the game."

It was just the start of things for Harris. As a youngster, his mother didn't want him to play football. She didn't know anything about football. She was an Italian war bride who married Franco's father, a Black Army sergeant, while he was stationed in Italy. He was one of nine brothers and sisters who were raised in Mt. Holly, New Jersey.

Franco's mother is a very religious woman. She looked upon her son's catch as a miracle. Moments before his game-winning reception, she had put on her favorite record, Beniamino Gigli singing "Ave Maria." It was her faith. Who can deny her that?

And no one could deny that Harris was a dominating force in Pittsburgh's resurgence. In 1973, nagging injuries limited Harris to 698 yards. Still, they made the playoffs for the second time. In 1974, Harris gained 1,006 yards, and the Steelers won their first Super Bowl. The following year, he ran for 1,246 yards, and they won their

second straight Super Bowl. Pittsburgh became the capital of the pro football world.

There was no diminishing Harris's contribution. Through his running, the Steelers were able to control the game. His presence on the field helped make Bradshaw a better quarterback. The combination presented a problem for opposing teams.

Like the 1975 Super Bowl game against the Minnesota Vikings. All week long Harris didn't feel well. He was troubled by a nagging head cold. But when the game was over, the Vikings had a nagging headache. Harris set a Super Bowl record by running for 158 yards in 34 carries. He was unmistakably the difference in the 16–6 victory. And he was unaware that he had set a record.

"I can't believe I made 158 yards," beamed Harris. "You have to be kidding. I had a head cold the last few days and I felt crummy. They say there is no remedy for the common cold, so I didn't look for one. Well, now there is. All you have to do is win a Super Bowl. I feel great now."

He felt even greater the following year when the Steelers

defeated the Dallas Cowboys, 21–17, to win their second straight Super Bowl. There was talk of the Steelers becoming the first team in history to win three straight when the 1976 season began.

Harris did all he could to make it happen. He finished the season with 1,128 yards and led the AFC with 14 touchdowns. After a slow start, the Steelers won their last 10 games in succession. They were coming on strong.

But they couldn't do it without Franco. He stood on the sidelines and watched the Raiders romp, 24–7. It was the only way to stop Harris . . .

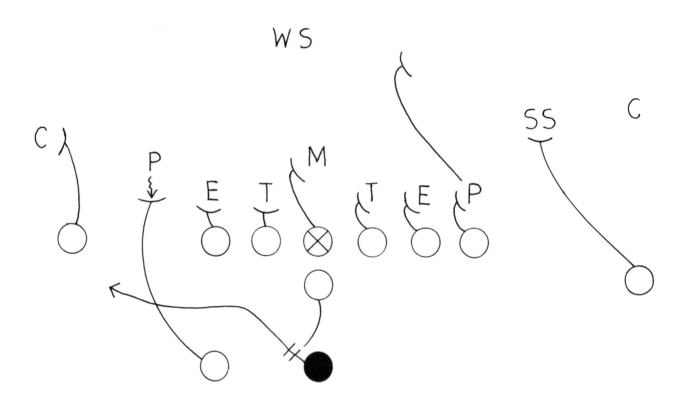

Diagrammed by Coach Chuck Noll

Lawrence McCutcheon

He didn't know what to think. He tried not to let it bother him. But it was difficult. They wouldn't let him. Almost every day they would ask him his feelings about the situation. And every time he would shrug his shoulders and dismiss it. He was determined not to worry about it all. Outwardly, he didn't appear upset. He was only concerned about getting ready for the 1976 season, which was less than three weeks away. And, as the season approached, the rumors persisted that he would be traded. It reached such a distracting level that the owner of the Los Angeles Rams, Carroll Rosenbloom, issued a statement to the press that he was not about to acquire O. J. Simpson from the Buffalo Bills.

That brought some relief to Lawrence McCutcheon. But he couldn't be certain it wouldn't happen. In the trade talks with the Rams, the Bills had insisted on getting a top running back in return as part of the deal. By now, everyone knew that had to be McCutcheon. After all, he had led the Rams' running attack in all three seasons that he played. Not many runners can equal that. Not even O. J., and he's the best.

It was no secret that Simpson wanted out at Buffalo. He hadn't even reported to training camp. He had insisted that he would retire rather than go back to Buffalo. O. J. had made it known that he wanted to play football only two or three more years and that he would like to finish his career with a contending team near his hometown. It just so happened that Simpson's home is Los Angeles.

And playing before his hometown fans, the popular O.J. would sell more tickets at the gate.

That was what McCutcheon had to contend with. It had to leave him wondering somewhat. It certainly wasn't the best atmosphere to be exposed to in training camp. The probability of his being traded was the subject of headlines in the Los Angeles newspapers. And everybody reads newspapers or watches television. That kind of speculation can only create pressure, something that McCutcheon handled quite well.

"I don't want to go to Buffalo," disclosed McCutcheon. "I love it right here with the Rams. I'm not going to get worked up over something that may never happen. It it happens, then I'll say something about it. I've tried to come to camp with the best mental attitude possible. Football is such a mental game. And if I let myself get down, it will affect my play. And I won't be helping the team if that happens."

Then he smiled that soft smile of his.

"I just turned 26," he said, "and O.J. says a runner doesn't enter his prime until he becomes 26. Well, I'm just entering my prime. I should have my best season this year."

Well, Simpson wasn't traded to the Rams and McCutcheon did, in fact, have the best year of his career. Not that he should be embarrassed by any of his other three campaigns. It's just that in 1976 McCutcheon gained 1,168 yards to finish third in the National Football Conference. He also scored more touchdowns than in any other season, nine rushing and two receiving. Still, the Rams, despite McCutcheon's finest year, failed once again to reach the Super Bowl.

Ever since McCutcheon began playing for the club in 1973, the Rams have come close to the big game. It certainly was no fault of McCutcheon's that they didn't make it. In 1973, he gained 1,097 yards. The following year, he set a club rushing record with 1,109 yards. And in 1975, he ran for 911 yards, missing a chance to achieve another 1,000-yard season when he was hurt and didn't play in the final game of the season.

However, in the opening game of the 1975 playoffs, McCutcheon returned to the lineup and had the biggest day of his young career. In fact, McCutcheon established a new NFC record by rushing for a remarkable 202 yards, coming off an injury just two weeks earlier. Nobody expected him to run for so many yards against the St. Louis Cardinals. Certainly not the Cardinals. Especially in the first series of downs.

The Rams opened the game on their own 21-yard line. Surprisingly, McCutcheon carried the ball the first four plays of the game. After quarterback Ron Jaworski completed a pass, he handed the ball to McCutcheon three straight times. When Jaworski was through, he drove the Rams straight down field 79 yards for a

touchdown. In the 13 plays it took, McCutcheon ran with the ball nine times and accounted for 51 yards.

That set the tempo for the game. Minutes later, the Rams intercepted a pass and scored again. Within eight minutes, they had jumped into a 14–0 lead. They not only had the momentum but they had McCutcheon and a strong defense to send against the Cardinals. When the first half ended, the Rams were on top, 28–0. McCutcheon had already carried the ball 20 times and gained 118 yards, an average of 5.9 yards a run.

The Rams' second-half strategy was now obvious. All they had to do was to control the ball on offense with McCutcheon and make the defense alert to what would in all probability be a St. Louis aerial attack. With quarterback Jim Hart and speedy receivers Mel Gray and J. V. Cain, the Cardinals were capable of the long bomb. They could score and score quickly from anywhere on the field.

Hart tried but it wasn't enough. When the game ended, he had thrown a total of 41 passes.

McCutcheon was given the ball 17 more times in the second

half for a total of 37 in the game. It was the most times he had ever
carried as a pro.

"I wasn't aware of how many yards I had," exclaimed
McCutcheon after the game. "I know that I had carried the ball a lot
because I got tired at the end. The most times I had carried the ball
previously was 39 times in college. We knew going in that St. Louis
had an explosive offense and that we had to take charge and control
the line of scrimmage. Since I didn't play the previous week, my legs
felt extra strong going in."

McCutcheon isn't a particularly big back. He is 6'1" and weighs
205 pounds. He didn't attract much attention at Colorado State. The
Rams waited until the third round of the 1972 college draft to pick
him. He had some leg problems his senior year, and a good many of
the pro teams were afraid to draft him. But the Rams were aware
that McCutcheon had gained a lot of yards behind a poor offensive
line. He was always getting hit pretty hard, but he always managed
to gain a few yards.

However, as a rookie with the Rams, McCutcheon didn't gain

anything. Tommy Prothro was coaching the team then, and he soured on McCutcheon in the exhibition campaign. He fumbled quite a bit, didn't block well, and was relegated to the taxi squad. McCutcheon felt lost.

"You don't always feel you're part of the team," remarked McCutcheon. "You work out all week, but then, come Sunday, everybody else is doing the playing and you're not even in uniform. It's a weird feeling. I did a lot of soul-searching that year. I knew I had the ability to play, but I had to take a long, honest look at the situation."

It's not that McCutcheon sulked. He's not the type. He is a quiet individual who comes from a large but poor family in Plainview, Texas. When most kids were looking wide-eyed at life at 12, McCutcheon was in the fields picking cotton. He remembers getting up at 4 A.M. and working until 7 or 8 P.M. He could have sulked about that.

So, that very first year with the Rams, McCutcheon learned how to block. He learned that without any blocking there isn't any running. And when the 1972 season was over, McCutcheon took pride in his blocking. The only action he did see was some duty on the special teams in which he had to block.

Within a year, fate smiled on McCutcheon. After the 1972 campaign, the Rams fired Prothro and hired Chuck Knox, who was an assistant with the Detroit Lions. Little did McCutcheon realize what the change would mean to him personally. But he found out long before the 1973 season began. One of the first things Knox asked McCutcheon was why he hadn't played more his rookie season. McCutcheon appreciated Knox's concern. No one had paid attention to him before.

"I told him that I didn't know," answered McCutcheon. "The coaches never gave me a plain answer as to why I wasn't playing. I questioned the coaching staff about it several times, and Prothro told me that it was very hard to bring a player off the taxi squad once the season began. That was the only answer ever given to me."

Knox was fond of McCutcheon. He apparently realized the youngster had a great amount of talent, upon viewing films of the Rams' 1972 season. In fact, he went out on a limb by telling McCutcheon that he was depending on him to do a lot of running during the upcoming season. That vote of confidence meant a great deal to McCutcheon. He looked forward to the year ahead.

"I think I can be the Rams' big runner this year," he exclaimed. "I know I have the ability to be. It's going to be a lot different for me this year. I'm going to make a name for myself."

And he did. In the opening game of the season against the Kansas City Chiefs, McCutcheon ran for 121 yards on 21 carries. That was just about six yards a carry. McCutcheon was off and running and improving with every game. After all, it was really his first active season on the club, even though he had been with the Rams for two

years. When he finished the year with 1,097 yards, he set a club record.

"All it takes is quickness and blocking," pointed out McCutcheon. "If you have our kind of blocking and my kind of ability, you should gain 1,000 yards every year. Quickness is the ability to hit between two blockers as soon as the hole starts to open in the line. Speed only helps on end runs. In this league, nobody gets outside very often. I think of speed as what it takes to get around the linebacker on the weak side sweep. But quickness, the ability to accelerate, is the key ingredient. The hole opens, and you are there.

"A runner may have 9.6 speed, or even 4.6 speed for the 40, and still not be a good inside runner because he isn't a particularly fast starter. A man's time for the 40 doesn't matter too much. In the NFL, he can run inside if he can hit his top speed with his second step. To a running back, quickness and acceleration mean the same thing.

"I like to get any tackler one-on-one because I feel I can beat him. But when I see out of the corner of my eye a teammate coming up beside me to get an angle on the blocker, I try to set him up. But consistency is what I'm aiming for. You can have a great game one week and then have a bad game the next week. That's not the way to do it."

McCutcheon has shown the way to do it. His first four years with the Rams he has demonstrated consistency above everything else. It is the main reason the Rams have been in the playoffs all four times. All that's missing is a Super Bowl, which McCutcheon is thinking about.

"I think that part of my desire to improve myself is that a football player leads a better life than a cotton picker," he smiled.

He probably was good at that, too . . .

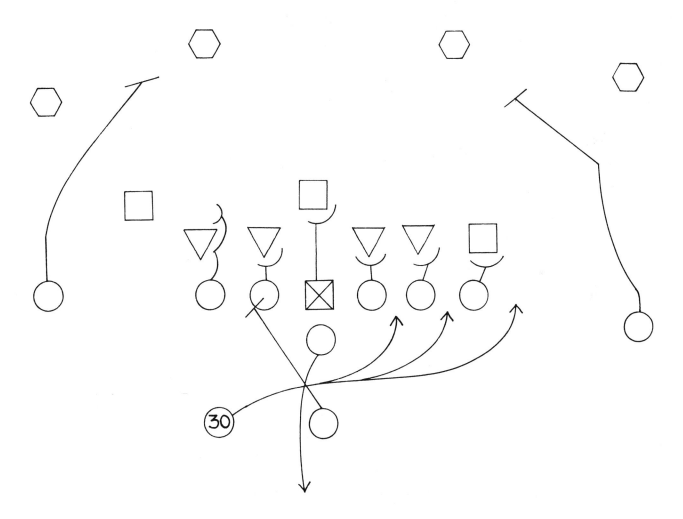

Diagrammed by Coach Chuck Knox

Terry
Metcalf

He is something special. He can do anything. Basically, he is a runner. But he is an extraordinary type. It is the way he runs. The different ways. Normally he lines up at halfback. But he can run back kicks and punts like no one else. And he can catch a ball. Occasionally, he can throw it, too. What makes him dangerous is that he can score from anywhere on the field. That's what makes him exciting. Every time he touches a ball he can go all the way. He is such a threat. One that can turn an entire game around. He is perhaps the most versatile back in the National Football League. That's what makes Terry Metcalf so valuable.

Ironically, the St. Louis Cardinals didn't think that highly of Metcalf in the 1973 college draft. They weren't the only ones. Neither did the rest of the NFL teams. They had trepidations about his size. He was 5'10" and weighed 180 pounds. Pro scouts snicker at that. So do the computers. They do wonders with big numbers. Little ones they chew up and spit out. Ask any little guy around the league. More than one has been victimized by the computer monster.

In 1973, the Cardinals couldn't afford to make a mistake with their draft choices. The year before, they had finished with a 4–9–1 record for the second year in a row. They had fired their coach and had hired one from a small college in California. They didn't realize it at the time, but when they named Don Coryell of San Diego State as their coach, they collected an instant dividend for the upcoming draft.

Metcalf's name didn't surface in the first couple of rounds of the draft. The Cardinals had four choices in the first three rounds. On the first round, they picked defensive end Dave Butz from Purdue. On the second round, they went for quarterback Gary Keithley of Texas–El Paso. They had two picks on the third round. They exercised the first one by selecting guard Fred Sturt from Bowling Green. Metcalf's name was still on the board.

Then, Coryell spoke up. He remembered the way Metcalf played at Long Beach State. In fact, he never forgot him. Long Beach was in a punting situation deep in its own territory. It was in the fourth quarter of a close game. Metcalf dropped back to punt. Instead, he took off with the ball and made his way for a first down. Long Beach kept its drive going and drove all the way downfield for a touchdown. They upset San Diego State, and the highly successful Coryell suffered a rare defeat. He never forgot the play that beat him. Coaches never do. And so, the Cardinals made Metcalf their second selection on the third round.

"I knew I wouldn't be drafted high," admitted Metcalf. "I was small and I was coming from a small college. I thought I could make it in the NFL, but I heard what all the scouts were saying about my size.

"They brought me to St. Louis for a visit; and I went to lunch with Coryell and George Boone, their chief scout. I didn't know where they planned to play me. I was hoping I'd be a running back, but I thought they might think I was too small.

"At lunch, Boone looked across the table and said, 'Terry, what do you think about safety?' But before I could answer, Coryell said, 'Uh, uh, Metcalf is my running back.' I knew right then and there that, if I made the team, Coryell and I were going to get along just fine."

Metcalf made the team and made it big. He showed just how explosive he was the very first time he touched the ball from the line of scrimmage. On Coryell's very first call as a pro coach, he signaled for Metcalf's number. The rookie responded by bursting up the middle for 50 yards. Coryell won't forget that either. Metcalf finished his first professional game with 133 yards.

When his rookie year ended, Metcalf had had a fine season. He had carried the ball 148 times and had gained 628 yards, averaging 4.2 yards a run. He had also caught 37 passes for another 316 yards. Despite the fact that the Cardinals finished with their third consecutive 4–9–1 record, they felt they were on the way back, primarily because of Metcalf's first-year performance.

Before the 1974 season began, the Cardinals decided to get the most out of Metcalf's explosiveness. In addition to rushing and catching passes out of the backfield, they wanted to have Metcalf run back kickoffs and punts. So that's what Metcalf did. He was kept quite busy, too. He rushed for 718 yards on 152 carries, an average of 4.7 yards a rush. Then he caught 50 passes for another 377 yards. In addition, he returned 20 kickoffs for 623 yards and 23 punts for 285. He ended the year with 2,058 combined net yards. What's more, the Cardinals started to win. They turned it around with a 10–4 record and an appearance in the championship playoffs.

"Something big happened in St. Louis," smiled Metcalf. "We changed a losing attitude into a winning one. I was happy to be part of it. It seems they expect me to get the big plays. That's the kind of responsibility I want. I'll try to do anything that's asked of me."

The Cardinals asked Metcalf to do it again the next season. And he did. Only this time he was even more involved. He carried the ball 165 times, gained 816 yards, averaged 4.9 yards a run, and scored nine touchdowns. Then he caught 43 passes for 378 yards and two touchdowns. Tirelessly, he returned 35 kickoffs for 960 yards and a touchdown. He handled 23 punts for 285 yards and another touchdown, giving him 13 total touchdowns for the season. What's more, when everything was added up, Metcalf had established an NFL record by producing 2,462 combined net yards. Metcalf did it all, and the Cardinals flew to an 11–3 record and their second straight Eastern Division title.

Metcalf had improved every year he played. He even added another dimension to his versatility in 1975. He threw a 51-yard touchdown pass. Metcalf became the first back in the NFL since Gale Sayers to account for a touchdown five different ways, passing, receiving, running, and returning kickoffs and punts.

In a game against the New England Patriots, he, more than anyone else, accounted for a 24–17 victory. It was not that he gained so much yardage. But he scored all three touchdowns, two rushing and one on a punt return. The touchdowns were scored in pressure situations, in that the Cardinals were behind at the time.

In the second period, the Cardinals were behind, 3–0. They appeared sluggish and needed a big play to get them going. Metcalf came through. He fielded a punt on his own 31-yard line and darted and dashed his way to a 69-yard touchdown.

Later in the game, Metcalf really erupted. The Cardinals were behind, 17–10, as the fourth quarter opened. Continuing a drive they had begun in the previous period, the Cardinals were threatening to tie the score. They had reached the Patriots' one-yard line. On second down, Metcalf broke through for a touchdown.

Midway through the fourth period, Metcalf came through for the third time. With the game deadlocked at 17–17, Metcalf swept around his right end to go in standing up from seven yards out. The come-from-behind triumph sparked the Cardinals to an 11–3 season.

Metcalf was St. Louis' newest hero. He was recognized in restaurants and deluged with autograph requests. A quiet person,

44   TERRY METCALF (RUNNING BACK)

Metcalf nevertheless worked a great deal with kids during the off-season. The youngsters all looked up to Metcalf.

"It's the glamorous part of football," remarked Metcalf. "Each person makes what he wants to of that. Really, I'm not an outgoing person. This is what I've always wanted to do, and I finally have the opportunity to do it."

Everything looked good in St. Louis. Since Metcalf and Coryell joined the Cardinals that same season, they began to turn things around. After so many losing seasons, the Cardinals had begun to win consistently. They won in 1974 and repeated their success in 1975. There was no reason to believe they wouldn't continue winning in 1976. The Cardinals did, but Metcalf didn't have the year everyone was expecting of him.

Something happened that off-season to Metcalf. It was a strange turn of events. It wasn't good. And it all happened so suddenly. The first incident took place on the way to the Pro Bowl game. His luggage was checked by security at the St. Louis Airport. The woman attendant discovered some firecrackers in Metcalf's carry-on bag. She asked Metcalf about them. He jokingly replied, "I'm going to blow up the airplane with firecrackers."

The woman panicked. She summoned the police. Before he knew what was happening, Metcalf was handcuffed and taken down to the station. He was fingerprinted and booked for disturbing the peace and making a false bomb report. A few hours later, Metcalf was released.

"When I got on that plane I couldn't believe what had just happened to me," exclaimed Metcalf. "Reporters, television cameras, handcuffs, fingerprints. All the questions over a few firecrackers. I didn't settle down until I got to New Orleans. When my cab pulled up to the hotel, there was John Gilliam standing outside and he said, 'Oh, oh, Terry, we've heard all about you. You were gonna blow up a plane.' I said, 'Wow, news sure travels fast.'

"Then, when I got to the dressing room, here was this thing in my locker. The trainers did it. They took one of those big tape cans, painted it red, stuck this string in the top for a fuse and put it in my locker. Everybody got a big laugh out of it, including me. They'd treated the whole thing as a joke, which is exactly what it was."

Several months later, Metcalf was on his way to the airport again. On the way, he stopped by a friend's house. When he went back to his car, he discovered that he had been robbed. He had lost clothing, jewelry, and some money. His total loss was about $1,800.

Shortly after that, he was playing basketball at Washington University. Metcalf's opponent was a little too aggressive. It reached a point where Metcalf couldn't take any more. After being knocked to the floor, he got right up and stung his antagonist with a right to the face. The punch broke the guy's nose. A couple of weeks later, the guy slapped Metcalf with a lawsuit demanding $5,000 in actual and $50,000 in punitive damages.

It wasn't a peaceful off-season for Metcalf. When he reported to training camp, he wasn't exactly mentally ready to play football. He was unhappy with his contract. He told the Cardinals that he didn't want to run back any more kickoffs or punts unless he was paid additional money to do so.

Metcalf was unhappy. It was reflected in his play. He was further irritated by a number of nagging injuries throughout the season. When the 1976 campaign ended, the Cardinals didn't make it to the playoffs. Metcalf had gained only 537 yards on 134 carries, an average of 4.0 yards a run. He had caught 33 passes for 388 yards. His touchdown total was only seven. He had only run back 17 punts and 16 kickoffs.

Metcalf can do a lot more than that . . .

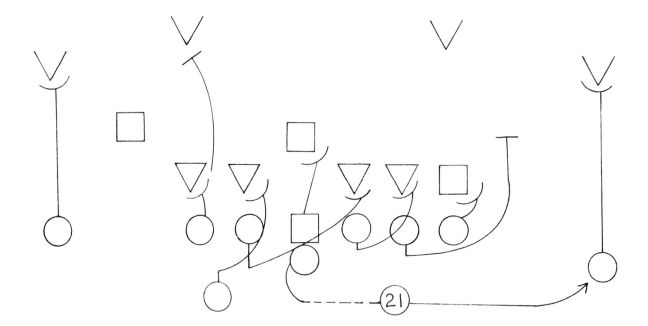

Diagrammed by Coach Don Coryell

Lydell Mitchell

They didn't want him. He was a second-round draft choice, a bona fide All-American. He had set two NCAA season records his final year at Penn State, 29 touchdowns and 174 points in running for 1,567 yards. He had played in the College All-Star game the day before he reported to camp. Still, they had made up their minds about him. The coach told him that he was three weeks behind and that he would never be able to catch up. It was unheard of. Then they started him in the third exhibition game against the Kansas City Chiefs. He led the club in rushing and to their first win. But that was it. One start and back to the bench. Just before the regular 1972 season began, the coach insisted that he be cut. Lydell Mitchell couldn't believe what was happening.

When Mitchell reported that year, the Baltimore Colts were on the verge of decline. They had won the Super Bowl in 1971 and had made the playoffs again that season as a wild card team. But now the club was starting to get old and the veterans were afraid of losing their jobs. They didn't want any hotshot rookies pressing them. The coach, Don McCafferty, respected the veterans. They had won for him and he stuck with them. He didn't want Mitchell on the squad.

But Joe Thomas, who had become the team's general manager earlier that spring, intervened. He refused to cut Mitchell. He insisted that he be kept on the reserve list. McCafferty and Thomas had bumped heads, and it wouldn't be the last time. Midway during the season, McCafferty wanted to keep an aging Johnny Unitas, who

was a Baltimore legend. Thomas instead traded him to the San Diego Chargers. McCafferty quit and an assistant coach, John Sandusky, replaced him.

Mitchell was finally placed on the roster the third week of the season. That was his introduction to professional football. It didn't leave him with a very good impression. He managed to play very little his rookie year. He carried the ball only 45 times for 215 yards, an average of 4.8 yards a run. He also caught 18 passes for another 147 yards. At least, Mitchell felt, he showed that he could play in the NFL.

In 1973, the Colts hired Howard Schnellenberger as head coach. Mitchell came to camp feeling that he would experience a new beginning. But it looked like 1972 all over again. Only this time he was given a chance to compete for a job. That he didn't mind. What happened afterward upset Mitchell. He had a fine pre-season, but it didn't matter.

"Schnellenberger called me into his office one day," remembered Mitchell, "and told me that he thought I had better ability than Don McCauley. He said that whoever had the better pre-season would be the starter once the regular season began. I led the team in rushing during the exhibitions. However, when the season started, his backfield was McCauley and Don Nottingham. It really bothered me."

For some strange reason Schnellenberger wanted to trade Mitchell. But Thomas once more intervened and refused. Instead, he forced Schnellenberger's hand. He traded Nottingham to make room in the lineup for Mitchell. It was a great move, too. Mitchell started the remaining 11 games on the schedule and ran for 963 yards. It certainly wasn't his fault that the Colts could only win four games.

Mitchell was on his way, even if the Colts weren't. In 1973, Baltimore planned to use Mitchell more as a receiver, coming out of the backfield. It worked. Besides gaining 757 yards rushing, Mitchell also caught an amazing 72 passes for another 544 yards. It was the first time in NFL history that a running back caught that many passes. Still, it didn't help the Colts to win. They sunk to their lowest depth in years, winning only two games. But at least the Colts had found themselves a player. Even if not too many others noticed. When you're playing for a losing team, the recognition isn't always there. Especially when the television networks don't think enough of your team to provide them with national exposure. Nobody wants to see a loser.

So, Mitchell operated in almost total obscurity his first three years at Baltimore. It wasn't something that he was accustomed to. He was philosophical about it. He could handle it.

"Being recognized as a star is something I'm used to," said Mitchell. "I've been a good player since I got into football. It's fun walking down the street with people recognizing you, knowing who you are and wanting to meet you. I don't get a big head about it, but it makes me happy, and every day I say to myself that I am glad of who I am and I'm glad of what I'm doing. I like to be recognized by kids, have them look up to me, to be able to tell them that they can be whatever they want, if they are willing to work hard enough at it."

Then something wonderful happened to the Colts. And Mitchell. Before the 1975 season began, Ted Marchibroda was named as the team's new coach. He was an offensive genius who knew and understood that phase of the game. He was one of those assistant coaches who never fully received the recognition he deserved, first at Los Angeles and then at Washington. But Joe Thomas knew of Marchibroda's talent and didn't hesitate in naming him the head coach of the Colts. They needed someone to lead them out of despair.

So what did Marchibroda do? He performed a miracle. He coached so well that the Colts finished the 1975 season with a 10–4 record. He made such an impact that he was named the coach of the year. He directed Baltimore to the most amazing comeback in NFL history. Only one year before, the Colts had finished with a 2–12 record. Suddenly, in one year, they were Super Bowl contenders.

It so happens that Mitchell enjoyed the greatest year of his career. He carried the ball an amazing 289 times and gained 1,193 yards, an average of 4.1 a run. He also found time to grab 60 passes for another 544 yards. Combined, Mitchell accounted for 1,737 yards of the Colts' total offense. The amazing thing is that he became the first 1,000-yard rusher in Baltimore history while finishing third in the NFL.

The 1975 season was a pivotal one for the Colts. It not only established the club as championship calibre, but it also developed quarterback Bert Jones and Mitchell as explosive offensive threats. Baltimore was coming on.

Now everybody knew about the Colts. And Jones. And Mitchell. They were the Cinderella team. From rags to riches in one year. Even Mitchell's critics had to rub their eyes. They had scoffed at him as a runner who didn't really have any speed—the breakaway kind, like O.J. Simpson. But for all-around performance, there is none better than Mitchell. Not really.

Mitchell gave his critics something to think about when he experienced his greatest day as a runner. Against the Kansas City Chiefs, he scampered for 178 yards on 26 carries. That's an average of 6.8 yards a run. But what was more important was that Mitchell broke loose on a 70-yard touchdown gallop. That showed some kind of speed.

"You can't imagine how much that run meant to me," signed Mitchell. "It's funny how you'll come into the league and people put labels on you, like, 'He's not fast; he can't do this or he can't do that.' I realize I don't have tremendous speed, but I've got good speed.

"It bothered me when they wrote that I wasn't good enough, that the Colts had to find an explosive runner. There was just one way to stop that talk and that was to finally break a long one. So I said to myself, 'I'll show them. I'll just show them. It'll happen one of these times.' And it happened.

"I think now that it's expected that I should get 1,000 yards. I get paid well, and they expect 1,000 yards from me. If I stay healthy, I know I'll get it. I'm looking forward to another season like this. I like to carry the ball a lot of times. If I go any less than 250 carries, I'll be upset."

Apparently the Colts felt the same way. In 1976, Mitchell again carried the ball 289 times. This time he gained 1,200 yards, which was second best in the AFC and fourth best in the NFL. He also caught 60 passes for the second straight year, which resulted in 555 yards. The number of receptions was not only third best in the AFC, but also third highest in the NFL. Talk about consistency.

"People have to understand the total situation," explained Mitchell. "In the past, our offensive line wasn't that good. Now we have one of the best fronts in the game and this has allowed us to open up our whole game. I only caught 18 passes my whole career at Penn State. But I always could catch a ball, and besides, it's fun going one-on-one against a linebacker.

"Sure, I felt I deserved more publicity as a pro. But that only comes with winning. Franco Harris made it big with the Steelers because their great defense keeps the offense on the field most of the time. Now it's getting that way with the Colts. But the big thing with me is that I have the respect of my peers."

Mitchell and Harris are close friends. It is one of the rewarding aspects of professional sports. They played against each other in high school in New Jersey and both attended Penn State at the same time. They have maintained their friendship even as pros. They frequently call each other to see what's going on.

Back in 1974, they made a friendly wager between them halfway through the season. It was obvious at that point that Simpson was going to win the rushing title. So Harris made a dinner bet with Mitchell. He contended that whoever finished second behind O. J. would pick out the restaurant and whoever finished third would pick up the check. Needless to say, the friends ate Italian food after the 1974 season but soul food after last year.

Even now, few appreciate what a durable runner Mitchell is. He isn't thought about along those lines, simply because he is only 5'11" and weighs 190 pounds. But the truth of the matter is that Mitchell hasn't missed a game since he was in high school. He's a slasher type of runner who knows how to take a hit.

"I see well all around me and I can sense when I'm about to get hit, so I protect myself," disclosed Mitchell. "It's very seldom that anybody gets a real solid, head-on shot on me. That's where runners get hurt. I take a shot on my arm or my side.

"And when I see I'm about to get hit hard, I sell out. I go down. You see too many runners get hurt when they're hopelessly stopped and still struggling. Then somebody else hits them and they get hurt.

"The biggest factor is that I always keep my legs moving, and that prevents injuries. It is when the leg is planted that knees and ankles give way on tackles. I've got to carry the ball at least 20 times a game to be effective. I get better; I am more conscious of what is going on the more I carry the ball. I feel the pressure more now that we are starting to win, because I know I am one of the key men. I like the pressure and I go out there realizing that, if I do the job right, we can win."

Apparently, he's doing just that . . .

Greg Pruitt

He loves to dream. He actually believes it helps him. Especially before a game. Like one night when he was still in college. Before a game against the University of Southern California, he had a good dream. He dreamed that he reversed his field and ran for an 80-yard touchdown. The next day it happened. It made him happy. Another time he dreamed he would be picked on the first round of the 1973 college draft. That didn't happen. He rubbed his eyes in disbelief. He was ready to cry. Greg Pruitt was a very disappointed young man.

Pruitt was a star at the University of Oklahoma. Apparently the computer didn't think so. The computer is what the pro teams swear by. But, when you're only 5'10" and weigh 185 pounds, the computer doesn't give high ratings. They like to be fed big numbers. Yet, Pruitt felt he was big enough and good enough to be a first-round choice. The day of the draft, he was filled with anxiety. Since he was a journalism major, he had access to the wire service machines that were in the department. So, Pruitt went over there that morning and began a vigil that lasted until the early part of the afternoon.

He waited and waited. Name after name appeared. It went on that way for hours. Finally the round ended. All 26 teams had made their first-round selections. Pruitt hadn't been picked by any of them. He couldn't believe it. He had to get away from it all. So, he went out on the golf course to relieve his frustrations. It wasn't until much later that a writer from a local newspaper caught up with him on the links to tell him that he had been picked on the second round by the Cleveland Browns.

"I had gotten all dressed and went over to the machines in the journalism department and waited for my name to come across the wire," recalled Pruitt. "I expected to be picked in the first round. But my name never came up. I thought about my size again and everything I had been told, and I felt embarrassed. I couldn't take the pressure, so I went out and played golf. I shot 180."

The reason Pruitt felt disappointed was obvious. The Browns had had two first-round selections that year, and they had failed to exercise either one of them on Pruitt. Instead, they first picked wide receiver Steve Holden from Arizona State. Then they selected guard Pete Adams from the University of Southern California. If it hadn't been for the club's owner, Art Modell, who had a hunch about Pruitt, the Browns would probably have passed him by. Because of his size, he wasn't getting many looks.

"All I heard through my career was that I was too small,"

grumbled Pruitt. "I despised it. I've developed a complex about my size. I've been trying to live it down all my life. It has made me give more effort to prove everybody wrong."

Pruitt had speed. Good speed. That was one of the things that impressed the Browns. They also figured that Pruitt had enough versatility to help the squad. He could run, catch passes, and run back kickoffs and punts. They really didn't expect Pruitt to make the starting lineup with Leroy Kelly, who was back for another season.

Like most rookies, Pruitt had to learn. He began before he even reported to the Browns. The first thing he wanted to do was to build up his strength. He went about this in an unusual way. He lost ten pounds and then started to gain it back by lifting weights. He figured the added muscle would help him tremendously and at the same time not affect his speed.

"I realize it will take time to learn how the pros do it," said Pruitt. "I compare this with my collegiate career in that it took me time to come around. I didn't start until the end of my sophomore season. I was nervous and made mistakes because I tried too hard. I'm older and more experienced now. It will take a while to adjust to a new system. I'm going to start off quietly and take it from there.

"First I want to drop to 175 pounds and work back up to 187 by lifting weights. That way I'll be solid for sure. I want to be stronger and cut down on my injuries. They've been saying that I've been too small ever since I walked out on a football field. Size is not a dominant factor. Because I'm smaller than most guys, I can go in different directions quicker than the bigger guys."

He had to learn quicker, too. After appearing with the College All-Stars, Pruitt finally joined the Browns' training camp several weeks later. Physically, he was ready. Mentally, he was not. He had to cram everything regarding the Browns' system just to be able to catch up. It was tough on a rookie trying to prove himself.

Cleveland's coach, Nick Skorich, didn't look upon Pruitt as a regular. He felt his backfield was set with Kelly and Bo Scott. He figured that Pruitt would play behind Kelly, learn the position, and then take over for the veteran in the next year or two after he retired. Skorich did manage to see Pruitt in a couple of All-Star games and was quite pleased with his ability.

"We'll use double wings and flood formations with Pruitt the same way we've been doing it with Kelly for a long time," explained Skorich. "Obviously, we've got to get Pruitt outside around the corners. You don't need guards who run a 4.6 forty in front of him. We just got to get him to the corner. If we get the sweep turned up field at the line of scrimmage, we've got yards. Jim Brown would get 30 yards for you, Kelly would get 25 or 30 yards. It all depends on the ability of the runner.

"Pruitt has fine ability. I remember seeing him play in the Hula Bowl in Hawaii. It rained, and the red clay soil in Honolulu was like

grease. Other runners on the field were slipping all over. But Pruitt ran like he was on dry ground. I said then that I hoped he was a flat-footed runner like Kelly. We feel he can be an explosive runner and receiver."

After being with the Browns for two weeks, Pruitt finally got to see some action. He was inserted late in the third quarter in a pre-season game against the Los Angeles Rams. The Browns were behind at the time, 21–7, and they had displayed practically no offense.

The first time he entered the game, Pruitt carried the ball four straight times. The next time he played, he handled the ball on seven consecutive plays. He finished the night with 40 yards rushing, a key pass reception, and scored the Browns' final touchdown as the game ended in a 21–21 tie. Still, Pruitt wasn't completely satisfied with his performance.

"My mind was running a thousand miles an hour trying to get everything down right in the game," disclosed Pruitt. "The crowd

bothered me. I had trouble hearing the calls at the line and listening for the 'live' numbers on the audibles."

Still, Pruitt was an exciting runner. He caught the fancy of the long-suffering Browns fans who hadn't seen a championship for ten years. Pruitt showed that he could not only run outside but also be effective inside where the yards are hard to get. But Pruitt was his own most severe critic.

"I'm still making mistakes, but I feel I'm making pretty good progress, too," he remarked. "It's different from college. They hit hard in college, but here you get hit harder more often. I was going out for a pass one game, and I made the mistake of getting too close to a linebacker. He let me have it. I was groggy for a couple of seconds, but learned a lesson. In fact, I've been learning with every game."

The Browns didn't use Pruitt much in the backfield his rookie season. He carried the ball only 61 times but gained 540 yards, an average of 6.1 yards a carry. He was used mostly for kickoff and punt returns. The following year it was the same, only he carried the ball more often. He ran for 540 yards on 126 attempts, averaging 4.3 yards a carry.

Pruitt still hadn't earned a starting role. It wasn't until Forrest Gregg replaced Skorich as head coach in 1975 that Pruitt got to play regularly. Pruitt relished the opportunity to become a starter.

"I know that some people say I'm too small to take the beating, but I don't think so," said Pruitt. "I don't try to run over people. I like to get around them. So I don't figure I'll take that much of a beating."

He didn't. What he did do was to run like no other back in Cleveland had for years. He gained 1,067 yards on 217 carries. He averaged 4.9 yards a run and scored eight touchdowns. He also caught 44 passes for another 299 yards and a touchdown.

Pruitt went over the 1,000-yard barrier with a memorable performance the next to last game of the season. He became only the third runner in Cleveland's history to do it, and he did it while playing with a cracked rib. Pruitt ran with the ball 26 times and gained 214 yards, a remarkable average of 8.2 yards a rush. He also scored three touchdowns in the 40–14 rout of the Kansas City Chiefs.

"I've been waiting and waiting, and it finally came around," smiled Pruitt. "I've gotten discouraged at times. So have other players and the coaches. It's hard not to when you lose the first nine games of the season.

"The game was the biggest one of my career. I think the linemen enjoyed the 1,000 yards more, though. All the linemen were keeping tabs. They kept saying, 'He needs 50. He needs 30. He needs 5.' The closer I got to it, the harder they blocked. That touchdown I scored to go over 1,000 was one of the biggest holes I ever saw. I was going to spike the ball; but, to be truthful, I just forgot to spike it, I was so glad to get it."

In 1976, Pruitt again gained 1,000 yards, but just barely. He hit the big number in the final game of the season, one in which he played in a great deal of pain. He had injured his ankle midway in the season, against the San Diego Chargers.

The Browns didn't know how much they could get out of Pruitt the following week in a crucial game against the Cincinnati Bengals. Although the Browns lost, 21–6, Pruitt had an excellent day. He ran for 124 yards on 18 carries, averaging 6.9 yards a trip. He also caught four passes for another 28 yards. He played the entire game in pain.

"Whenever I'd get hit, it would sting," revealed Pruitt. "A couple of times I had the opportunity to outrun the safety, but I couldn't accelerate fast enough or put a move on him. On one pass, I was caught by a linebacker. That's the first time that ever happened. A couple of times, holes opened, but I didn't hit them quick enough. I had a chance to go all the way. On Tuesday, I felt I could play. But Thursday and Friday it stiffened up, and Sunday I had to keep moving on the sidelines or it would have stiffened up again."

Pruitt couldn't play very much or very effectively the rest of the season. He had been shooting for 1,500 yards when the year began. Against Kansas City in the final game of the year, he needed 46 yards to reach 1,000. He just made it on a two-yard run and limped off the field afterward.

"A little guy has more incentive," remarked Pruitt. "It has made me give more effort to prove everybody wrong."

Indeed he has . . .

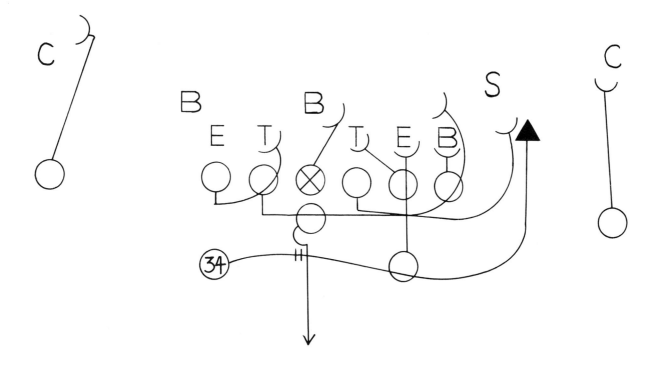

Diagrammed by Coach Forrest Gregg

O. J.
Simpson

The rain was coming down hard. It was damp and dark. He sat alone at the end of the bench. He just sat there looking straight ahead, his head snug against his shoulders under a parka. He really didn't see what was going on in the closing minute of the game. Instead, his thoughts reflected on the season that was coming to an end. In the half-empty stadium, he was at peace with himself. It had been a long season. Too long. It gets to be that way when a team finishes 2–12.

The only solace for O.J. Simpson was that, on that gloomy day, his spindly legs had carried him to a second straight rushing title. It was personally rewarding. He had run for 1,503 yards over a tortuous season that had weighed heavily on him, both physically and mentally. So much so, that on this final day of the 1976 season, Simpson's teammates wanted so much for him to win the rushing title once again. He was their main man.

Before the final game against the playoff-bound Baltimore Colts, Simpson was second in the run to glory. Walter Payton of the Chicago Bears was leading O.J. by nine yards. All season long Simpson had chased the Bears' star, and now he was that close to overtaking him. There is pride among losers, which perhaps doesn't make them that at all. Buffalo's offensive line wanted to salvage something from a disastrous year. They wanted Simpson to finish number one.

When the game began, the Bills fell quickly behind. Which wasn't unusual. It had been that kind of a season. But the Bills' offensive line had a mission; and the rain, mud, and impending defeat

wouldn't discourage them. That's pride. The Bills were trailing, 17–6; but Simpson at that point in the game had taken over the rushing lead. He had accumulated 65 yards while Payton could muster only 21 yards against the Denver Broncos.

As the rain began to come down, the game began to seem like an eternity. Baltimore had built its bulge to 41–6. Still, the Buffalo blockers wouldn't quit. Simpson was now over 100 yards. They urged quarterback Gary Marangi to keep giving the ball to O.J. Somehow, there was still life in Simpson's tired legs. He broke loose for a 44-yard gain that swelled his total to 171 yards. Nobody was certain to catch O.J. now. His linemen achieved satisfaction in that. They congratulated Simpson on the sidelines when the defense took over.

Then they thought of something else. Something that would cover O.J. with still more glory. Word had reached the Buffalo bench that Payton was injured and through for the day. It ensured Simpson's rushing crown. O.J.'s blockers wanted him to go for 200 yards. That would make him the first running back in NFL history to

gain 200 yards in three consecutive games. The thought was appealing. Certainly the 29 yards were within Simpson's grasp.

No one cared that the score was now 58–20. O.J. talked the situation over with his coach, Jim Ringo. They talked briefly. But when the Bills got the ball for the last time, O.J. did not come back into the game. Instead, he sat on the far end of the bench alone with his thoughts as the season finally came to an end. Later in the dressing room, Simpson explained why he preferred to end the game on the bench.

"The Colts had the second team on the field," observed O.J. "I didn't want to go for a record against a second team.

"Besides, I had the rushing title won after we learned that Payton got hurt. Payton's a genuine star. He's not one of those young guys that will make people say, 'Hey, remember Payton, he had that one big year.' He's what I call one of the insane runners, the kind who can make the moves without having to stop and think."

Then he smiled.

"I wasn't thinking about the rushing title before the game started, simply because we didn't exactly want to be distracted about our playoff plans."

That's all Reggie McKenzie had to hear. He is Simpson's closest friend on the Bills. The two have a deep brotherly love off the field. On the field, McKenzie shows it by leading the blockers in pulling out from his guard position to clear the path for Simpson's outside runs. O.J. at times likes to put McKenzie on. But every once in awhile McKenzie gets a word in.

"O.J. couldn't forget about the title if he tried," remarked McKenzie. "The linemen wouldn't let him."

When the season first began, there were a great many of the Bills who had started to forget about O.J. It was a season that might not have been. Simpson seriously thought about quitting football. It was a sickening thought. O.J. was the franchise. But he was determined to leave the game and pursue his acting career and other business interests unless he was traded to the Los Angeles Rams.

Born and raised in San Francisco, Simpson had deep California roots. His wife did not want to keep taking their children out of school, moving to Buffalo and then returning to California once the football season ended. She had done this in previous years. But now the children were getting older, and she remained in Los Angeles while O.J. went east. The seasons were long and lonely for both.

O.J. missed the entire training camp and all the pre-season games. He was a determined holdout. So much so that the Buffalo Bills' 1976 press guide omitted Simpson from its pages. Certainly, if Simpson was going to play in 1976 it wouldn't be with the Bills. The Bills did have trade discussions with the Rams. How serious they were, no one will ever know. But negotiations did break down, and 48 hours before the season began, Simpson was still at home resigned to retiring.

The Bills had an empty feeling. Their pre-season home games did not draw well. Their season ticket sales were down. They faced the prospects of still smaller crowds once the regular season began without O.J. in the lineup. Buffalo owner Ralph Wilson made a hurried trip to Los Angeles on a Friday night. On Saturday, he met with Simpson and his wife and, in an impassioned plea, got O.J. to sign a new two-year contract for more money perhaps than anyone who ever played football.

O.J. flew on a plane all night and joined the Bills for the first time on Sunday. He arrived in time for a late afternoon workout as the Bills made final preparations to open the season on Monday night against the Miami Dolphins. Simpson's last-minute appearance spurred ticket sales in Buffalo and also helped ABC-TV's ratings for the night. The Bills without O.J. aren't exactly audience binding.

But things had changed. Suddenly a great many of the Bills' players were strangers to O.J. During the pre-season period, the Bills

had traded a lot of players. A great many were Simpson's friends, Ahmad Rashad, Earl Edwards, and J. D. Hill.

Others looked at him differently. Tony Greene, for one. Bob Chandler, for another. And most importantly, Jim Braxton, O.J.'s friend. All three were seeking better contracts when Simpson arrived and was signed for heaven knows how much money. They all figured that they would now get the short end of the stick. They had worked and sweated all during training camp to support their cause.

The first time O.J. approached Braxton, the big 245-pound full-back, who does a ton of blocking for Simpson, turned and walked away. It hurt O. J. This was his friend, one to whom he always gave credit for his blocking, one whom he affectionately calls "Bubbie."

"Hey, Bubbie," said Simpson softly. "I don't want to take anything away from you. Let's work together, and I'll do everything I can to help you get your share later."

Braxton smiled. It broke the tension and any resentment that Braxton might have harbored. It was very important to Simpson. But as fate would have it, Braxton was hurt in the opening game against the Dolphins and was lost for the season. When they lost their quarterback, Joe Ferguson, a few games later, the Bills' season was doomed to failure. But still the tension remained. It reached such a high level that the coach, Lou Saban, quit after the season was only five weeks old.

"We really didn't resent O. J. trying to get more money or place himself with a better team," admitted center Mike Montler. "I tried that myself when I moved from the New England Patriots to Buffalo. And when you look at what some just average basketball players are getting, you can't begrudge anything to an O. J. The only hard feelings weren't toward the Juice, but toward the way it was handled.

"We'd been working our butts off in camp, trying to salvage something. But to the fans we were unnoticed, anonymous. Then O. J. arrived and everything was 'Rah, Juice.' No matter how professional you try to be, that has to hurt."

What also had to hurt were the boos that O. J. was hearing for the first time. The Bills were losing. O. J., with no pre-season training whatsoever, got off to a slow start and the fans made him their target. It's easy to pick out a high-priced commodity and vent your frustrations. In his first three games, Simpson gained 28, 38, and 39 yards for a paltry total of 105 yards. No one thought about a rushing title. More important, Simpson didn't let the angry boos affect him. He looked at it philosophically.

"They went in one ear and out the other," claimed Simpson. "People are fickle, but they have a right to be. I was fickle when I tried to get traded, so how can I blame them? It was up to me to win them back."

In his first seven games, Simpson managed only two 100-yard games. It appeared that nothing could save him from a disastrous season, not since his early days with the Bills when he was misused, confused, and depressed.

But suddenly, pride surfaced. It first appeared among the offensive linemen. O. J. had always attributed his success to them. The year he ran for a history-making 2,003 yards, he brought every one of them to his post-game press conference and praised them. He was known as the Juice, but they were called the Electric Company. They were the ones who turned on the juice. That's the way it was. And the Electric Company was turned on again, this time by criticism.

"In mid-season, a jerk in Buffalo wrote that we offensive line-men couldn't block our own driveway," revealed Montler. "He had the nerve to write, 'Where is their pride?'"

O.J. didn't quit either. The first half of the season was like a conditioning period for him. He had to get in top shape, and he had to pay for it along the way with the bruising tackles that made his

body ache afterward. But O.J. was willing to pay the price. That's pride.

"For the first half of the season I was in shape to run with the ball, but I wasn't in good enough shape to improvise if there was no hole," explained Simpson. "If there was no hole, I couldn't shimmy or bounce out of trouble the way I wanted to. Some of the guys were telling me that I was getting sharper, and they'd get the rushing title for me. But when I got kicked out of the New England game for fighting, I figured I'd be damn lucky just to get a thousand yards. What I didn't figure was what the linemen would do for me."

Everybody else soon did. In a nationally televised Thanksgiving Day game against the Detroit Lions in a meaningless meeting in Detroit, O.J. ran for 273 yards. Nobody, but nobody, among the great runners of pro football had ever reached such heights. That made a 1,000-yard season a reality and the rushing title a possibility. The Juice and the Electric Company were turning on the lights in dreary Buffalo. It was the only action in town.

In many ways, the 1976 season was the greatest in Simpson's brilliant career. He overcame so many adversities not only to gain 1,503 yards but also to win a second straight rushing title. And he did it because his teammates wanted him to. Against the odds, too, facing defenses that were designed specifically to stop him. The Buffalo offense had nothing else.

"I don't know how I can sum up this season," reflected Simpson. "We lost so many good players, we lost coach Lou Saban, we lost 12 games. What can you say about a season where the high point is setting a rushing record against Detroit on Thanksgiving when we lost the game by two touchdowns?"

Only that O.J. Simpson is the greatest runner of all time. Enough said . . .

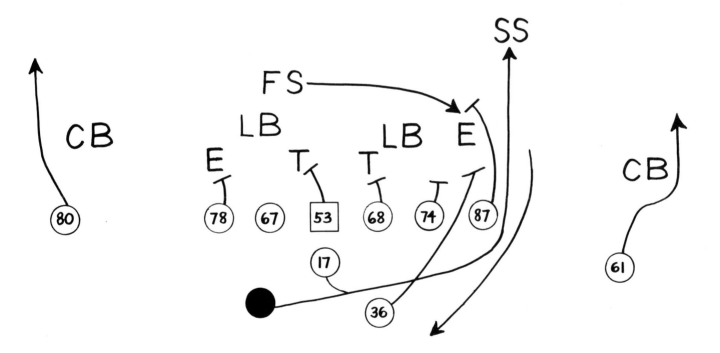

Diagrammed by Coach Jim Ringo

Mike Thomas

He doesn't like rookies. They are untested. It is as if they don't even exist. That's how much he's turned off by them. Instead, he prefers veteran players. He likes them experienced. The more experienced, the better. He is known to have some vintage players on his squad. He has won with veteran performers. That is the mark of his success. And he's loyal to them, too. He'd sooner go with a veteran than anyone else. That's George Allen's way. The coach of the Washington Redskins believes that the future is now. It is the main reason why he trades draft choices for proven players any day. It is also why, down through the years, the Redskins have had very few draft choices.

Like in 1975. Their first choice was on the fifth round of the college draft. It's not considered a round for blue-chip players. Those are usually chosen in the first three rounds. When you get down to the fifth round, a player's chances are about 50–50 that he will make the squad. That's with a normal NFL team. With the Redskins, it's probably nothing more than a free plane ride and then back home. So, when the Redskins made Mike Thomas their first pick in 1976, 107 other players were drafted ahead of him. Suffice to say, his selection seemed insignificant except for the fact that he was Washington's first choice. That's the only reason it was noted for the records.

Thomas wasn't highly regarded by most of the NFL clubs. In fact, some teams didn't regard him at all. The word on him was that he was a disciplinary problem. No professional team wants that. His college career had taken a number of detours. First he played at the University of Oklahoma, but quit after his sophomore year. He went back home to Greenville, Texas, and started to attend the University of Texas at Arlington. Then he received a scholarship offer from the University of Nevada at Las Vegas.

He quickly left town. He had to attend summer school to make up some credits so he would be eligible in the fall. Which Thomas didn't mind at all. He couldn't wait to leave Greenville. He had seen too many of his high school buddies walking the street with nothing to do and nowhere to go. Thomas didn't want that kind of life.

"I didn't tell my mother or anyone what I was doing," disclosed Thomas. "It was time I made up my own mind. I had to break loose. Time was running out."

Thomas was living in the shadow of two older brothers. Both had finished college, both had played football, and both had made it to the pros. Earl played with the St. Louis Cardinals, and Jimmy with the San Francisco 49ers. They were heroes around Greenville when Mike was growing up. Reputations can hurt.

"I realized the background that Mike had," said Larry Kennan who recruited him for Nevada. "It was hard for him to adjust. We tried to temper him a little. We tried to understand him, and we asked him to try to understand us. He still was a problem for us at times. He had some personal difficulties which affected him, and sometimes he didn't abide by the team rules. There we had to discipline him."

The Nevada coach who did the disciplining was Ron Meyer. Thomas never cared much for him. Midway through Thomas's senior year, Meyer kicked Thomas off the squad. Thomas's teammates quickly reacted. They went to the coach and asked that Thomas be put back on the team. Just 12 hours after he was suspended, Thomas was reinstated.

"I was overwhelmed by what they did," confessed Kennan. "I mean, Mike was a prima donna; and they knew it. But they loved him. I've never seen anything like it. He could fire them up at practice just by putting out. Whatever he did, they imitated him."

One day at practice, Thomas wasn't working out because of a sore ankle. One of the defensive players was bragging out loud that nobody was going to run through his hole. Thomas finally heard enough. He trotted onto the field and asked for the ball. He ran three straight plays right at the guy, and he never touched Thomas.

It so happened that Mike Allman, the Redskins' Director of College Scouting, was at the practice. He remembered what he saw. That's why he was ready for the 1975 draft. He was just hoping that Thomas would last until the Redskins got their chance to pick.

"We were just waiting," said Allman. "Coach Allen said, 'Wouldn't it be great if we could get another Larry Brown like we did on the eighth round in 1969?' Well, long before that day, I had told Allen about Mike Thomas. I go way back with Mike.

"When the fifth round started, Roosevelt Leaks and Thomas were still there. I said to Allen, 'It'll be tough to pass up Leaks, even with the question about his knee. But I got to check on Thomas. Either he's in jail or paralyzed. He should be picked by now.' I called Larry Kennan, and he told me that Mike was healthy and anxious to play. That's all we needed to know. Baltimore picked ahead of us and went for Leaks, and we got Thomas."

It might have been a stroke of luck. Kennan had tried to convince the pro clubs that Thomas wasn't hard to handle, that he was a victim of a bad rap. They conceded that he had ability, but they questioned his attitude.

So, Thomas had something to prove. He was on his own now and making the Redskins team was what mattered to him. He kept quiet in training camp and did what he was told. It was a long way from Las Vegas and Greenville to Washington, but Thomas was determined. Even if the odds were big.

"I kept hearing that Coach Allen wanted to keep four or six running backs, and I knew that was all we had in camp," said Thomas. "But I also knew that he liked to go with veterans, that rookies rarely make it. I didn't think I was on the squad until we broke camp and went to Washington."

He was on the squad but not in the starting lineup. Maintaining his coaching philosophy, Allen employed two veterans, Larry Brown and Moses Denson, as his starting backfield. In his first pro game, Thomas ran for only two yards in three carries against the New Orleans Saints in the opening game of the season.

Brown was injured in that game and couldn't play the following week against the New York Giants. Allen looked around and nominated Thomas to start against the Giants. It was only the second time that Allen had ever given a starting assignment to a rookie. He handled himself like a veteran. When Brown returned to action, he was switched to fullback just to accommodate Thomas. That's how much Allen was impressed with Thomas.

Thomas had an outstanding rookie year. So outstanding that he was named the NFC's rookie of the year. No one could remember the last time a Redskin had been honored as rookie of the year, until it was discovered that wide receiver Charley Taylor had gotten the award in 1955. Thomas was a busy rookie. He carried the ball 235 times and gained 919 yards, an average of 3.9 a run. He also caught 40 passes for another 483 yards. He scored seven touchdowns to lead the Redskins in that department.

Near the end of the season, Allen had ample praise for Thomas. And remember, Allen isn't one to get excited about rookies.

"Mike is our big-play man," remarked Allen. "He has speed; he's tough; and he breaks tackles."

Thomas reminded many of Brown, who was the team's star running back before he was felled by knee injuries. And, as Brown did, Thomas got most of his yards inside, on quick bolts between the tackles.

"To me, that's where I prefer to go," claims Thomas. "The quickest way to get anywhere is to run straight, the off-tackle play. If that one goes, then you get there in a hurry. Once you're past the line of scrimmage, you already have six or seven yards.

"I don't mind going wide; but then you've got the pursuit coming, and your blocking can get strung out. Then it's a mess. Some people say, 'Man, you're too little to run inside.' But that's the best kind of running. The big guys are up so high, sometimes they can't even see me."

Thomas picked up where he left off in the opening game of the 1976 season. He scored the biggest touchdown of his young career, one that gave the Redskins a come-from-behind 19–17 victory over the Giants. It was a dramatic way to open a season.

There were only 49 seconds left in the game. The Giants were in front, 17–12. Veteran Redskins quarterback Billy Kilmer had just completed a clutch pass. On a fourth-and-ten situation, he had hit Roy Jefferson with a 19-yard pass on the Giants' five-yard line. Blood was still dripping from Kilmer's nose. Only minutes before, he had needed five stitches to close a gash from a blow that had almost knocked him out. Kilmer called for a pass to one of the backs, whoever got open.

"I just came out of the backfield and so did Brown," explained Thomas. "Whichever one of us had man-to-man coverage has got to get open. I was the one. I had linebacker Pat Hughes on me. As I went to make my move, my leg gave way. It felt like I pulled a groin muscle. I went down. I got up. I don't know how, but I did; and Billy hit me."

Hughes disclosed that the Giants were in a zone and not man-to-man coverage. "I gave Thomas a shove and then fell back to an outside zone on the left side," said Hughes. "Thomas just circled in

deep and went over the middle. It was a good throw. It had to be high, and it was a good catch."

Later that season in another big game against the St. Louis Cardinals, Thomas once again was the deciding factor. Thomas had a busy afternoon. He carried the ball 31 times and gained 195 yards to set a Washington single-game record. He averaged 6.3 yards a run and scored the Redskins' only touchdown in their 16–10 triumph. His touchdown run came in the third quarter when his team was behind, 7–6. On a third-down-and-two play, Thomas found an opening inside right guard and broke loose on a 22-yard touchdown gallop.

Thomas had an exceptional year. He lugged the football 254 times and produced 1,101 yards, an average of 4.3 yards a run. He also caught 28 passes for another 290 yards and finished the year with nine touchdowns. He was now a veteran in Allen's eyes.

"The way I look at running is that the offensive linemen have a job blocking," explained Thomas. "They're not going to block a great defensive player every time. You run for a designated hole, but you're also looking the other way if it's not there. What happens with a move is instinctive, but you've got to have concentration to get there.

"I've always survived because of my quickness. You can't expect the linemen to hold open big holes every time. I'm going to be around a long time because size doesn't make any difference."

Not in Mike Thomas's case, anyway . . .

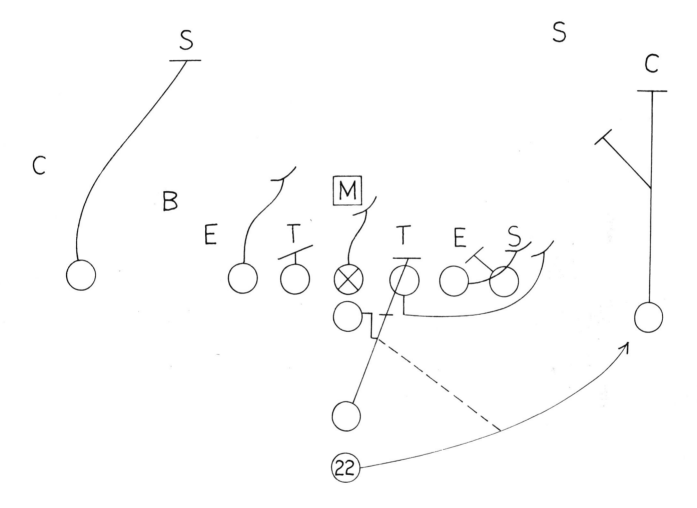

Diagrammed by Coach George Allen

Delvin Williams

He used to play football with a beer can. He used to run on a garbage-littered field pretending he was somewhere else. One time he was Lenny Moore. Another time he was Bobby Mitchell. At night he would go to bed dreaming that he ran for a touchdown or that he caught a touchdown pass. He never believed that he would ever play on a real football field. The odds were too great. That's how it is in the ghetto. But as long as one can dream, then there has to be hope. That's what dreams are made of. Making them come true is another thing. The ghettos are filled with kids who never get out. And Delvin Williams doesn't ever want to forget where he came from.

The star San Francisco 49er running back beat the odds. He overcame the hunger, the sickness, the poverty he knew as a child growing up in Houston. It was an experience he'll never forget. Fights were always going on in the streets. So were the dice games. The dope pushers were always around, too. Somehow Williams managed to avoid the temptations. He stayed away from trouble, even though it was on his doorstep. In his case, the odds were even greater.

Williams never remembered his father. He had left his mother and the other children when Williams was only four years old. In fact, for his first 13 years, Williams lived with his grandmother. He was the oldest. After his grandmother died, he returned to live with his mother, two other brothers, and a sister who was mentally retarded. Every so often he talks about it.

"My grandmother had been living off Social Security," recalled Williams. "But she would try her best to give me anything I wanted. The things she said stuck with me. She taught me to say my prayers, which I still do, every night. She told me to respect my elders.

"We went through some hard times. You had to be tough to live in the neighborhood. I would come home from school and see the dice games and the dope pushers and all that. I never remember having a family doctor. We didn't eat well. When I lived with my grandmother, we had rats and roaches. When I lived with my mother in the housing project, we only had roaches because rats couldn't eat brick.

"Sometimes I used to go with my uncle, who was a landscaper, and cut white people's lawns. I'd see the white kids playing on bicycles and living in air-conditioned houses, and sometimes I used to wonder why we didn't have those things. During all that time, I always said this is not the kind of life I want. I think that's what kept me going. I always wanted to do better."

He turned to sports. It was his security blanket. But it wasn't easy. He tried to play in junior high school, but they told him he was too small. He tried the following year, and they told him they didn't have any more uniforms left. It was enough to discourage any kid. But Williams didn't give up. He finally got a chance to play his final two years in high school.

Williams started out as a flanker and defensive back. However, when all the running backs got hurt, Williams was made a runner. It was something he had wanted to do all along. The first time he got his hands on a ball, he ran for an 87-yard touchdown. He was an overnight hero.

"When I first started playing football, it was just for the fun of it," revealed Williams. "I had no idea of going to college. I just wanted to finish high school, not get drafted into the service, and get a job."

In his senior year in high school, Williams exploded. He ran for 1,806 yards and scored 26 touchdowns. That was enough to attract college scouts from as far away as California. His mother wanted him to stay fairly close to home, so Williams accepted a scholarship to the University of Kansas. When he got to Kansas, Williams received a setback. It was discovered that he wasn't academically eligible. That meant that he automatically lost his scholarship.

Instead of feeling rejected and returning home, Williams got a job at a milk carton factory to earn money for his tuition. He also worked hard and made the necessary grades scholastically. His scholarship was restored for his remaining three years. Williams earned his degree in four years and finished with close to a B average. He was proud of that accomplishment.

"I just wasn't ready for university work," admitted Williams. "I didn't have enough background. Everyone was taking notes in class, and I didn't know what they were doing. I couldn't even write a theme for my English class because I didn't know what a theme was.

"I just wasn't from much of an academic environment. Fifty percent of my education came from the streets, 25 percent from school, and 25 percent from existence. I had a 1.8 grade point average my first semester, which was below a C. At Christmas time I thought about not coming back, but I've always been one to complete what I set out to do. I had a 2.7 the next semester and knew I could finish school. I'm proud that I licked the problem to graduate in four years."

Williams didn't have a spectacular career on the football field. He was always slowed by bothersome injuries like hamstring pulls and ankle sprains. Still, he showed enough talent when he played that the 49ers selected him on the second round of the 1974 college draft. The 49ers' first choice that same year was another runner, Wilbur Jackson of the University of Alabama.

The injury jinx followed Williams to San Francisco. In his rookie season, Williams broke his wrist. He was presented with the choice of undergoing surgery and being sidelined for the year or wearing a special brace and playing. Having gotten this far, Williams wasn't about to quit. He decided on the brace.

He didn't see much action. Williams got to carry the ball only 31 times for 201 yards, which averaged out to 5.6 yards a run. But one particular run caught the eyes of the 49er coaches. In a game against the Oakland Raiders, Williams broke loose on a 71-yard touchdown gallop.

"If I had it to do again, I would play with a brace," exclaimed Williams. "I wasn't about to miss a year of football."

In 1975 Williams managed to see a lot more action. It didn't start out that way. But Jackson started to fumble a lot early in the season, and Williams took his place. He became a starter the third game of the year and never left the lineup. He finished with 631 yards on 117 carries, an average of 5.4 yards a run, which was second only to O. J. Simpson. Williams was the 49ers' top rusher, and he also caught 34 passes for 370 more yards. He also enjoyed his first 100-yard game in his brief career against the Chicago Bears, finishing with 106. It earned him his first game ball.

"That was one of the happiest days that I have had since I became a pro," remarked Williams. "I couldn't have accomplished it without a lot of help. I only wish that I could have split the ball with the backs and the linemen, too. I didn't feel I rightfully deserved it all by myself. You have to try and be consistent; and when you get a chance, you have to take advantage. I've always been confident that I could do the job as a starter."

Williams more than got the chance in 1976. The 49ers hired a

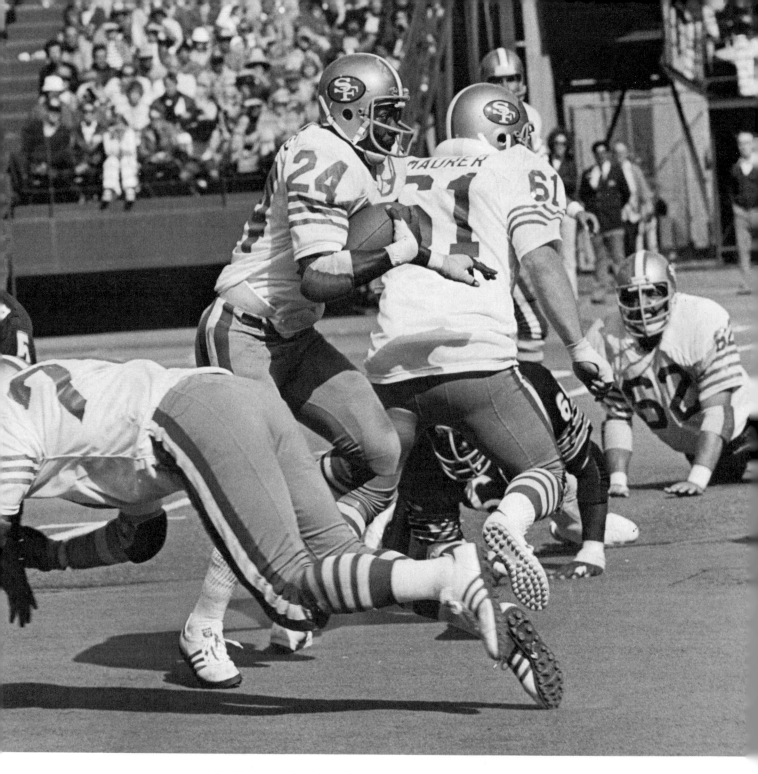

new coach, Monte Clark, who was a strong exponent of the running game. Clark had been with the Miami Dolphins, who were successful in the years he was there with Larry Csonka running the ball. Clark took Williams aside and told him he would get the chance to run a great deal more in his run-oriented offense.

And did Williams ever run. He carried the ball 248 times for 1,203 yards, second best in the NFC behind Walter Payton of the Chicago Bears, and third highest in the NFL. Williams averaged 4.9 yards a run and scored seven touchdowns. He also caught 27 passes for 283 more yards and two other touchdowns. Williams did it all, despite missing one entire game and half of another with a dislocated toe. He led San Francisco to a record, their finest season in four years, as he became the first 49er to gain 1,000 yards since J.D. Smith did it in 1959.

Williams set a one-game rushing record when he gained 194 yards in 34 carries in a 23–20 overtime loss against the St. Louis Cardinals. In that game he averaged 5.7 yards a run as he scored all three 49er touchdowns. By the half, he had already rushed for 108 yards.

In the first 49er scoring drive, which covered 80 yards, Williams carried the ball eight times and picked up half the yardage. In the second drive, which took 60 yards, Williams only carried the ball two times but broke loose for 33 yards. In the final scoring march of 64 yards, Williams ran only three times and gained only five yards.

The following week against the Washington Redskins, Williams erupted again. He rushed for 180 yards, caught four passes for 99 more yards, and once again scored three touchdowns. He tallied on runs of 80 and 22 yards and on an 85-yard pass from quarterback Jim Plunkett in another losing effort, 24–20.

His 80-yard run brought the crowd to its feet. It also left the Redskins with their mouths wide open. Williams took a handoff from Plunkett and started to go around his right end. The Redskins had the play figured and began to converge on Williams. Quickly, Williams reversed his field and cut back to his left. He got around end Dennis Johnson and then cut back inside linebacker Chris Hanburger. Williams got open in the middle of the field and sped untouched for the touchdown.

Although the 6'0", 198 pounder does possess excellent speed, his greatest attribute is instinct. It is something the great runners have. It can't be taught. They are born with it. O.J. Simpson is the greatest personification of it. And he's the greatest of them all.

"Instincts to me are not something you can define," explains Williams. "It's a feeling to go this way or that way. Instincts are when you are running and you can 'feel' a guy on you. You can't really see him, but you can 'feel' him. There is just something in you, and you can tell that he is close to you and that you should make a break. It just happens, and it happens quick, so that often you can't describe it after it's over.

"Maybe I'm gifted a little bit more in that I've got more speed to go with the instincts and moves and quickness. The big key to it is experience. You can have all the ability in the world and not have knowledge of the game, or you can have all the knowledge in the world and no ability; and either way, you won't be able to play. I think it is very important that you learn how to do everything. Running the ball, catching it, blocking. You have to be able to do everything to be a complete back.

"I don't want to think of myself as just a runner. I want to do

everything asked of me. If I don't carry for much yardage but get good blocks so others can do it, I'm satisfied."

There's another thing that Williams does by instinct. Every once in awhile he returns to the ghetto he escaped from.

"I pray that I never in my life forget where I came from," emphasized Williams.

The way he runs, he never will . . .

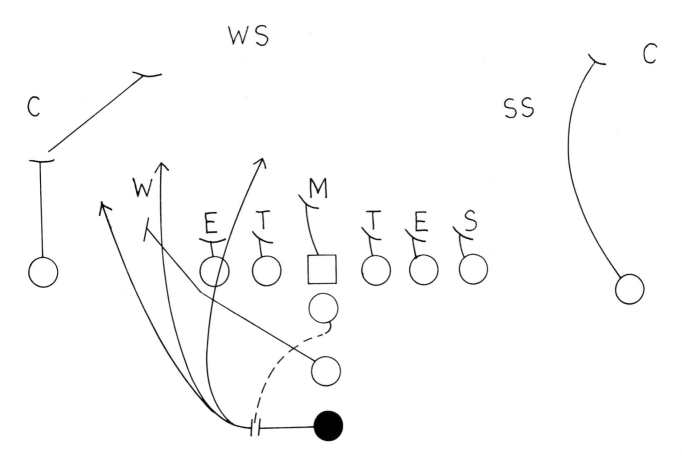

Diagrammed by Coach Ken Meyer

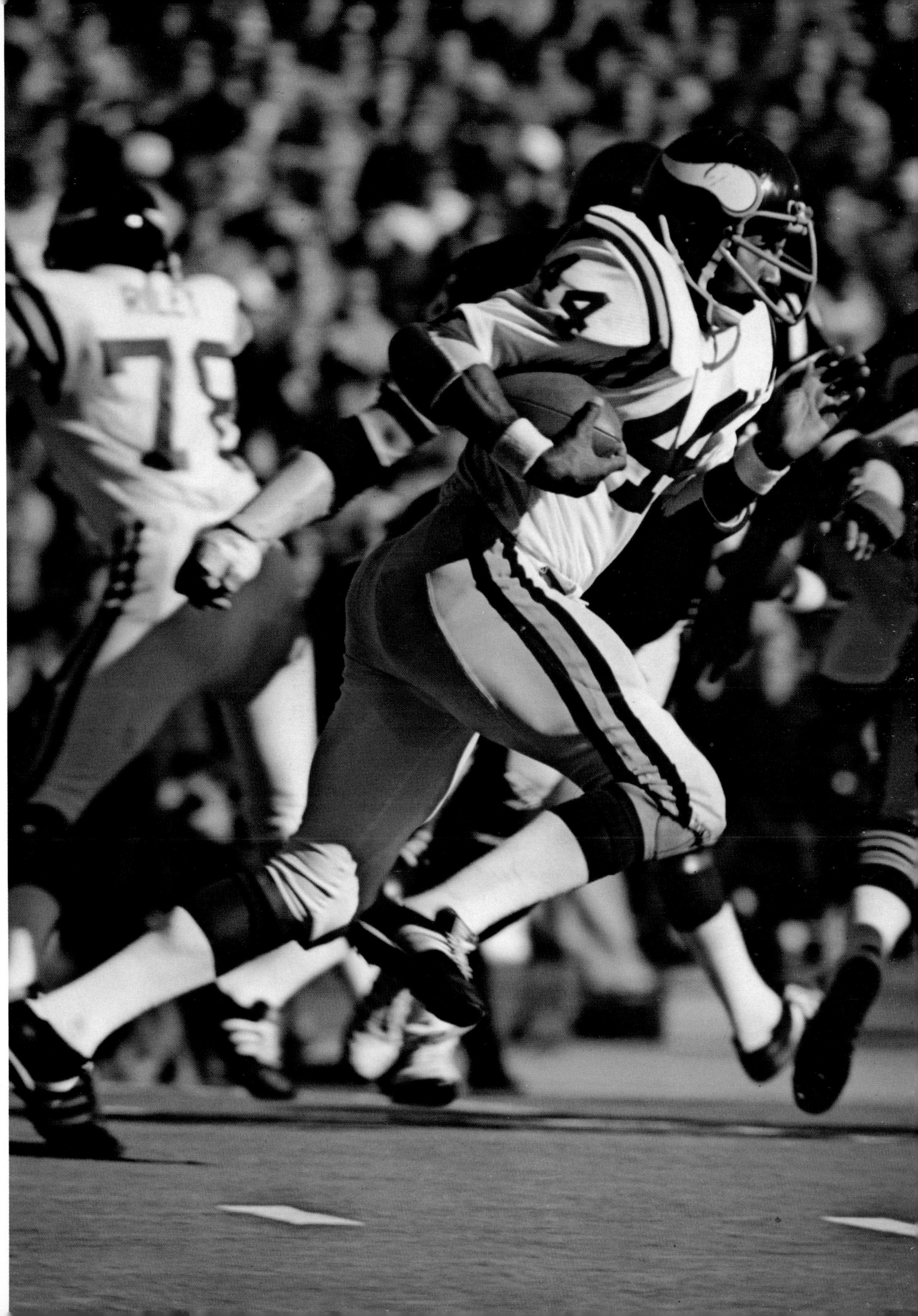

Chuck Foreman

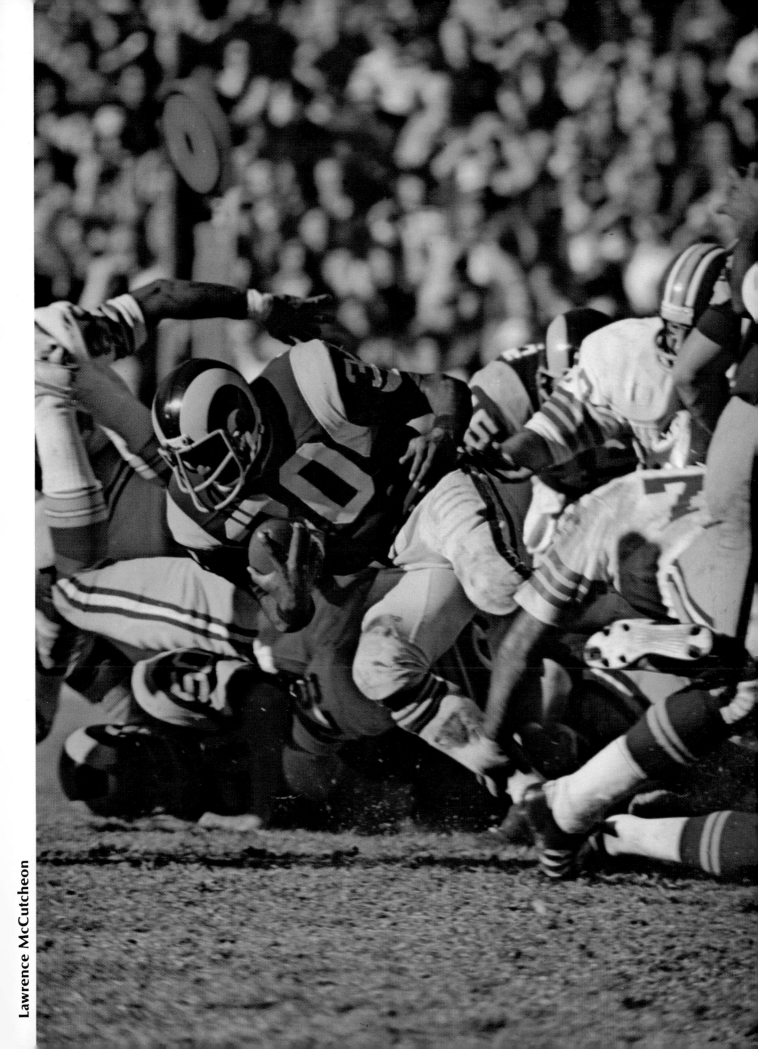

Lawrence McCutcheon

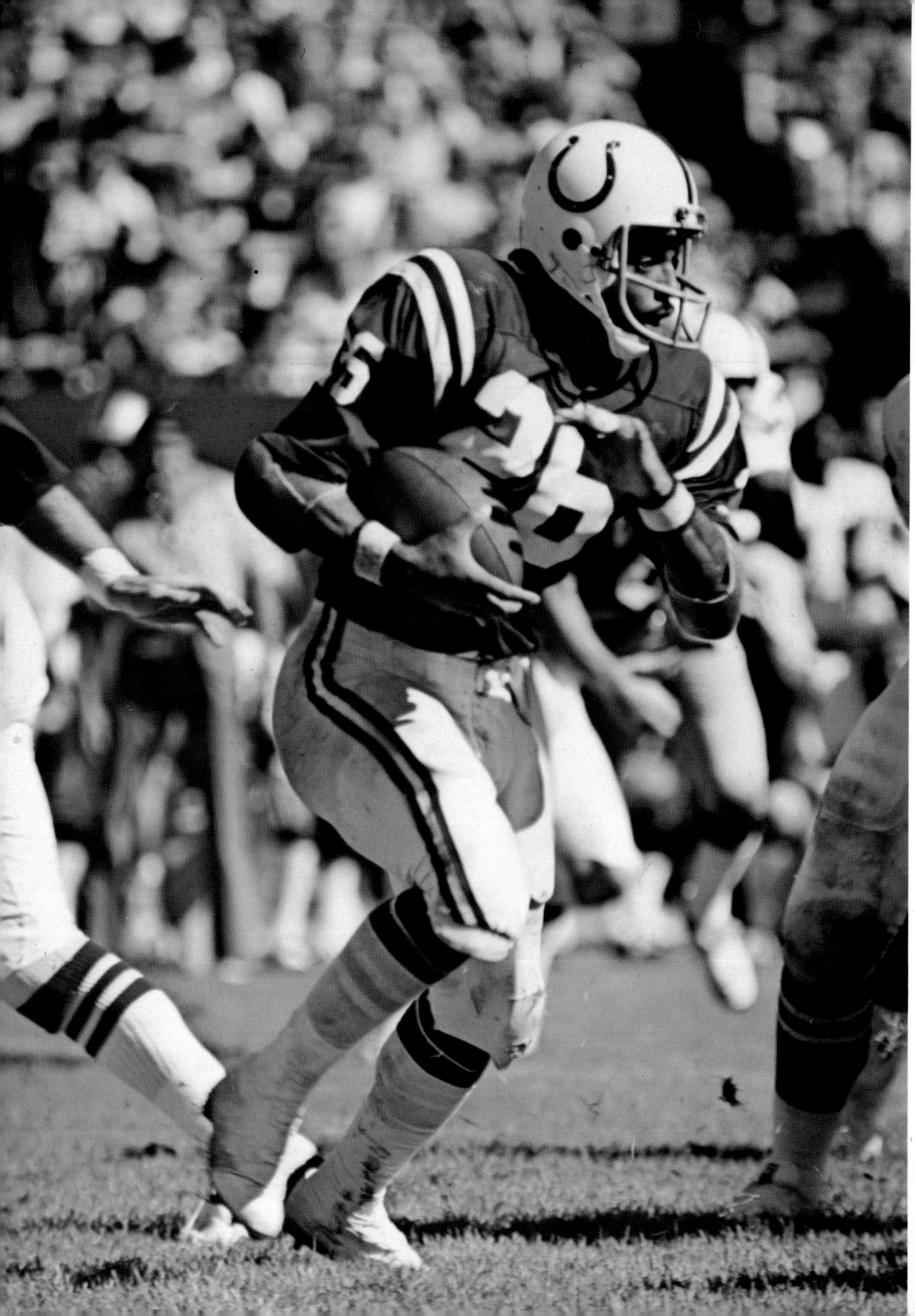

Lydell Mitchell

O.J. Simpson

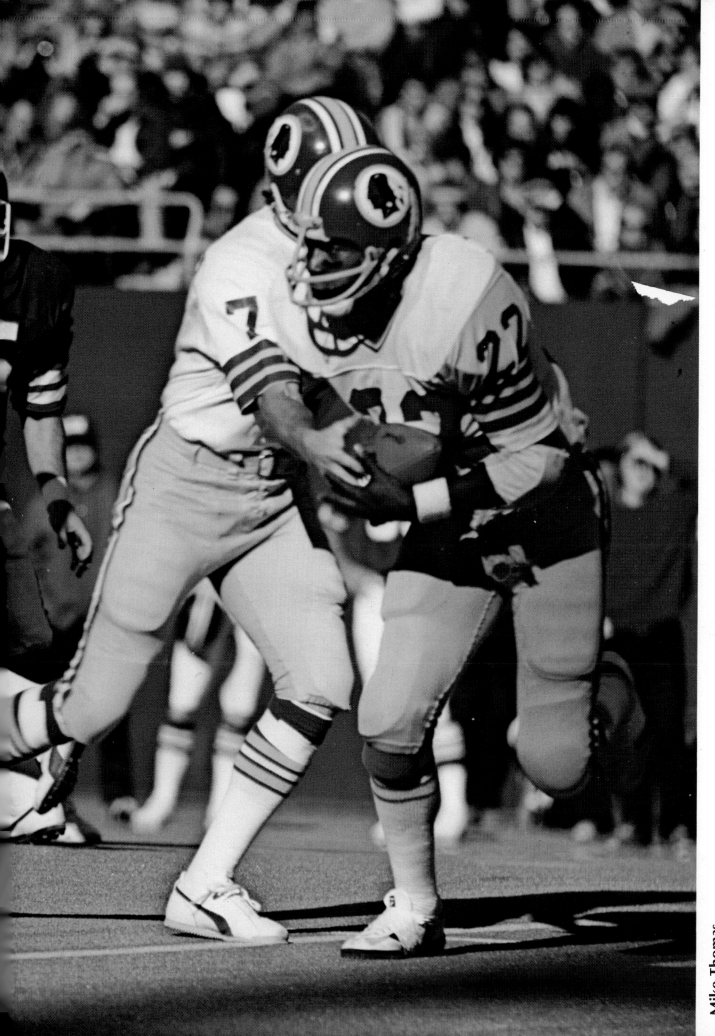

Mike Thomas

Ken Anderson

He was everything his coach wanted in a quarterback. He had size, a good arm, intelligence, and discipline. Mechanically he was sound. His attitude was good, too. He looked like the kid next door, the all-American type with the boy scout image. He was quiet, well mannered almost to the point of being humble. But that's the way Paul Brown likes his quarterbacks.

Ken Anderson was his type of quarterback. And nobody knows quarterbacks better than Brown. When he was coaching in the glory days of the Cleveland Browns, he developed one of the greatest in Otto Graham. He also made a star out of little known Milt Plum. Then when Brown returned to football after a three-year hiatus to build the fledgling Cincinnati Bengals, he had another bright prospect in Greg Cook. However, after leading the league his rookie season, Cook's career was abruptly ended by arm miseries.

All the while, nobody had heard of Anderson. Nobody except the cagey Brown. And, understandably so. Anderson played his college football at tiny Augustana College. And nobody, but nobody, from the professional world scouts Augustana for football players. In fact, only 1,700 students knew that Augustana was in Rock Island, Illinois. That's how remote it is.

But Brown was a sly fox. He knew about Augustana and Anderson. He had received some encouraging reports on Anderson from some of his backwoods scouts. So, while Anderson was still only a junior, Brown began to scout him. Quietly, too. He didn't want

anyone to know. First he sent his son, Pete, to look over Anderson. He reported that Anderson had a "great arm and brilliant mind. A first-round choice if he had gone to a big school. A worthwhile first-round pick for us."

The report aroused Brown's curiosity even more. Next he dispatched his quarterback coach, Bill Walsh, to check on Anderson. He, too, had high marks for Anderson, "an excellent prospect equal or better than Dennis Shaw, Mike Phipps, or Terry Hanratty."

"Anderson was hurt on one of the first plays of the game," continued Walsh. "He got a badly bruised hip pointer. He was hobbling badly and could barely handle the handoffs. He could have quit, because it was obvious that his team was going to lose. But he began getting stronger and had a very fine day considering everything.

"He gave us clear-cut evidence that he could stand up under adversity. That's a major concern when it comes to small-college prospects. He had everything else we were looking for. He was big and strong. He was a clear thinker who made decisions on his feet, and he had a quick release."

Still, Brown wanted to be certain. So he instructed another son, Mike, the club's assistant general manager, to observe Anderson. Mike also reported back favorably. "The best quarterback prospect I have seen in college, more accurate than Greg Landry and Roman Gabriel were at this same stage."

Brown was convinced. Anderson was the quarterback he needed. He carefully plotted his strategy for the 1971 college draft. There were a number of glamour quarterbacks available, Archie Manning, Jim Plunkett, Dan Pastorini, and Lynn Dickey. Surely, Anderson would be missed. Brown decided to go for linemen on the first two rounds and then select Anderson on the third round. It worked.

"When we got to the third round," recalled Brown, "we decided that we had stretched our luck far enough and took Kenny. It was a good thing. We found out later that Atlanta, which picked before us on the next round, would have taken him."

Although he tried for two years, Cook never did recover from his injury. Virgil Carter had replaced him at quarterback in 1971. But by the following season, Anderson had established himself as the number one quarterback. He quietly got the job done, without any hoopla or fanfare. That's another thing that Brown likes.

"You can look at charisma if you want to," remarked Brown. "But, I look at a man's arm, his head, and his heart. Kenny is an all-American boy in an era where most quarterbacks are the publicity-seeking, swinger types. Kenny may be quiet and unassuming, but don't let that fool you. He has the respect of his teammates and he has my respect. He's my kind of guy."

Anderson was getting a grip on things. In 1972 and 1973, he began getting noticed. Not *too* much. But people were beginning to hear about Anderson. In 1974, no one could help hearing about Anderson. He led the league in passing with a 64.9 percentage, one of the highest on record. He didn't stop there. He came right back in 1975 to lead the league again, this time with a 60.5 figure. Ken Anderson was for real.

"Statistics don't mean anything to me," exclaimed Anderson. "The only one I am concerned about is the won-and-lost record. I'd rather be completing only 40 percent of my passes and be 8–0 than be leading the league while the team is 5–3.

"I think I'm a good quarterback. However, I've still got things to learn. But I feel comfortable out there now. I've become more disciplined. I know our passing game better, and I know where everyone is going to be. I feel I am making better decisions about who I throw to. I wouldn't classify myself as a superstar but I think I'm as good as any other quarterback in the league."

He was being modest. It was typical of Anderson. He most defi-

nitely had attained superstar status. Very few quarterbacks in the history of the NFL have ever led the league in passing two consecutive years. And Anderson accomplished this with a young team that was still building. He had carried the youthful Bengals into the playoffs in 1973 and again in 1975. It enabled him to silence his critics, specifically the Bengal fans themselves.

Anderson wasn't too popular with the Cincinnati crowd his first few years with the club. Quiet and colorless, he didn't appear to be a take charge leader on the field. The fans expressed their feelings by booing him. It would have affected any other young quarterback with a struggling team. But Anderson was different. He ignored the criticism and kept working to improve. And he did.

"I became immune to the boos," revealed Anderson. "You have to. I was always confident of myself. And the Bengals stuck with me. It all started coming together with experience. Like mathematics, there's a lot of logic involved in football. You take a problem step by step until you come up with a solution."

Walsh recognized the situation. He also knew that Anderson would make it.

"Bengal fans had been spoiled," pointed out Walsh. "First, there was Cook, who was brilliant as a rookie. But then he hurt his arm and Carter came along. Virg led us to a divisional title in 1969 and was extremely popular with the fans. Ken just wasn't that colorful. But he was developing the rudiments of discipline that would pay off later. His first couple of years was like finishing school."

In the Bengal system of doing things, discipline was accepting the plays sent in from the sidelines and making them work. It was something Brown did throughout his coaching career. He did it by alternating his guards on every play. The quarterback would wait for the messenger guard to bring in the play from the bench. Only on rare occasions was he allowed to change it.

It was strictly a Paul Brown innovation. He was successful with it and he never changed. It took a certain type of quarterback to accept this method. That was discipline. Still, it's not looked on too favorably by others. They feel that Anderson is not a complete quarterback in that he doesn't call his own plays. It's unfair.

The Bengals' theory, advocated through Brown, is that it's the coaches' responsibility to call the plays. They contend that their system relieves the quarterback of a great deal of unnecessary pressure. It also eliminates any second-guessing of the quarterback when some plays don't work. It makes sense.

Anderson isn't upset by it. Not at all. In fact, he welcomes the system. He feels he has enough to do in preparing for a game all week long. Every night he spends two hours reviewing game films of the Bengals' upcoming opponent. He studies scouting reports that

are designed to relate specific trends by the same opponent. And on Wednesday, he receives the game plan for the battle, which he studies intensely, making certain he familiarizes himself with every facet. He contends all this is more important than actually calling his own plays.

"The worst place to see a game is on the field," reasons Anderson. "I'm happy to get all the help I can get. I'm happy to have others share the burden. Now, more and more they're starting to call plays for quarterbacks all around the league. The more complicated you want your offense, the tougher it is for the quarterback to call his own game.

"If you see a quarterback call his own game, it's more a basic game plan, without a lot of innovative stuff. And we do as many innovative things as anybody in football. So what I try to do is think about the defense we might be facing, rather than the play that might come in. And, don't forget, I always have the option to change it if I see something that will work better."

In one game against the Pittsburgh Steelers during the 1974 season, Anderson couldn't have passed the ball better. In fact, he was nearly perfect. He connected on 22 out of 24 passes for a percentage of 91.6 to set a new league record. In the previous game against the Baltimore Colts, he finished the game with eight straight completions. Then against the Steelers, he opened the game with eight more completions for a streak of 16 before he was stopped.

But Anderson is not one for statistics. Nor is he one to compare himself to other quarterbacks. He just wants to perform the best way he can and translate it into victories.

"The other quarterbacks have their attributes," he feels. "I don't do things the way Fran Tarkenton does. I can't throw the ball as hard as Terry Bradshaw. I can throw a ball hard if necessary. But a lot of times you can't throw the ball as hard as you like because it's got to go over people or around them. One of the hardest things I've had to learn is to put touch on the ball. And I probably can't throw as far as a lot of them. The thing is, most of the time you don't have the chance to sit back there and wait to throw the ball eighty yards, even if you could.

"People are always trying to make pro football players into something special, but we're not. We take out the garbage and go to the grocery store just like everybody else. We like to putter around the yard and chat with our neighbors."

Real folksy. Paul Brown's type of guy all the way . . .

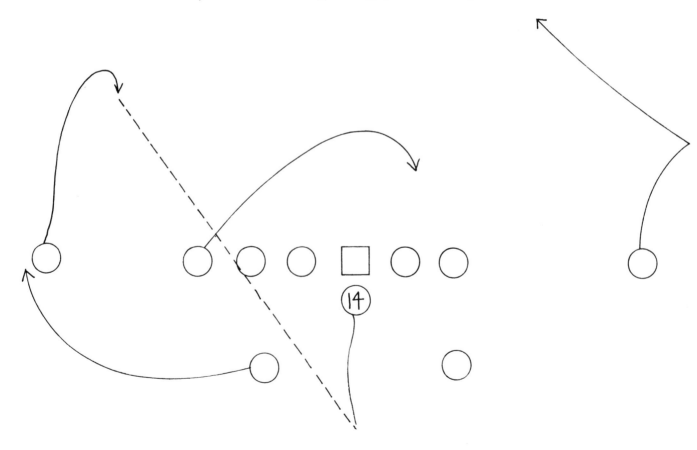

Diagrammed by Coach Bill Johnson

Terry Bradshaw

The words came a little more slowly. He still appeared a bit glassy-eyed. He was already dressed in a sports shirt and slacks. The room was hot and overly crowded. He stood on a platform with the bright television lights directly over him. It caused him to perspire. Yet, despite his discomfort, he answered the questions directed at him. He answered them as well as he could. And then he was led away when he became tired, heading to the hospital for precautionary X-rays.

Terry Bradshaw couldn't actually remember the final few minutes of the 1976 Super Bowl game. He didn't know that the Pittsburgh Steelers defeated the Dallas Cowboys 21–17, until after the game had ended. While his teammates were celebrating the victory, Bradshaw sat in the trainer's room slowly trying to regain his senses. He had been knocked out with three minutes left in the game, one that the Steelers could not have won without him. Bradshaw's accurate passing and flawless play calling enabled the Steelers to capture their second straight world championship. And the one play that sealed the victory was blurred from Bradshaw's mind.

It was the biggest play of the game. At the time, the Steelers were leading 15–10. They had the ball on their own 36-yard line. There was exactly 3:02 remaining in the game. Bradshaw was faced with a tough call. It was third down and he needed four yards for a first down. Should he fail, the Cowboys would have ample time to drive for a game-winning touchdown.

There was no play sent in from the bench. It was Bradshaw's call all the way. The pressure was on him, too. The situation dictated a pass. And he knew that the Cowboys would be coming after him, applying a big rush in an effort to prevent him from gaining the necessary time to complete a pass.

Bradshaw was faced with the biggest decision in his six-year career. The final outcome of the struggle could very well depend on his play selection. In the huddle, his teammates looked up, awaiting his decision. Bradshaw firmly announced "69 Maximum Flanker Post." It was a long pass, a post pattern designed for wide receiver Lynn Swann. Bradshaw was going all the way. Instead of a first down, he was shooting for a touchdown. It was a gutsy call.

As he anticipated, the Cowboys came with a rush at the snap of the ball. They came faster than he expected. Dallas linebacker D.D. Lewis exploded on a blitz. Bradshaw reacted, took a step to his right, and ducked under Lewis's charge. It gave Bradshaw an extra second to look for Swann racing downfield. He needed it, too. Storming in right behind Lewis was safety Cliff Harris. Dallas had attacked with a double blitz.

Bradshaw had his arm primed, ready to pass. Just as he released the ball, he was pulverized with a crushing blow to the head by Harris. Bradshaw dropped right on the spot, from the force of the hit. The ball was on its way and Swann caught it for a 64-yard touchdown reception that gave the Steelers' their final points. It was a picture book play.

Yet, Bradshaw never saw it. While the big crowd in Miami's Orange Bowl was cheering loudly, Bradshaw lay unconscious on the ground. By now, some of his teammates had come over to help him but the quarterback didn't move. He was out like a light. The Steelers' trainer finally succeeded in reviving Bradshaw. Still dazed, Bradshaw got to his feet. He had to be helped off the field, as his legs were wobbly and his steps unsure. Bradshaw was through for the rest of the game. But he was the hero nevertheless.

He had brought the Steelers from behind to accomplish the triumph. Dallas had jumped into the lead with a first-quarter touchdown. However, on the ensuing kickoff, Bradshaw had calmly moved his team 67 yards for the tying touchdown. It was the only other touchdown the Steelers had scored, but again Bradshaw made it happen.

Driving deep in Dallas's territory, Pittsburgh had a third down and one on the Cowboys' seven-yard line. Bradshaw looked up over the huddle and detected the Cowboys bunching up tight to play the run, in an effort to prevent a first down. If anything, Pittsburgh was in position to kick a field goal. But Bradshaw wanted to get the tying touchdown.

Bradshaw didn't have to audible. The Cowboys stayed in their short yardage defense. He yelled out the signals clearly, dropped back quickly, and set up to pass. He watched his tight end, Randy

Grossman, run his pattern accurately. Grossman took one step inside and then broke outside to his right. Bradshaw delivered the ball into his waiting arms for the touchdown.

It was a big touchdown. If the Steelers hadn't scored, they would have been forced into a situation of playing catch-up football. As it was, Dallas led at the half, 10–7. The touchdown kept them close. And it was obvious that the pressure would be on Bradshaw all day. Dallas had structured its defense to stop the running of Franco Harris. At the half, they had succeeded in holding him in check. The Cowboys were willing to challenge Bradshaw instead. It was his game, and he broke it open with his last-minute touchdown pass to Swann. The one Bradshaw never saw.

"I was in the locker room, and the game was just about over when I understood what happened," remembered Bradshaw. "I didn't know it was a touchdown until then. I didn't see the catch. I'm still a little hazy about things. I got hit from the blind side, and I heard bells ringing. I wanted to go deep all day. On the Swann play, I barely got the ball off. They were coming on a blitz. I got hit right here on my left cheek.

"Our strategy first was to run the football, then to mix it. Then I decided to throw more on first down, and then throw some more. I had lots of time out there, great protection. I felt we were in control even though we were behind most of the game."

Yet, during the early years of his career with the Steelers, Bradshaw never was quite in control. The Steelers risked their future on him. They had first pick in the 1970 college draft, and they exercised it to choose Bradshaw from little-known Louisiana Tech. It was the first time in the NFL's draft history that a small college player was made the first selection.

What the Steelers liked about Bradshaw was his size. At 6'3", 215 pounds, he was big for a quarterback. They liked his arm even more. Bradshaw had a strong arm and could throw the ball a mile. Because of his small-college background, there was some consternation among the Steeler hierarchy about selecting Bradshaw. The Steelers were haunted by the failure of past first-round picks. Their trepidation was understandable. In fact, several weeks before the draft, they entertained thoughts about trading their first-round position.

The offers were attractive. They were tempted to take several proven veterans for an untested college rookie. And the way the Steelers were playing back then, they needed all the help they could get. Finally, Art Rooney, Sr., the patriarchal owner of the Steelers since their inception in 1933, illustrated a point.

"All I'm going to tell you is this," emphasized the 67-year-old Rooney to his sons. "If we trade the guy, if we give away a guy who turns out to be great, just make sure we get front-line players. We're experts on quarterbacks, you know. We've had Sid Luckman, Johnny Unitas, Len Dawson, Jack Kemp, Earl Morrall, and Bill Nelsen, and we got rid of them all, every single one of them."

Bradshaw walked into a tough situation. The Steelers were in a vast rebuilding program. The year before, they had won only one game and lost 13. It was through such ineptitude that they were able to draft Bradshaw number one. The Steelers were also committed to Chuck Noll. They had hired him as coach in 1969 and believed in his program. Noll felt that the only way to build a club was through the draft. That's why Bradshaw's selection was a big one.

An enthusiastic youngster, perhaps Bradshaw was overzealous in his approach to professional football. It so happens that success is not achieved overnight. He didn't realize it then, but he had adjustments to make and a great deal to learn. In his rookie year, Bradshaw completed only 83 of 218 passes. He threw 24 interceptions and was sacked 25 times. It was a rough beginning. Bradshaw had appeared confused at times during the course of the season. So much so, that at one time he was benched. The move shocked Bradshaw. He felt his whole world had fallen apart.

"The longer the season went on, the more I was losing my confidence," admitted Bradshaw. "It wasn't the team. Everyone was doing his job. It was I who wasn't doing mine. When the season ended, I just wanted to get away from Pittsburgh. All I wanted to do was go home to Shreveport. I wanted to get away from sports, football particularly. I wanted to relax and get football out of my mind. The way I felt then, I didn't know if I wanted to play football anymore."

Bradshaw improved somewhat his second season in 1971. He completed 203 of 373 passes but still threw too many interceptions, 22. He still hadn't put it together yet. During the 1972 season he improved. He accounted for only 12 interceptions as he completed 147 of 308 passes. Although his percentage was down, he was learning not to force the ball.

In 1973, Bradshaw looked like he had arrived and was ready for stardom. After a fine start, he was injured in the seventh game of the season. He was sidelined for five weeks with a shoulder separation. However, he returned for the final two games, led the Steelers to a 10–4 finish and their first playoff appearance in 40 years. Bradshaw and the Steelers had found joy.

But the Steelers also found another quarterback when the 1974 season began. Joe Gilliam, another strong-armed thrower, had a hot pre-season, hitting on 62 percent of his passes and 12 touchdowns in six games. Noll decided to stay with him when the regular season opened. Bradshaw was disillusioned. After a good start, Gilliam began to flounder. Noll handed the ball back to Bradshaw in the seventh game of the season.

"I felt I never lost my job," exclaimed Bradshaw. "There was just another guy who showed up with a hot hand. Noll never gave up on me. He just had to go with the guy who had the hot hand. I accepted that. I didn't like it, but I accepted it."

The turning point for Bradshaw and the Steelers came in a Monday night game against the New Orleans Saints.

It's not so much that Pittsburgh won, 28–7, but it was the way in which Bradshaw handled the team. The players noticed a different Bradshaw. He had control of what he wanted to get done. He had become the team's leader. By the season's end, he had led them to the Super Bowl for the first time.

"Terry really came of age two weeks after New Orleans, against the New England Patriots," disclosed center Ray Mansfield. "Just things he said and did. He had complete control of the game. He knew it and we knew it. He's been that way ever since. There were times when he wasn't so sure of himself out there, but that's not the case anymore."

Terry Bradshaw has lived up to what was expected of him. He has a couple of Super Bowl rings as a reminder . . .

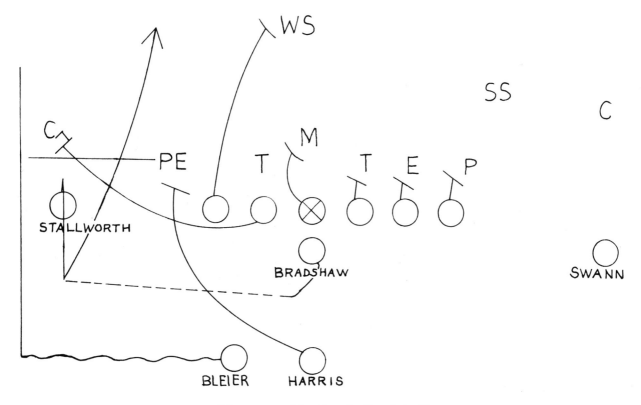

Diagrammed by Coach Chuck Noll

Bob Griese

He was the victim of two eras. The first was the hardest part, the expansion years. Expansion clubs in the National Football League don't win many games. They're not expected to. Not the first year or the second year or the year after that. A guy could get quite depressed in such an atmosphere. And nobody could blame him if he did. There's no joy in losing. Especially when it seems you're on a treadmill to nowhere. When one season is no different from the next. And each year the losses are harder to take. That's the way it was for Bob Griese.

But then another era began for the Miami quarterback in 1970. That's when Don Shula took over as coach of the maligned Dolphins. And suddenly, the three years of despair and frustration that Griese had suffered were nothing more than a nightmare. Football was fun again. It was fun because, that very first season under the coaching genius of Shula, the Dolphins began winning. Nobody expected it. The Dolphins won so many games that they wound up in the championship playoffs. Nobody would have believed it. Not for a team coming off a 3–10–1 season the year before.

But that 1970 season was the turning point, not only for Griese but for the Dolphins as well. It is significant that, as Griese developed into an outstanding quarterback, the Dolphins became successful. Not without some trying moments. After winning four of the first five games, the Dolphins went into a tailspin. They lost three straight games and were shut out in two of them. Griese was in a

115

slump, but Shula stuck with him. It was a major decision in his development. If Shula had benched him, it could very easily have destroyed the young quarterback's confidence. It was a bold move by Shula, and it paid off in dividends for both Griese and the Dolphins.

"I guess a lot of quarterbacks have gone through this," reflected Griese. "It just seems to have happened all of a sudden. People often lose confidence in a hurry. It seems the quarterback gets a lot of credit when things are going right, and then some fans want to use him as a pin cushion when they aren't.

"During that one stretch, I felt I had a couple of bad games. When you start winning, everybody expects you to win every game. The players feel that way, too. But when you lose, some of the fans quickly forget what you did before. I just expect the fans to give me a fair chance. I do feel the pressure around me, but I have to try to ignore it.

"I'm throwing the same way I always have. It's just that sometimes you get the breaks and sometimes you don't. I feel that things will turn around soon, and I'll throw a bunch of touchdown passes all of a sudden. I'm too far along in my career to start changing the way I throw. Like I said, when the team is going good, the quarterback gets the credit. When things go bad, he takes the blame. That's the way it is. The big thing for us to realize is that the three losses are behind us. I haven't lost confidence in myself, and I don't think the others have either."

It was without question a critical stage in Griese's career. It was also his low point. But Griese rose to the occasion and put it all together. He led the team to six straight victories and a spot in the playoffs. It didn't matter that they lost. They were a young team, and there was always next year. The important thing was that Griese established himself as the team's leader.

In 1971, Griese finally silenced his critics. His play calling was excellent, and his passing was outstanding. He led the AFC in passing with 145 completions in 263 attempts, for a percentage of 55.1. He also threw the most touchdown passes, 19, in the conference. He led the Dolphins into Super Bowl VI against the Dallas Cowboys. Although the young Dolphins lost, they had arrived as a championship contender.

They proved that in 1972. Did they ever. They produced a year that no other team in the long history of professional football ever did. Not even the Green Bay teams of the immortal coach Vince Lombardi accomplished what the Dolphins did. They went through an entire season unbeaten, winning all 17 games they played! It was unheard of and very likely will never be equalled again.

But the season was not without tension. In the fifth game of the season against the San Diego Chargers, Griese suffered a broken ankle. The chances of the Dolphins reaching the Super Bowl again were now in the hands of Earl Morrall, a veteran 38-year-old quarterback. He miraculously picked up where Griese left off and carried the Dolphins into the playoffs. However, in the AFC championship game against the Pittsburgh Steelers, Morrall had trouble moving the Dolphins. At halftime, the score was tied at 7-7.

In the dressing room, Shula made a dramatic decision. He decided to start Griese in the second half. He approached Griese.

"Are you ready?" he asked.

"Yes, I'm ready," replied Griese.

It was that simple. Shula and Griese are never ones to mix words. They have a great understanding between them. Nobody in Pittsburgh's Three Rivers Stadium knew of Shula's big decision. The Steelers took the second half kickoff and moved downfield for a field goal. The Steelers edged in front, 10-7, and an upset appeared in the making.

When Griese trotted onto the field, the big crowd roared with surprise. After being sidelined for almost three months, Griese was injected into a pressure situation. There was no tomorrow. This was a game he had to win to reach the Super Bowl. The 15-0 record the Dolphins had produced meant nothing at this point. Shula had faith that Griese, despite the long layoff, could get the Dolphins moving. It was a daring maneuver.

Griese put the ball in play on his own 20-yard line. He faced a big challenge. He not only had to move his team 80 yards but, in so doing, had to stop the Steelers' momentum. Everybody waited to see if Griese could do it. The whole season rested on his shoulders. He had to make it happen. He was the leader.

Taking control, Griese coolly moved the Dolphins 80 yards for an important touchdown that gave Miami a 14-10 lead. Then, midway through the final period, he marched them 49 yards for another touchdown that put the game out of reach. It mattered little that the Steelers scored at the end. Griese had returned from a long period of inactivity to lead the Dolphins into Super Bowl VII, 21-17.

"I don't think anyone can play quarterback without being a leader," stressed Griese. "There is no way. The players on our offense feel I am well prepared. They understand I'm ready to play. I'm not a rah-rah type person. The way I lead is by my presence on the field."

But there was still one more game left. The one that counted. Miami had to beat the Washington Redskins in the Super Bowl to truly make the season a success. Oddly enough, the Redskins were established as two-point favorites. The Dolphins were 16-0 and the Redskins were 13-3, and yet the experts figured they could beat Miami. What made them feel that way was that in their two playoff victories, the Redskins hadn't yielded a touchdown. They had beaten Green Bay, 16-3, and had defeated Dallas the following week for the NFC championship. 26-3.

On the first two series of the game, Griese played it tight. Al-

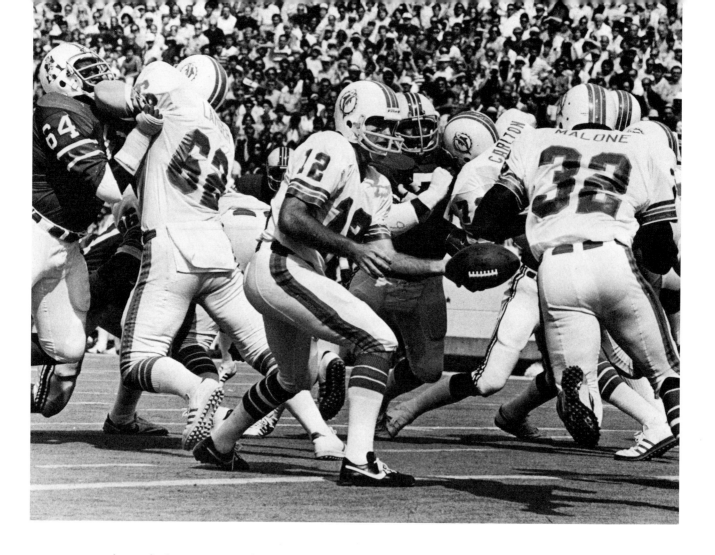

though he appeared extremely confident against the Redskins' tenacious defense, Griese didn't take any unnecessary chances. He was probing, keeping the ball on the ground. Suddenly, without any warning, Griese opened up. He had a third down and four yards to go on Washington's 28-yard line.

The Redskins figured Griese would play it safe and position a field goal. However, in the huddle, Griese called a pass play. Not for a first down, but a deep one for a touchdown. And he didn't go to his prime receiver, Paul Warfield, but to his other wide receiver, Howard Twilley. The cagey Twilley broke down the right sideline, and Griese hit him perfectly as the crowd jumped to its feet. With only one second remaining in the first quarter, the Dolphins exploded into a 7–0 lead. Griese provided the Dolphins with the spark they needed.

Miami had the momentum now. It carried over into the second period. Griese displayed his confidence. It was infectious. The rest of the squad felt the same. He had the Dolphins moving, utilizing both his ground attack and his passing game. He threw a picture perfect 47-yard touchdown pass to Warfield that was nullified because of a penalty.

It didn't shake Griese in the least. He brought the Dolphins right back. With only 46 seconds remaining in the half, he hit tight end

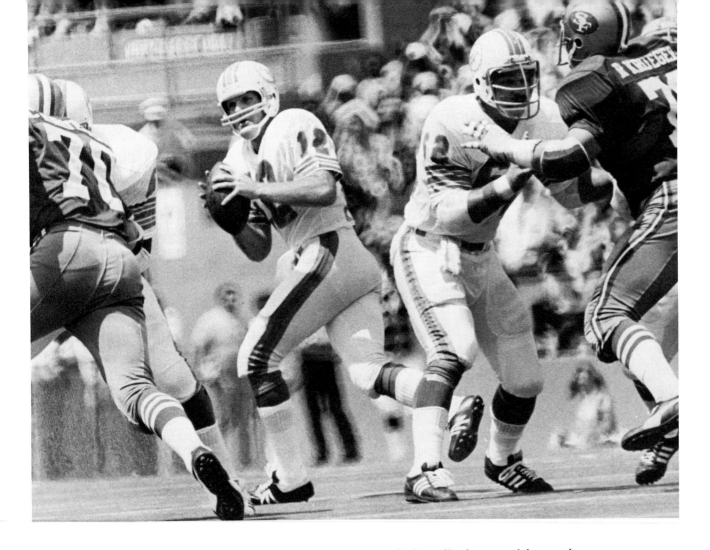

Jim Mandich with a 19-yard pass. Mandich rolled out of bounds on the two-yard line to stop the clock. The Dolphins were close to another touchdown. Running back Jim Kiick moved closer by gaining a yard. Then, with only 21 seconds left on the clock, Kiick followed a solid block by fullback Larry Csonka that enabled him to score Miami's second touchdown to give the Dolphins a 14–0 half-time lead.

Griese was perfect in the first half. He threw six passes and completed every one of them. He had two other completions called back because of penalties. More important, he was in total control out there. Against a veteran, opportunistic club like the Redskins, that was needed. Washington was a team that prided itself in forcing the other team into costly mistakes.

But not this day. Griese kept command the rest of the game as he guided the Dolphins to a 14–7 triumph that enabled Miami to conclude a perfect 17–0 season. He did it coming back from a broken ankle when they needed him most.

"One of the big things as a quarterback is knowing what we are capable of doing and then doing it well," emphasized Griese. "I understand the abilities and the inabilities of our club. We used to throw a lot when we lost ten games a year. Now we are throwing less and enjoying it more.

"I'm not selfish about wanting to throw 35 times a game. We've got both the running and the passing attack. And if we mix them up, and the opposing team doesn't know what to expect, we're tougher to defense. All I want to do is win games. I just want to do whatever we have to do to win. I don't want to throw more touchdowns or fewer touchdowns. I just want to score more touchdowns as a team. I don't care if, on the two-yard line, we run it across or throw it across.

"If a team is tough against the run and we have to throw 35 times, then we'll do it. If we are beating them with the running game and just mixing the passes, then we'll do it that way. There's much more fun in winning as a team than in losing as a successful individual. We had all that a few years ago."

Griese is a quiet leader. He is not one for flair. It is reflected in his psyche. He is a very private person, more of an introvert than an extrovert. But he gets the job done, coolly and effectively.

That's all anyone could be expected to do . . .

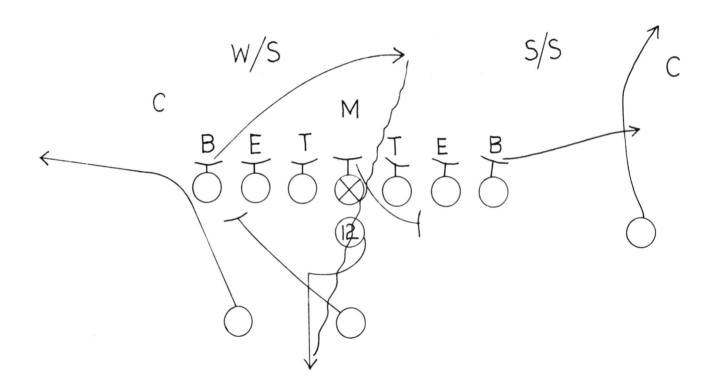

Diagrammed by Coach Don Shula

Steve Grogan

He was depressed. He kept to himself. Most of the week he was walking around with his head down. In the opening game of the 1976 season, he didn't play very well. He had looked forward to the new season with great expectations. So had everyone else for that matter. But he threw four interceptions against the Baltimore Colts. It was enough to give the Colts the opportunity to produce a 27–13 victory. Interceptions are the one thing quarterbacks hate the most. Four in one game is horrendous. It is something you don't forget. Especially when you lose. And when you're young, it can easily destroy your confidence. The way he took the loss personally, nobody knew if Steve Grogan would bounce back.

It was a crucial period. The New England Patriots' success for the 1976 season would be determined in the first month of the season. The Patriots faced the toughest schedule of any team in the National Football League. After Baltimore, they had to play the Miami Dolphins, the Pittsburgh Steelers, and the Oakland Raiders. It was like facing a firing squad without a blindfold. Nobody beats those teams without a quarterback. And the Patriots rested all their hopes on the shoulders of Grogan. They thought so highly of the second-year quarterback that they had traded Jim Plunkett long before the season began.

A few days before the Miami game, Grogan received a letter in his mailbox at Schaefer Stadium. It wasn't the normal type of fan mail. This one was different. It was from the owner of the team, Billy

STEVE GROGAN (QUARTERBACK)   123

Sullivan. That made it even more unique. Owners of football teams don't usually go around writing letters to their players. That's an area they don't get involved in. The players are the coaches' domain.

"I was down," admitted Grogan. "I felt that I had let the team down with the way I played against Baltimore. I got a letter from Mr. Sullivan, and it lifted my spirits. He told me to go out and do my best because he and Coach Fairbanks were behind me. He emphasized that I was the quarterback, and I had to come back from disappointment.

"Then Coach Fairbanks took me aside after I had been throwing bad in practice one day and said, 'Good quarterbacks have bad days as well as good days,' and that he had confidence that I was a good quarterback. I had a lot of confidence going against the Dolphins."

There were other things happening before the game, too. The night before, there was a special team meeting. That also was an unusual event. Team meetings don't usually take place that early in a season. But the Patriots realized how important the next three weeks of the season were. They had to win at least two games if they were going to drive toward a playoff spot.

The reassurance was all Grogan appeared to need. Against the Dolphins, he completely reversed his opening game performance. He completed 16 of 27 passes for 167 yards without throwing a single interception. He also ran for 76 yards. When it was all over, Grogan had thrown three touchdown passes and had scored another himself. The Dolphins had been slapped with their worst defeat in years, 30–14.

Then, to complete the unique happenings revolving around the game, Sullivan was presented with the game ball. It was only the third time he had received one in 16 years. The first one he had gotten was years earlier when the Patriots upset the Dolphins in 1970. He received the other the following year, after the first game in Schaefer Stadium.

"I had read some of Grogan's comments after the game with the Colts, and I could see that he was losing his confidence," disclosed Sullivan about the letter. "I just wanted to tell him the two people who had the confidence in him were his coach and the man who signs his paycheck.

"I even went to see the coaches during the week. I told them I was with them all the way and knew they were doing a good job. I didn't want them to get down, because I felt we had the best team in the club's history. They called me in the press box to come down after the game, and I couldn't get there fast enough. This was the best because we really needed it."

It was a big hurdle to overcome. The biggest one was the following week. The Patriots were facing the world champion Pittsburgh Steelers in Pittsburgh. The Steelers were so good that they were picked to win a third straight championship, something no

team in professional football ever achieved. The Steelers were so strong that they were rated a two-touchdown favorite against the Patriots.

Grogan was far from impressive in the first half. It was a wonder that the Steelers were in front, 13–9. They had fumbled the ball an alarming six times, and all six times the Patriots had recovered. Still, Grogan couldn't take advantage of the mistakes and score any touchdowns. He had to settle for three field goals.

Coming off a strong game against Miami only the week before, Grogan was strangely ineffective the first half. He threw 23 passes and only completed seven of them for 65 yards. What's more, two of his passes were picked off by the Steelers. He couldn't seem to do anything right. He couldn't get a running attack going and the entire offense of the Patriots in the first half consisted of 87 total yards and only five first downs.

It appeared that the Steelers had finally settled down. The first time they got the ball in the third period, they scored. They pushed their advantage to 20–9, which seemed safe enough for their strong defense to hold. The Patriots were on the verge of collapse. The Steelers had moved easily on them, going 74 yards in only five plays. Grogan had to do something fast before the game could turn into a rout.

A good kickoff return gave the Patriots comfortable field position on their own 38-yard line. Two running plays gained 16 yards. Grogan kept on the ground and reached the Steelers' 37-yard line. On a third and one, he sent his big fullback off left tackle to get the first down. But he was thrown back for a one-yard loss.

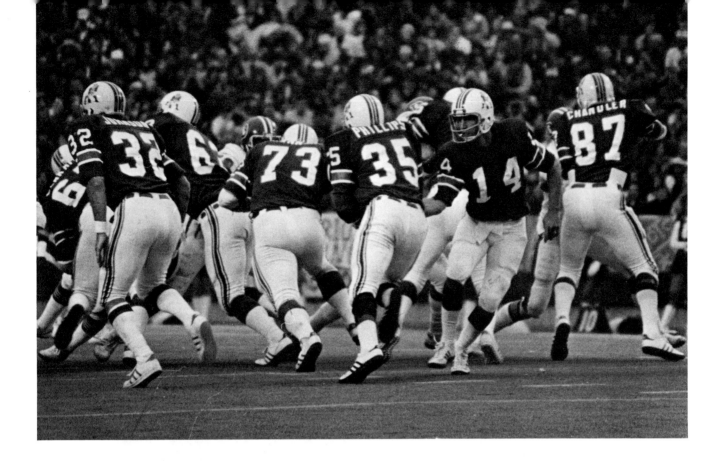

It was now fourth down and two on the 38-yard line. It was too far for a field goal try. However, instead of punting, the Patriots decided to go for it. Grogan called a pass play. He sent his tight end Russ Francis deep and hit him with a 39-yard touchdown pass. It was the shot in the arm the Patriots needed. Suddenly Grogan exploded to cut Pittsburgh's margin to 20–16.

The next time the Patriots got the ball, however, they were in a difficult field position. A Steeler punt had pinned them deep in the shadow of their own goalposts on the seven-yard line. On the first play, Grogan lost a yard. But he kept his poise even after Cunningham dropped his second down pass. On a key third and 11 play, Grogan rifled an 18-yard pass to Francis for a first down on the 24-yard line. Grogan had moved his team out of trouble.

Still, Grogan had to keep them moving. After Francis dropped a pass, Grogan faced a third and eight on his 26-yard line. He dropped back to pass and hit Andy Johnson coming out of the backfield for a first down at the 42. In the huddle, Grogan implored his team to go all the way. He wanted to stun the Steelers with a bomb. He sent wide receiver Darryl Stingley deep down the sidelines and connected on a 58-yard touchdown pass. The bomb put the Patriots in front, 23–20.

Grogan had the Patriots fired up. By the time the third quarter had ended, he had moved his club all the way down to the Steelers' six-yard line, the big play being a 48-yard pass to Francis. On the first play of the final period, Grogan kept the ball and ran around right end for a touchdown that gave the Patriots a 30–20 lead.

When the game ended, Grogan had brought his team back for a

30–27 victory. He had made the difference between winning and losing, completing six of nine passes in the second half for 192 yards and two touchdowns, while scoring the other touchdown himself. The victory was considered the biggest one in the history of the club. The club had overcome an 11-point deficit and poor field conditions to achieve it.

"I was really upset with myself at the half," exclaimed Grogan, "particularly with those two interceptions. But suddenly I thought, 'Hey, you're playing a super team, you gotta make a few mistakes.' So, I decided to keep a clear head and do my job. You know who they are and how good they are. You've got to be a little intimidated by them. But you can't let down. You've got to keep working."

Grogan had shown his team other qualities of leadership that do not appear in the statistics. At one point near the end of the game, a frustrated Dwight White had spit in Grogan's face. Fearlessly, Grogan spit back at the Steelers' big defensive end. On his touchdown run, Mean Joe Greene was drawing a bead on Grogan. To avoid the big tackle's grasp, Grogan stuck his hand in Greene's face and delivered a stiff arm that frustrated his pursuer.

That one game pulled the Patriots together. The following week, Grogan hit on 10 of 14 passes for 165 yards to lead the Patriots to a 48-17 rout of the Oakland Raiders. He tossed three touchdown passes and ran for two others. The Patriots were the talk of the NFL. They had won three straight games against some of the best teams in the league. Grogan made sure they kept winning. The Patriots finished with an 11–3 record and made the playoffs for the first time since 1963. It took a last-minute touchdown by Ken Stabler of the Oakland Raiders to stop the Patriots in the opening game of the playoffs, 24–21.

Grogan finished his first full season by completing 145 of 302 passes for 1,903 yards. His completion percentage was only 48.0, but he had 18 touchdown passes and was intercepted 20 times. These are all areas he will improve upon because he is young and short on experience.

"I think it takes any player a few years just to experience what's going on," believes Grogan. "You have to be in a situation just to learn how to react. You have to experience things, and sometimes it can hurt a young player's confidence. But that player has to realize that he won't always play super and he won't know everything right off the bat."

Apparently the Patriots knew a lot about Grogan. He was a fifth-round draft pick from Kansas State University in 1975. When he reported to the Patriots that summer, he was listed as the number four quarterback behind Jim Plunkett, Dick Shiner, and Neil Graff. His chances of even making the team were worse than 100-1.

Although he had size (6'4") and a strong arm, other clubs shied away from Grogan. After a good junior year, he was bothered by a pinched nerve in his neck his final season and didn't play well. The other pro teams wrote him off. Grogan didn't think too highly of his chances.

"With all the quarterbacks the Patriots had, I never unpacked my bags in training camp," revealed Grogan.

But Shiner retired, Plunkett got hurt, and Graff flopped in his two chances to take over. When Plunkett came back, he got hurt again the fifth game of the season. Instead of Graff, Fairbanks gave the shot to Grogan for the rest of the season.

"Right now, I just want to be more consistent," pointed out Grogan. "I've played some bad games, and I still have a lot to learn."

One thing about Grogan, he's a fast learner . . .

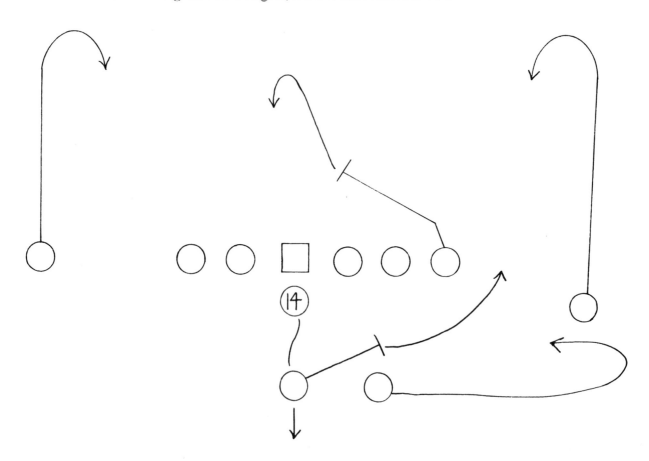

Diagrammed by Coach Chuck Fairbanks

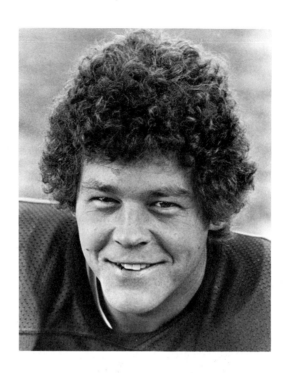

Jim Hart

It was an informal dinner. And it was an unusual one, too. They quaffed a couple of beers and talked. When they finished eating, they viewed films of the 1972 season. There weren't many highlights to dwell on. There never are when a team wins only four games. So they drank a few more beers and talked some more. The evening lasted about three hours. That didn't make it unusual. What did was that a coach and quarterback were sitting and rapping in a St. Louis restaurant away from the stadium, away from the regimen that is professional football.

Oddly, each was trying to establish his identity. A short time before, Don Coryell was named as the new coach of the St. Louis Cardinals. Nobody really knew him. He had been quite successful as a college coach at San Diego State. But San Diego State to the National Football League is something else again. So he took the time to get acquainted with some of his players who lived in the St. Louis area. One was Jim Hart, the much maligned quarterback. He had suffered through two straight losing seasons with the club. When a team loses that much, the quarterback often takes much of the abuse.

The fact is, Hart had absorbed a great amount of criticism since he joined the club in 1966. He had played for two different coaches during those years and never really knew where he stood. And now, there was yet another coach. And with it, more uncertainty. The only difference was that this coach made it a point to talk with Hart.

Nothing formal, like in the coach's office where authority is clearly defined. Rather, in a quiet restaurant where they sat and let it all hang out. And Coryell told Hart a very important thing. He made it clear to him that he was his quarterback. Not only that, but he emphasized to Hart that they were going to win. And if he or any other player didn't believe him, then they might as well leave.

It was quite different from what Hart had experienced during his seven previous years with the Cardinals. Or the first time he joined the team, for that matter. Hart had played at Southern Illinois University. But he didn't impress anyone. During his last two years in college, Southern Illinois only experienced seven victories. And Hart just happened to throw a great many interceptions those two seasons. They were so noticeable that Hart was passed over by both the National Football League and the younger American Football League. He was a bit disappointed by it all.

"I had been led to believe that I would be drafted," said Hart. "I had gotten some information from the Dallas Cowboys. Of course, I found out that the Cowboys send that kind of information to just about anyone who's got two legs and throws or catches a football. But they weren't the only team. Two others, the Los Angeles Rams and the San Francisco 49ers, really showed a lot of interest in me. The Rams called me the week before and asked if I would be around at the time of the draft and for me to expect to go in the upper rounds. So I was very excited, and when the first day's rounds went by and nothing happened, I just waited for the later rounds. Still nothing. I was very dejected, but I still thought I could play somewhere."

If it wasn't for the fact that Hart's coach, Don Shroyer, was joining the St. Louis coaching staff, Hart may never have made it to the pros. About a week after the draft, Hart saw Shroyer at a basketball game. The two talked for a few minutes. Shroyer told him about his new position and left Hart with some hope. He told his quarterback that he would call the Cardinals the next day and suggest that they give him a tryout. The way he figured it, the tryout wouldn't cost the Cardinals anything.

A few days later, Hart got a call from the Cardinals. Oddly, it wasn't from one of the coaches. Instead, it was from the club's ticket manager, Ed Howald. They arranged a meeting. Hart wasn't feeling that well when he met with Howald later that night at a motel in Carbondale. Howald offered Hart a thousand-dollar bonus to sign. Hart asked for more. Howald told him that the front office wouldn't go any higher, but that he would be willing to call and ask. Feeling tired, Hart told him not to bother, that he would accept the offer. So, for a thousand-dollar bonus and a $12,000 contract, Hart signed with the Cardinals. It wasn't exactly a star's salary. Hart didn't know what to expect when he reported to training camp.

"I went to training camp as the fifth quarterback," remarked

Hart. "Charley Johnson was the starter, and they had Buddy Hum-
phrey and Terry Nofsinger behind him. The other rookie was Gary
Snook from Iowa, the fourth-round draft choice. And then there was
me. I felt I could make the team, but I didn't know if I would. I
figured at least I'd enjoy the experience, and if I was cut early, I'd
have time to go somewhere else. I felt I was the better of the two
rookie quarterbacks, and I was hoping that the money that the Cardinals invested in Gary Snook wouldn't enter into it, but I didn't
know."

Snook went into the Army and Hart made the team. He sat and
sat and sat. Finally, in the last game of the season, Hart got to play.
Coach Charley Winner handed him the football in the fourth quarter after Johnson had to leave the game with an injury.

"I ran 17 plays," recalled Hart. "The coaches told me to throw
the ball, so I threw 11 times, but only completed four. I guess I was
just too nervous."

Those weren't exactly the kind of statistics to build dreams on.
Yet Hart dreamed about playing. He felt he could play well if he was
given the opportunity. But that didn't seem a reality. Johnson was
solidly entrenched as the club's number one quarterback. If anything, all Hart could dream about was just playing more. And that
was possible if he listened and learned.

Four days before the 1967 season began, the Cardinals, Johnson,
and Hart all experienced varying degrees of shock. Johnson was ordered into the Army as an officer. He was speechless, and so were
the Cardinals, who were now without an experienced quarterback.
They hurriedly made phone calls to try to get one. Anyone with
some experience. Unsuccessful in their search, they were forced to
go with Hart. After handling the ball a total of 17 times the year
before, Hart was now the starting quarterback.

"I was in my room when the word came," disclosed Hart. "It
was in the evening, and Charley Johnson came by and said, 'Well,
tomorrow, I've got to go.' Charley had said that Charley Winner had
told him that he probably would go with me at quarterback, but I
said to myself, 'No, I don't think so. He'll probably try to find someone else.'"

It was Hart's job. He had to learn the hard way. Johnson was in
the service, and there weren't any veteran quarterbacks around to
help him. It wasn't easy. The most difficult part was learning to read
defenses. It was painful. In his first full season, Hart led the NFL in
interceptions with 30. It's a negative the fans don't let you forget.
The following year, Hart was responsible for 18 more interceptions.
His passing yardage also suffered as he threw for a thousand fewer
yards. It didn't exactly endear him to Cardinal fans, even though he
led the team to nine victories after a shaky beginning. He was learning.

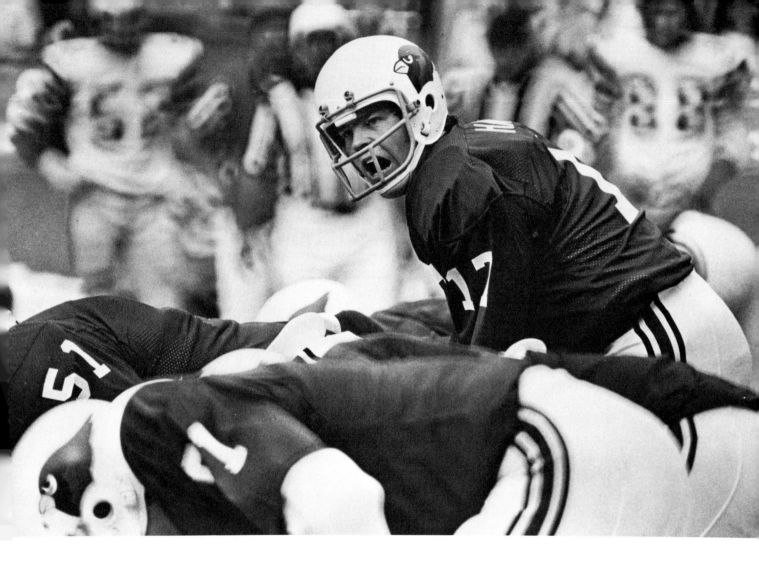

"When you make up your mind about who you're going to throw to, and you go to him regardless of the situation, it causes an interception," explained Hart. "It's really very simple. Sometimes you're bullheaded. You get back there and you think, 'There's no way that defensive player is going to get there . . . I can get the ball there quicker than those guys can get there.' It's a lack of respect, sometimes, for the defensive personnel. It's really a sickening feeling when it happens.

"The worst part is when you hit the defensive player right in the stomach with it. A lot of times you don't see it. A linebacker is running like sixty from the middle of the field. He has a lead on it and knows where you're going to throw, and he's out of your vision for an instant. And just as you let it go, you see him and you think, 'Oh my gosh, it's going to go right into his hands.' That's really embarrassing, because you know that the fans sitting in the stands saw the linebacker coming the whole time. You wish you could explain it somehow. But there's a hole in that helmet, and you know all those boos are meant for you. It is like those fans are throwing spears and they're aimed only at you."

Johnson returned in 1969 and shared the quarterback duties with Hart. It wasn't a good situation. Neither quarterback benefited by it. Johnson spoke out and asked to be traded. The Cardinals sent him to the Houston Oilers after the season, but it didn't make it any easier for Hart. The next three years the Cardinals brought in one quarterback after the other. It was tough on Hart and on the rest of the squad. When the Cardinals had two losing seasons in a row in 1971 and 1972, the boo birds became vociferous. Internally, the team was ripped apart by racial strife and dissension.

"The mental strain we had here in the early 70s was almost enough to make me give up the game," admitted Hart. "The regime we had didn't believe in me, and it was frustrating with the losses and all of that. There were fleeting thoughts in my mind like, 'What am I doing here? I should be doing something else more worthwhile.'"

That all changed when Coryell arrived. After a losing season in 1973, the Cardinals won three consecutive Eastern Division championships. Hart was finally established as the club's regular quarterback and leader. He had his finest season in 1976, finishing fourth among the NFC quarterbacks. Hart hit on 218 of 388 passes, a percentage of 56.2, which was a club record. He threw 18 touchdown passes, tops in the NFC, and his 2,946 yards gained was second best and third highest in the NFL. The boos had finally turned to cheers. Hart had earned them.

Never more so than in a game against the Los Angeles Rams near the end of the season. Hart brought his team from 15 points behind to beat the favored Rams, 30–28, in Los Angeles. He did it with a remarkable demonstration of passing and leadership. Hart completed 20 of 33 passes for 324 yards and a touchdown. But it was in the second half, with the Cardinals trailing, 21–6, that Hart gave an extraordinary performance.

With the pressure on him, Hart connected on 13 of 16 passes for 226 yards, including a 25-yard touchdown throw to J. V. Cain that cut the Rams' lead to 28–27. Two of the passes that were incomplete were deliberately thrown away when Hart's receivers were too well covered. Both occurred on the final drive that began with only 1:39 left to play. Hart coolly directed the Cardinals from the Rams' 48 to the eight-yard line. Then with only four seconds showing on the clock, Jim Bakken booted a 25-yard field goal to give the Cardinals a dramatic 30–28 triumph. The win was a big one for the Cardinals. It left them with an 8-2 record and a solid hold on the division lead.

"You don't have time to be nervous in a situation like we were in," said Hart. "It may have been the best second half performance that we have had since I became a player."

And to think nobody wanted him . . .

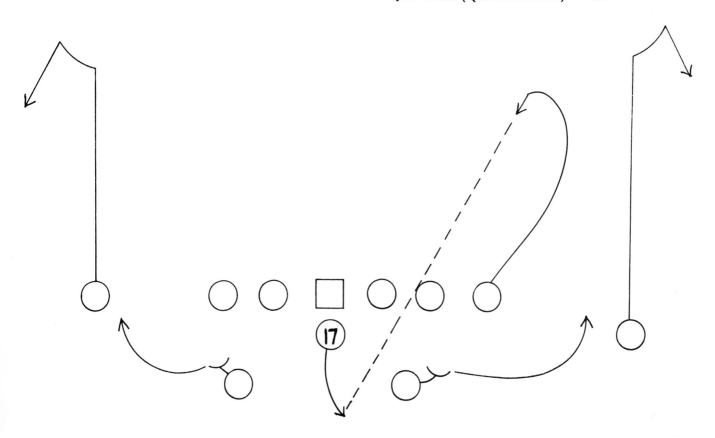

Diagrammed by Coach Don Coryell

Bert Jones

His ribs ached. Every time he took a deep breath, he would flinch. Others would have quit. And without any criticism, either. The score was already 28–0, and it was only the first half. A loss seemed inevitable. No one would fault him for leaving the game. But he wouldn't think of it. All he was concerned about was pulling his team together. The disparity in the score didn't matter. He was being looked upon as the team leader. In only his third season, he had taken it upon himself to be just that. He had to produce. If the team was going anywhere, he had to make it happen. And he did. By the time the half ended, Bert Jones had brought the Baltimore Colts to within a touchdown of the Buffalo Bills, 28–21.

The game was very important to the Colts. After a season opening win in 1975, they had dropped four straight games. They managed to win their next two games, and midway into the season they were 3–4. They had one chance in a hundred of making the playoffs. Jones wanted that chance. When the game finally ended, Jones had brought his young Colts all the way back to a 42–35 victory. It was the greatest comeback in the team's history. The triumph firmly established Jones as the team's leader and made contenders of the Colts. They finished the year with nine straight victories, the Eastern Division championship, and a spot in the playoffs for the first time in four years.

That one game was the turning point of Jones's young career. And for the young Colts, for that matter. It was not unusual that the

success of each intertwined. Under general manager Joe Thomas, the club had undergone an exhaustive turnover in personnel in three years. Thomas was thoroughly committed to a youth program. He disposed of such Colt legends as Johnny Unitas and was scorned and ridiculed. But Thomas stood tall.

What he did was to blueprint that Colts success around Jones. It was a calculated risk that Thomas was certain of. He knew quarterbacks. In building the Minnesota Vikings, he picked Fran Tarkenton, and in doing the same for the Miami Dolphins, he selected Bob Griese from the college ranks. He coveted Jones who was big, 6'3", 212 pounds, had a strong arm, and was an All-American at LSU.

In order to ensure getting Jones in the 1973 college draft, Thomas designed a trade. He traded defensive end Billy Newsome and a fourth-round pick to the New Orleans Saints for their number one choice. Since the Saints had drafted Archie Manning the year before, they didn't feel they had a need for Jones, even though he was a local hero in nearby Baton Rouge.

"This is one of the best young quarterbacks to come out of college in years," claimed Thomas. "We've got the kind of player who can make a franchise. He can run, call plays, take punishment, and when it comes to throwing the ball, I'm not sure that he doesn't have a cannon for an arm."

However, Jones didn't exactly make the Colt fans forget about Unitas. Not hardly. He started the first five games of the 1973 season but was benched. During that stretch, the Colts were 1–4, and their fans were already growing impatient. Jones finished the season on the sidelines, not even playing in the final four games as the Colts completed a 4–10 campaign.

Baltimore's fortunes weren't any better in 1974. In fact, the club finished with a worse record, 2–12. By now, Colt fans were angry. However, significant changes took place. The first was that Howard Schnellenberger was fired as the coach after losing his first three games. He was replaced by Thomas. It didn't take Thomas long to install Jones as the club's regular quarterback. He had unabashed faith in his potential. In the final game of the season, Jones made a significant breakthrough. He completed 36 of 53 passes for 385 yards against the New York Jets. He also set an NFL record in the process by completing 17 successive passes.

Immediately after the season, Thomas stepped down as coach. He quickly began a search for a new coach. He didn't look far. He already had his eye on Ted Marchibroda, the offensive coordinator of the Washington Redskins. Within a month, Marchibroda became head coach of the Colts, which was another significant step.

In the next couple of months following his appointment, Marchibroda spent countless hours reviewing game films. He was evaluating his personnel and spending the majority of his time looking at Jones. A former pro quarterback himself, Marchibroda was well

acquainted with the demanding position. After making notes and formulating judgments, Marchibroda decided to have Jones spend some time with him in the spring. For six weeks, Jones and Marchibroda practically lived together, breaking down films and getting to learn the new coach's philosophy on offense. It was a whole new game for the young quarterback.

"We had to adjust to take advantage of what Jones does best," pointed out Marchibroda. "We didn't try to program him. The six weeks we had him going over our formations and ideas helped him immensely. I wanted him to be himself and let him work his own talents into the game plan. I think he was relieved we weren't trying to shape him into a model of some quarterback who played before him.

"The first thing I told him was to be himself. I didn't want him

to be a robot. I think that's exactly what he wanted to hear. It's unusual to find people with talent like Bert who are willing to work hard. Some think they have the ability so they don't need to spend hours looking at film and preparing themselves. Bert is just one of the exceptional people who's willing to do as much as he has to to be the best.''

No one knew what to expect of Jones and the Colts for the 1975 season. Baltimore fans were sort of resigned to losing with a young team coming off a 2–12 year, and now with a new coach. The best they could hope for was a .500 season. After all, that would be five more victories than they had had the year before.

The Colts looked impressive in opening the new season with an easy 35-7 win over the Chicago Bears. But then they lost their next four games in succession, and it looked like 1974 all over again. But

Marchibroda never lost his faith in Jones, and the youngster hung tough. That's why the almost unbelievable comeback against the Buffalo Bills was so important. Jones had to stamp himself as the leader without any doubts. And he did, with a sensational performance.

There is no telling how much further the Colts would have gone if Jones hadn't gotten hurt in the opening playoff game against the Pittsburgh Steelers. He left the game after his ribs were reinjured after the first series of plays. He didn't return until the fourth quarter. When Jones returned to the game, the Colts were behind, 21–10. He quickly moved them all the way down to the Steelers' three-yard line. However, dropping back to pass, he was hit on the blind side by Steeler linebacker Jack Ham. Linebacker Andy Russell picked up the loose ball and ran 93 yards for the game-clinching touchdown with Jones, of all people, in pursuit.

The 10–4 finish by the Colts, coming off a 2–12 season, was the most remarkable in NFL history. It established the club as a championship contender. And Jones established himself as the league's new glamour quarterback. He completed 203 of 344 passes, a percentage of 59.0. His passes gained 2,483 yards, he threw for 18 touchdowns, and he had only eight interceptions. He finished third among the AFC passers and fourth in the NFL.

"I don't throw any better than I ever have," remarked Jones. "The difference is mental preparation. I can recognize every defense used against us. I realize what I should be doing against it, how to attack it. And the reason I'm prepared is Ted Marchibroda."

Jones's relationship with his coach is almost fatherly. It is just what he needed. Jones has a deep relationship with his own father, Dub Jones, who played with the Cleveland Browns. He, too, is in the NFL record books by scoring six touchdowns in one game against the Chicago Bears in 1951. Jones needed someone to guide him on the field, which Marchibroda did. Nobody realizes it more than Jones.

"We felt that he would be a fine quarterback," said Marchibroda, "but we felt it would take longer. His play calling has been excellent, and he's making the big play more often than you would expect a third-year quarterback to make. Bert can throw the bomb, and he can make the big play, so you have to build your attack and philosophy around that. And he has one other quality that every great quarterback has had, and that is mental toughness. All the great ones—Norm Van Brocklin, Bobby Layne, Bart Starr, Johnny Unitas—they all had it, and so does Bert."

Jones and the players were faced with a sudden crisis just before the 1976 season began. It exploded out of nowhere. Right after a pre-season game only a week before the regular season was scheduled to open. It was big enough to rip a club apart. That was something Jones didn't want to happen.

What had happened was that the team's owner, Robert Irsay, stormed into the dressing room after the game. He was unhappy with his club's performance and got into a shouting match with Marchibroda. Tempers were so violent that Irsay fired Marchibroda on the spot. It was a shock, to say the least.

Jones kept a cool head. He went to Thomas to rectify the situation. Thomas said that he couldn't. Then the next day, Jones called the players together for a meeting without any coaches or anyone from management present. They voted to back Marchibroda and issued a statement to Thomas to that effect. Jones added a personal aside by telling Thomas that, if Marchibroda was not back as coach, he would not return to Baltimore after the season. There wouldn't be a future without Jones, let alone a season. It was obvious that, if Marchibroda didn't return, the team would fall apart.

Within 48 hours, Marchibroda returned. No one knew what

emotional effect the entire incident would have on the players. But this was a young team that had grown together with Jones as their leader. They played the season for their coach and won the Eastern Division championship for the second straight year. And, for the second straight time, they were victimized by the Steelers in the opening round playoff game.

Jones had his finest year ever. He finished right behind Oakland's Ken Stabler, who led the AFC passers. Still, Jones was second best not only in the conference but in the NFL itself. He hit on 207 of 343 passes for a leading 3,104 yards and a percentage of 60.3. He also connected on 24 touchdowns and had only nine passes intercepted. It was some kind of year. Jones almost disdains his accomplishments.

"The big thing now is how well I utilize the other players on the team," he remarked. "I need to make my team better. Football is so much a team game.

"I think it's important to improve in recognizing defenses. Different teams have different systems. Our concept of the passing game is to attack the weakness of the defense. Some teams try to make things happen. We try to take advantage of weaknesses.

"We just play basic football. We line up, they line up, and we attack their basic weakness and hope we win. I can't run any better or throw any better than I do now."

If he could, he would be Superman . . .

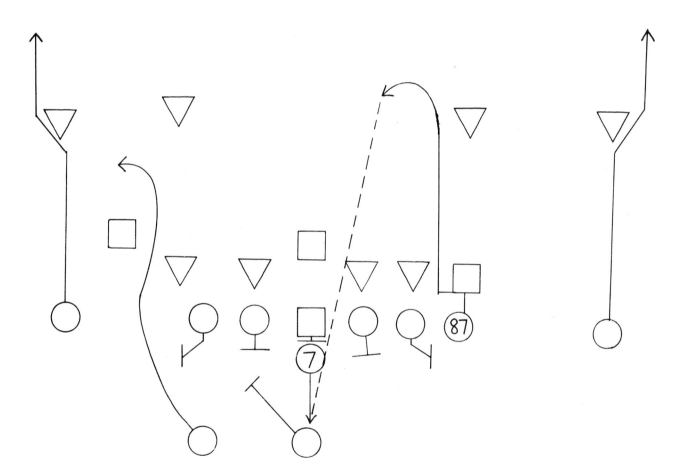

Diagrammed by Coach Ted Marchibroda

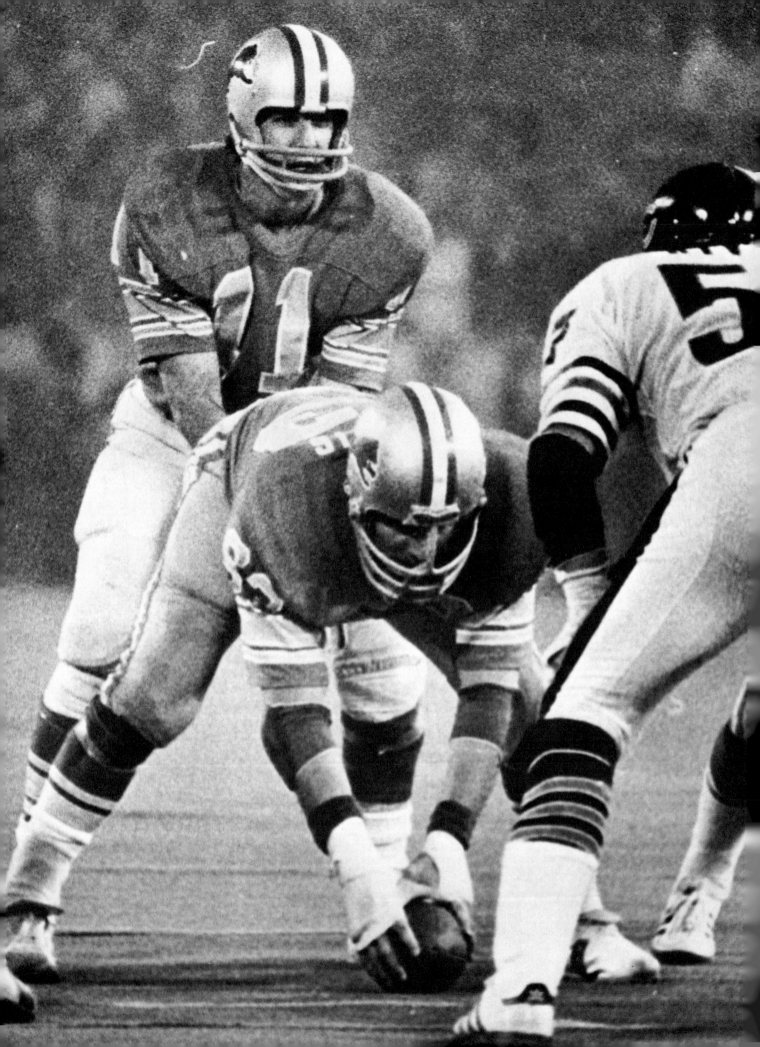

Greg Landry

The room wasn't strange to him. He had been there before. For three straight years now. Three years of pain and frustration. It's a period of time he'll never forget. The surgical scars are there to remind him in case he ever does. But it's the mental part that hurts the most. Lying helplessly in a hospital bed isn't the greatest thing for one's morale. Especially when one feels unwanted. That's the greatest hurt of all. A guy gets to do a lot of thinking when he's alone with himself away from the maddening crowd. The cheers are for the heroes. It was a feeling Greg Landry knew.

Landry was a fallen hero. The Detroit quarterback had missed most of the 1973, 1974, and 1975 seasons. His once flourishing career was ebbing. Unexpectedly, he had plummeted. In those three seasons, he had played in only a total of 18 games. That's not how heroes are made. They have to play. And when Landry played, during the four years he wasn't hurt, he was one of the best. He was so good that he set a club record by starting in 41 consecutive games at quarterback. Not since the days of Bobby Layne did the Lions have a quarterback they depended on.

Nobody knew for certain if the Lions could depend on Landry again. On a cold, gray day in January, 1976, Landry had just undergone a second knee operation. He felt the pain all through his leg. It hurt him so much that he had to have a painkilling injection. All he wanted was sleep. He wanted to close his eyes and wake up without pain. Even the Super Bowl game between the Pittsburgh Steelers and the Dallas Cowboys couldn't take his mind off the pain. He tried to watch the televised spectacle. But his eyelids grew heavy, and he dropped off to sleep. Landry had temporary relief from reality.

Only two short years before, Landry faced the reality of being traded. His name had been mentioned consistently in trade rumors. But that was before he hurt his knee for the first time. Injuries can change a lot of things. But not how a person feels.

"I've been aware of the trade rumors," said Landry the next day. "I think around the country I'm still considered a pretty good quarterback. Even though I've had some bad luck the last couple of years, I think I'm considered a pretty good quarterback around the league.

"I'm happy with the results of the operation. My knee joint has been unstable. I just hope this ends all my injuries, and hopefully the Lions won't trade me. The idea of it doesn't bother me as much as it did for a number of reasons. With this operation, it will be hard for them to trade me. Besides, it's part of the game. You learn to have your suitcases packed. It could happen at any time.

"The trade talk upset me before. Hey, three years ago I was a little younger. I'm more mature now. I'm feeling older. I don't care to go to bars anymore. If I have a date, we're more likely to go to the theater or out to dinner. I'd hate to be living out of a suitcase again. I don't want to be traded this year."

Landry was sincere. He had been under a great amount of pressure the past three years. Management had looked upon him with a suspicious eye. He had played out his option, had been wooed by the Canadian Football League, and had often said what he thought with refreshing candor. He was far from being the ideal company man. Nevertheless, Landry was well respected by his teammates.

The treatment he received from management was far from exemplary. It hurt him. Others would have been bitter and would have lashed back. Amazingly, Landry didn't let it upset him. He could have been caustic and vindictive. Instead, he remained quiet and unyielding.

In the deathly quiet of the hospital room, Landry had done a lot of reflecting. He thought of how suddenly he went from a hero's role to that of a villain. He remembered the ridicule and the scorn. The abuse he suffered was worse than any physical hurt.

"It's hard for me to be bitter," remarked Landry. "But then again, I guess I have a lot to be bitter about. The last three years, I was always getting a knife stuck in me. There were a few frustrating years for me. I had three knee operations and one shoulder operation, and there were two coaching changes in the three years."

Bill Ford, the owner of the club, had personally vented his frustrations over losing seasons directly at Landry. Quarterbacks are always the center of conversation whether it's about failure or success. In a moment of pique, Ford made a disparaging remark about Landry. That hurt plenty.

"The only way one of Landry's passes could hit the ground is because of the law of gravity," exclaimed Ford. Landry remained quiet.

"I'll never forget that statement," said Landry from his hospital bed.

There were other indignities. But Landry rose above them. Like the time he was injured and couldn't play. Still, he wanted to accompany the team to St. Louis. He was told that he couldn't go, that it was not the club's policy to take injured players on road trips. That, too, had to hurt. Everybody likes to feel wanted.

Landry wasn't dissuaded. He purchased a plane ticket to St. Louis with his own money. He didn't tell anyone and flew by himself on a commercial jet instead of the team charter. He sat by himself at the game and visited the locker room when the game ended. The same club official, who had spurned Landry's request earlier in the week, was shocked to see the quarterback standing there.

"Greg, what are you doing here?" he asked. "Since you're here, you can fly back to Detroit with the team."

"No, thanks," answered Landry.

Those were some of the bitter memories Landry harbored inside of him following the operation. Shortly after he was released from the hospital, he worked hard to rehabilitate his much-scarred knee. He faced an uncertain future in the approaching 1976 season. He didn't know if he would be traded; and worse yet, he didn't know how well he could play. Not that he had lost any confidence. They were just nagging doubts that any player coming off an operation faces.

Landry had to face it alone. It was that much tougher because management wasn't exactly enamored of him. The fact that he hadn't played a full season since 1972 also added to the doubts. But in his early years with the Lions, Landry had good years, even great ones. That's what he reached back for to keep his confidence high during the lonely workouts he went through in the months before the 1976 season.

The Lions had a high regard for Landry when they drafted him in 1968. Detroit selected him on the first round of the college draft. He was the first quarterback picked that year. When a quarterback is 6'4", weighs 210 pounds, and can throw a football, he won't last very long in the open market.

Landry didn't play much that first season. The Lions had acquired veteran quarterback Bill Munson from the Los Angeles Rams. Professional football teams always favor experience at quarterback. Somehow quarterbacks are always looked upon as rookies for a couple of years.

The following year, Landry saw more action. He got to play in

ten games and managed to complete half of the 160 passes he threw. He also displayed an uncanny knack for running. But running quarterbacks were not in vogue then in the NFL, and coach Joe Schmidt preferred Landry to remain in the pocket.

When the 1970 season began, Munson was still the number one quarterback. However, in the eighth game of the season, Munson was replaced by Landry. The Lions were floundering at that point and were 5–3. In his first start against the Minnesota Vikings, Landry almost upset the Vikings, losing 24–20. However, in the next five days, Landry beat two strong teams, San Francisco, 28–7, and Oakland, 28–14 (on Thanksgiving Day). Landry went on to win the final three games of the campaign as the Lions finished with a 10–4 record. Landry had led the Lions into playoff action for the first time in seven years.

In 1971, Landry had his biggest year ever. He completed 136 of 261 passes for a percentage of 52.1. His passes gained 2,237 yards, 16 of them going for touchdowns. Landry also ran for 530 yards and scored three touchdowns himself. He was selected for the Pro Bowl and, at the tender age of 24, was the premier quarterback in the National Football Conference.

Landry continued to progress in 1972. He hit on 134 of 268 passes for a 50.0 percentage. His passes accounted for 2,066 yards and 18 touchdowns. His running was another factor. He rushed for 524 yards and scored nine touchdowns, giving him a total of 27!

It all came to an end in 1973. Halfway through the season, Landry injured his knee and was through for the year. It was just the beginning of a discouraging series of injuries. In 1974 it was his shoulder, and in 1975 it was his knee again. Injuries had knocked Landry off the mantle. His future was cloudy at best.

That's how the Lions felt as Landry was preparing for his crucial 1976 season. Would he ever return to the greatness he had displayed before he was injured? Or was Landry finished, victimized by a crippling number of injuries?

Landry wasn't even listed as the team's number one quarterback when the season began. Enjoying that stature was Joe Reed, who took over for Landry in the final ten games of the 1975 season. Landry had to prove himself all over again.

It didn't take Landry long to assert himself. Once he got the opportunity, he made the most of it. He looked like the Landry of old. He even survived still another coaching change in mid-season. Although the Lions failed to make the playoffs for the sixth consecutive year, it was no fault of Landry's.

When the 1976 season ended, Landry made one of the biggest comebacks in pro football history. Although he played far more than James Harris of Los Angeles, Landry just finished behind the Rams' quarterback as the NFC's number one passer by two-tenths of a point. Landry completed 168 of 291 passes, a completion figure of

57.7, which was second to Minnesota's Fran Tarkenton's mark of 61.9. His passes gained 2,191 yards, which was fourth best in the conference, as he threw 17 touchdown passes. Only Jim Hart of St. Louis threw more—18. Many considered the year Landry's finest season.

"I was happy with my season, and I have no doubts anymore," pointed out Landry. "I believe I'm better now than I was in 1971. Experience is one word you can use. Experience is knowing a little more about the defenses, their strengths, their weaknesses.

"Almost 30 is a long time to be on one team. At 30, you recognize your limitations. Your assets are probably on the mental side rather than the physical side. At 30, you're not going to outrun defensive linemen who are 22. Now I'm having a lot more fun after lying in a hospital bed for three years."

It was almost as if he were never away . . .

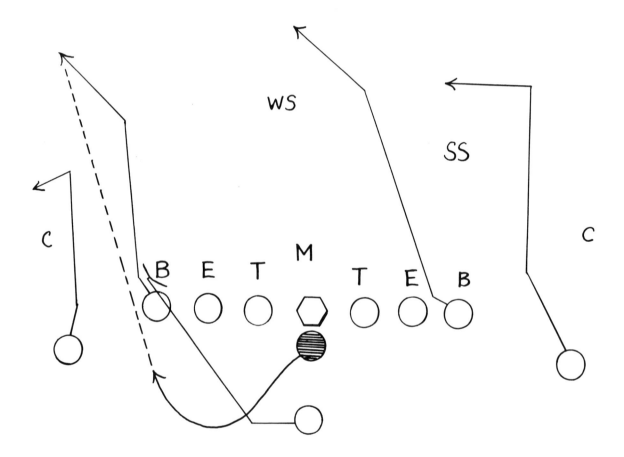

Diagrammed by Coach Tommy Hudspeth

Dan Pastorini

It was getting to him. So much so that he wanted out. All the years of frustration had finally erupted. Before he had sulked. He didn't say anything. He kept his feelings masked. But he finally had enough. The losing was getting to him. He wanted to be traded. He made his feelings known publicly. It didn't endear him to the fans. Not when he expounded openly about wanting to play for another team in the middle of the season. Houston fans began to boo him. Their feelings grew stronger every week. The love affair they once had with the quarterback was now over. The boos became louder. The fans displayed their anger with banners during the game. Dan Pastorini couldn't wait for the 1976 season to end.

Emotionally, it was the worst season that Pastorini experienced. He was mentally drained. The anguish affected his play. Once regarded as the team leader, Pastorini couldn't rally his teammates and lead them to the playoffs. Not that he didn't try to. The club got off to a good start, winning four of its first five games. Everybody began thinking in terms of making the playoffs for the first time in a decade. But then the Oilers went into a slump and lost their next three games. After an embarrassing 38–14 loss to the Baltimore Colts in a nationally televised Monday night game, Pastorini voiced his displeasure. When you lay an egg on national television, it hurts.

"This team just isn't working together," snapped Pastorini. "I had high hopes when I came here in 1971 that we'd build something, maybe even a dynasty. But we haven't built anything."

The Oilers opened the 1976 season with so much promise. Especially for Pastorini. It was reflected in the very first game against the Tampa Bay Buccaneers, an expansion team playing the first game in its history. Although the Oilers won easily enough, 20–0, it was the way that Pastorini took command that made the Oilers overly happy. It was one play in particular that impressed them, one that resulted in a touchdown. Those are the things coaches and players notice and appreciate. They make mental notes of it.

At the time, the Oilers were ahead, 10–0. They had the ball on the Buccaneers' 42-yard line. As Pastorini was calling out his signals, he detected that the Tampa Bay safety had moved in a few steps. Pastorini felt that he was going to blitz. So, he switched plays by calling an audible. He continued his cadence and took the snap from center Carl Mauck. Pastorini quickly dropped back and fired a spiral to his favorite receiver, Ken Burrough. Without breaking stride, Burrough cut into the middle of the field, reached up and caught Pastorini's perfectly thrown pass. Burrough sped 42 yards for the touchdown that broke the game open.

"Dan and I have played together so long I can read his lips on an audible," smiled Burrough. "I can get the call even when the crowd makes it impossible to hear him. I didn't read his lips on that particular call, though. I knew he'd change the play. I saw the safety come up. I knew that Dan would come through."

Pastorini and Burrough have an excellent rapport during a game. They are one of professional football's deadliest passing combinations. Pastorini has a strong arm and Burrough has speed. When they are in consort, they can score with sudden explosiveness. Pastorini and Burrough are the epitome of the bomb play. They are skilled artists in that regard. So much so that they can quickly change the complexion of a game.

Pastorini's passing skills began to improve when the Oilers hired King Hill as their quarterback coach in 1972. A former pro quarterback, Hill has worked closely with Pastorini. They have a fine teacher-pupil relationship. Hill has closely studied Pastorini's progress. As a former player himself, he, more than anyone else, has appreciated Pastorini's play perception.

"With the defense we have now, Dan is less apt to force things to happen now," analyzed Hill. "Up until we started playing great defense, Dan knew we had to score four or five touchdowns to win a game. Dan has always had a certain amount of arrogance, a feeling that his team will win. It's not that he feels he's better than anybody else. It's never been that.

"He's been chosen captain the last two years. That says a lot. That's more a tribute to him than to his position. He used to say things he thought a leader should say. Now he doesn't lead by saying. Now he's a leader by playing. Having running backs who can catch gives Dan a new dimension with the offense. He can manipu-

late more now, too. He knows the running backs, he knows the wide receivers, and he knows a good portion of the offensive line. He has more of a feeling of what the offense can do.

"He's also seeing more on the field, too. He doesn't have to look to throw deep all the time when he's pressured. He'll look right in front of him now. He can think about finding any receiver who's open, he can be coached to do it, and he can watch it in films. But he's got a feeling for doing it in a game now because of his experience."

Pastorini never looked better than in the sixth game of the season against the San Diego Chargers. The Oilers, who were 4–1 at the time, were expected to win. However, they lost a heart-breaking game in the final two minutes, 30–27. What made it such a tough loss was that Pastorini had one of the finest afternoons in his six-year career. He connected on 25 of 39 passes for 329 yards and three touchdowns. Not many quarterbacks have ever enjoyed a 300-yard day. He did it despite being pressured in the final period of play when he brought the Oilers from an 11-point deficit to take the lead.

On a key third down and two call, Pastorini hit Burrough with a quick pass from the Oiler 33-yard line. The swift wide receiver caught the ball on the 44 and sped the rest of the way for a touchdown. The entire play covered 67 yards and cut the Chargers' edge to 24–20.

The next time the Oilers got the ball, they scored again to take a 27–24 lead. This time the touchdown was even more dramatic. Houston had the ball on the San Diego 32-yard line. Pastorini faced a fourth down, needing five yards for a first down. He called a deep pass to his other wide receiver, Billy "White Shoes" Johnson. Seeing Johnson in the end zone, Pastorini deftly delivered the ball into his arms. It was a money play. It appeared that the Oilers would pull out a fourth-quarter triumph. But when the Chargers rallied in the final two minutes for the victory, the Oilers were shaken.

The defeat seemed to have a lasting effect on the Oilers. Two days after the loss, Pastorini escaped serious injury when his camper truck went out of control and struck several trees on a Houston street in the early morning hours. Hospitalized with cuts and bruises, he was released after one day and reported to practice on Wednesday to begin preparation for a key game against the Cincinnati Bengals that Sunday. Both Houston and Cincinnati were deadlocked for the Central Division lead with identical 4–2 records.

"I just lost control," explained Pastorini about the accident. "I was just coming down the street, and I didn't see the median. I used my hospital time to look at Cincinnati films, so it wasn't a complete waste. I'm not going to complain as long as I'm healthy."

Pastorini was healthy indeed. He was off to his best start as a pro. He had completed 55 percent of his passes for 1,219 yards and eight touchdowns. But after the auto incident, stories circulated around Houston about Pastorini's early morning escapades. The press had a field day with it, and the fans didn't let Pastorini forget about it either. Especially after they took a 27–7 beating from Cincinnati. But Oiler coach Bum Phillips defended his quarterback.

"Dan took a bad rap," remarked Phillips. "I never asked him where he was or what he had been doing. All I wanted to know was if he was okay. But he came into my office and told me he was out for a perfectly good reason. Then the stories came out, making it sound as though he had been fooling around all night. Dan reacted the way most of us would if we knew we hadn't done anything wrong. He fought back, said it was nobody's business."

The following week, the Oilers didn't fight back. They proceeded to lose six straight games. During that stretch, Houston's famed defense was practically nonexistent. They had allowed 179 points, an average of 30 points a game. Nobody wins anything with that kind of defense. The Oilers had fallen apart.

In the game following the Monday night Baltimore debacle, Pas-

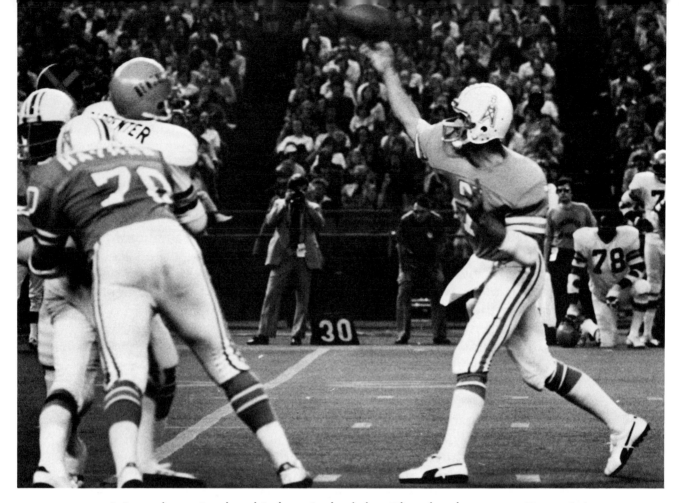

torini got hurt. In the third period of the Cleveland contest, Pastorini suffered injured ribs. He sat out the next two games with a cracked rib. Even though he had expressed his desire to be traded, he had also emphasized his intention to play and to help the Oilers salvage something out of the season, even if it was only pride. He was now in the unfamiliar role of a sideline spectator. His pride was wounded.

"I was told I was the first-string quarterback before the season," lamented Pastorini. "I'm number two now, and the reason hasn't been given to me. I want to do everything I can to help us win. Some people have said that I'm not loyal to this team, and that's not true."

The Oilers finished a dismal season. They lost eight of their last nine games for a 5–9 record. Only the year before they were 10–4 as their rebuilding efforts seemed to have been fulfilled. It had begun in 1971, after a woeful 3–10–1 season. Their primary need in the college draft that year was a quarterback. Their chances were excellent, too. The 1971 draft was the year of the quarterback. The New England Patriots opened the lottery by selecting Jim Plunkett. The New Orleans Saints didn't hesitate in taking Archie Manning. Picking next, the Oilers quickly named Pastorini.

Although he went to a smaller school, Santa Clara, and didn't attract the national publicity Plunkett and Manning did, Pastorini was highly regarded. He had size, 6'3", 215 pounds; he was tough; and he could throw a football farther than anyone. The Oilers had wanted him all along. Not only was he an excellent passer, but he was also an outstanding punter.

In his early years with the Oilers, it was amazing that Pastorini survived. The Oilers were not a good football team. They won only four games in 1971, and then only one in each of the 1972 and 1973 seasons. During that time, Pastorini was sacked more than any other quarterback in the NFL. In 1973 alone, he was sacked 53 times. The Oilers were so bad that they had three different coaches in three years.

Significantly, when Phillips was named coach for the 1975 season, Pastorini experienced his finest year. He guided the Oilers to their finest season since 1962, with a 10–4 record, just missing a playoff spot. Pastorini completed 163 of 342 passes for 2,053 yards and a completion percentage of 47.7. He also managed to throw 14 touchdown passes.

That's why the Oilers looked to 1976 with such great anticipation. Pastorini and the team's finest start ended up in total chaos. Still, Pastorini completed 167 of 309 passes, for a percentage of 54.0, while displaying flashes of brilliance. His passes gained 1,795 yards and 10 touchdowns. He was almost a forgotten man in the end.

"I guess I'm in limbo right now," remarked Pastorini after the season was over.

You'd better believe he won't be there long . . .

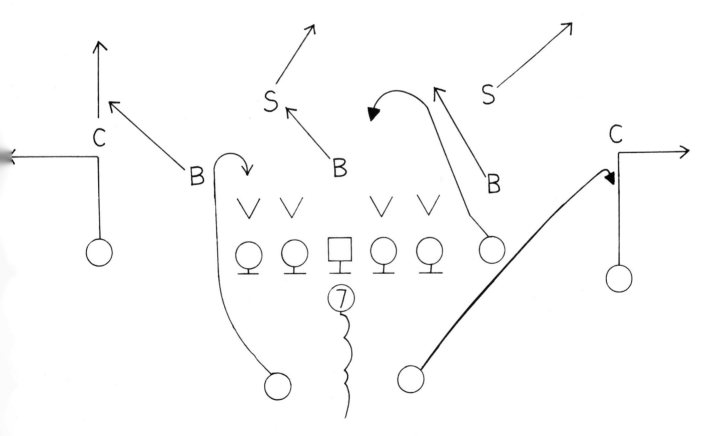

Diagrammed by Coach Bum Phillips

Ken Stabler

It was a moment of fulfillment. He had come the full cycle. There was no remorse now. He was completely relieved. It was a great feeling. Gone were the pains of yesterday. The ones of the beginning. The beginning was filled with pain. There were hurts. There was confusion. And then despair. It lasted for two years. It was like a nightmare. It was enough to shatter a dream.

Only Ken Stabler knew the feeling. He had been there. But at this very moment he was at the summit. He had just finished leading the Oakland Raiders to a relatively easy 32–14 victory over the Minnesota Vikings in the 1977 Super Bowl. But there was no time for champagne. That would come later. Minutes after the game had ended, Stabler was answering question after question in a makeshift pressroom underneath the stands of Pasadena's glorified Rose Bowl.

It wasn't a big room. Stabler stood on a wooden platform surrounded by a cordon of reporters. It seemed as if he couldn't answer the questions fast enough. As soon as he satisfied one, he would be asked to answer another. He stood with his back against the concrete wall, his face sweaty and his hair wet from perspiration. There was no immediate relief. Not for now. It was the price of fame.

Stabler had performed with excellence. Far beyond the statistics of 12 pass completions in 19 attempts for 180 yards and a touchdown. Football goes beyond statistics, especially for a quarterback. Stabler was in total control of the game from the opening kickoff. He set the tempo. He passed when he should have run and then threw when he was expected to hand the ball off. His confidence was contagious. His teammates made the game a rout. It was the most one-sided victory in the history of the Super Bowl.

Stabler was in such command that he didn't call a single automatic throughout the game. It was a tribute to his play calling and leadership. He executed so proficiently that the outcome of the game was practically determined by halftime. There was no drama. All that remained unanswered was how many points would the Raiders ultimately score. That's how brilliantly effective Stabler was.

"I don't have to answer to anyone now," exclaimed Stabler. "We won the big one. That's how they rate quarterbacks. It's the bottom line in our business."

Too many times Stabler and the Raiders did not win the big one. Only once before did they appear in the Super Bowl, almost ten years to the day. They lost to the Green Bay Packers, 33–14, in 1968; and they had been trying ever since for another chance. In nine of those ten years, they have won the championship of the Western Division of the American Football Conference. It is unmatched in the history of pro football.

In 1976, Stabler had his greatest year ever in his seven-year career. He completed 194 of 291 passes for a phenomenal completion percentage of 66.7. His passes accounted for 2,737 yards and 27 touchdowns. It was the best in the league. And Stabler accomplished it all under great pressure throughout the entire 1976 campaign as he led the Raiders to a 13–1 record.

Throughout their winning years, the Raiders' offensive philosophy was to establish a strong running game and pass off the run. With such power running fullbacks as Hewritt Dixon and Marv Hubbard, they were able to control a game offensively. They would make their opponents respect the run and then hit them with the pass. But before the 1976 season began, Hubbard injured his shoulder for the third time in less than a year and was lost for the season.

With the ground attack uncertain, coach John Madden made a crucial decision. He decided to reshape his offense to the pass. He confronted Stabler with the plan, and the quarterback accepted the challenge.

"Ken, we're going to change things around this year," disclosed Madden. "We're going to throw the ball more. I'm not sure about the running game, but I do know what we can do with the passing attack. There may be more pressure on you than ever before because you have to make things happen if we're going to the Super Bowl."

"I'm ready," remarked Stabler. "Don't worry. We'll get there."

Madden put it all on Stabler's left arm. He had to. The toughest part of the Oakland schedule was in the opening half of the season.

They were scheduled to open the season at home against the defending world champions, the Pittsburgh Steelers. Then they had to play five straight road games against the Kansas City Chiefs, the Houston Oilers, the New England Patriots, the San Diego Chargers, and the Denver Broncos.

What motivated Madden's thinking was the fact that Stabler was the NFL's most accurate passer. In three years, 1973, 1974, and 1975, Stabler had completed 512 of 863 passes for a percentage of 59.3. His aerials produced 6,762 yards and 56 touchdowns. There weren't many around who could match his consistency. Madden depended on it. The pressure was on Stabler to deliver.

He didn't wait long to do so. With only five and a half minutes left to play in the season's opener against Pittsburgh, the Raiders were trailing 28–14. Stabler had to overcome the renowned Pittsburgh defense. It seemed an impossible situation, but Stabler is something else.

Just 2:56 from the end, he hit tight end Dave Casper with a ten-yard bullet. It gave Oakland life. A minute later they got hope. With just 1:47 remaining on the clock, the Raiders blocked a Steeler punt on the 29-yard line. They were in striking distance. Stabler knew what he had to do. And so did the Steeler defenders. They deployed into a pass prevent defense and positioned an extra defensive back into the secondary in a determined move to avert a tying touchdown. There was no time to run. Besides, there was no runner to depend on.

So, Stabler dropped back to pass. Three straight times he threw the ball, and all three times it fell untouched on the ground. The rabid Oakland crowd moaned. But Stabler was not through yet. He had one more down. Once again he called pass. Perhaps for the last time. He set up quickly and threw the ball to his swift wide receiver Cliff Branch. Without breaking stride, Branch clutched the ball on the ten-yard line and sped to the two before he was brought down.

Oakland had a big first down. What's more, they were only two yards away from tying the game at 28–28. Stabler didn't hesitate. On the very next play, he kept the ball in his left hand and ran around left end for the game-tying touchdown. The moans of the crowd had quickly turned to cheers.

The dramatic comeback against the powerful Steelers reached its climax moments later. The alert Oakland defense picked off a Terry Bradshaw pass on the Steelers' 12-yard line. Coolly, Stabler completed the kill. He called two running plays designed to position a game-winning field goal. There was nothing the Steelers could do. Only 18 seconds from the conclusion of the game, Fred Steinfort booted a 12-yard field goal to provide Oakland with a pulsating 31–28 victory.

The triumph held special significance for the Raiders. It established Stabler as the key to the Raiders' success for the 1976 season.

Any hopes for the Super Bowl rested prominently on his arm. Bringing the Raiders from behind in a seemingly hopeless situation clearly established Stabler as the team's leader. He was the one individual who could lead them to the Super Bowl.

But it wasn't always that way. Not at the beginning. Stabler endured more frustration than any other Raider. He reported to the Raiders in 1968 full of hope. Oakland also had high hopes for Stabler. They drafted him on the second round of the college draft from the University of Alabama where he had starred for three years. He had played in three bowl games—the Orange, Sugar, and Cotton—which was unique, and was a bona fide All-American. They

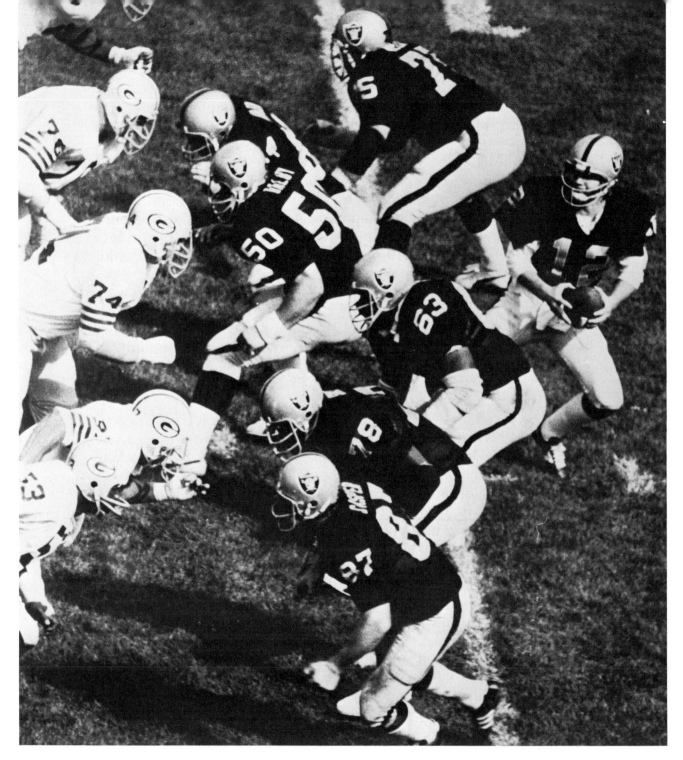

were golden years at Alabama as the Crimson Tide produced a 30–2–1 record. Stabler was the state hero.

With the Raiders, Stabler was just another quarterback. Oakland had a solid quarterback in Daryle Lamonica who led the Raiders to a 13–1 record in 1967 before losing to the powerful Green Bay Packers in the Super Bowl. The reserve quarterback was ageless veteran George Blanda, a miraculous 41-year-old who also performed the Raiders' field goal kicking.

After playing in a pre-season game against the Dallas Cowboy rookies, Stabler reinjured a knee that had troubled him and slowed his development. Instead of having him sitting around, the Raiders made arrangements with Spokane of the Continental League to have Stabler work himself into shape. Disillusioned, Stabler reported to Spokane; but his knee never did regain its mobility. Stabler had to have an operation he wanted to avoid, and his rookie season was a bust.

Stabler returned the following year, hopeful of starting all over again. But he never could get it together. Personal problems forced him to walk out of training camp and return home to Alabama once again. He never came back. He missed an entire season for the second straight year, and there were skeptics who wondered if Stabler would ever play professional football.

Only Stabler could answer that. The Raiders were willing to wait. They felt that Stabler needed time to adjust, to mature. The transition from college hero to pro quarterback prospect had overtaken him. Although Stabler was a free spirit, he was also a competitor. In 1970, Stabler came back to the Raiders. Nothing had changed. Lamonica was still the quarterback, and Blanda was still behind him; Stabler was number three on the roster.

He was resigned to not playing much. But he wasn't discouraged. He wanted to learn. He would sit beside Blanda during a game and ask him what exactly was taking place on the field. He especially concerned himself with observing the defensive formations. At times he innovated. He would call plays himself and have Blanda advise him if he was right or wrong. Stabler did this for three years, learning a lot and playing very little.

Stabler didn't complain. That is, until 1973. By then he had become edgy. He felt he was ready to become the number one quarterback. But coach John Madden decided to stay with Lamonica. Stabler wanted to play so badly that he asked the Raiders to trade him. When Lamonica could produce only one touchdown in the first two games of the season, Stabler was fit to be tied.

"I went to Madden and really raised hell," recalled Stabler. "I told him I wanted to play and that I was tired of going into games trying to make up points when we were behind. I told him I wanted to be traded if he wasn't planning to play me.

"I left the meeting and went out on the practice field feeling relieved. I was loose and decided to have a good time. I completed everything that I threw. I was popping the ball all over the field. After practice Madden came up to me and said, 'You're starting this week. You're our quarterback. We're going to win with you, lose with you, the rest of the year.'"

That was the chance Stabler needed. Against the St. Louis Cardinals in the third game of the season, Stabler started and completed a game for the first time since his senior year in college in 1968. It was a long time. But it had its rewards. He led the Raiders to their second consecutive Western Division title. During the course of the season, he showed signs of brilliance. In one particular game against the Baltimore Colts, he completed 14 straight passes, just one short of the record. He finished the game by connecting on 25 of 29 passes, establishing a new one-game completion record of 86.2.

Stabler finished the 1973 season as the number one quarterback in the American Conference. The Raiders discovered a quarterback, one that led them to the 1977 Super Bowl and their first world championship. The frustration was over, for Oakland and Stabler . . .

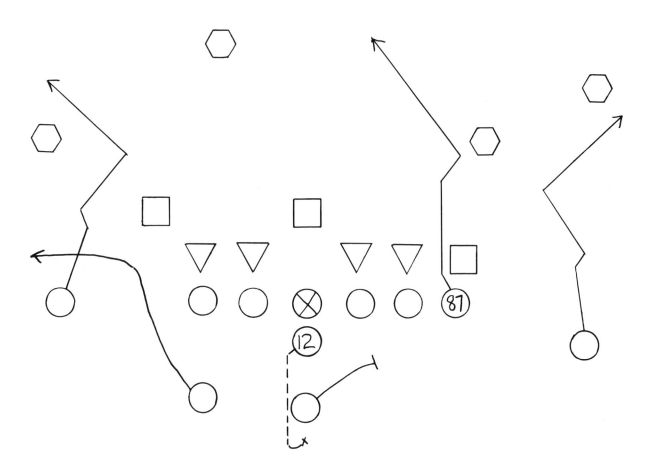

Diagrammed by Coach John Madden

Roger Staubach

The chemistry was wrong. It didn't seem to be working. First one quarterback would play and then another. It had become a guessing game. Who to start, who to keep ready, when to substitute one for the other. It had reached its zenith the week before. The coach had substituted quarterbacks on every play. That had never happened before in the history of the NFL. Even that ploy had failed. Everything seemed unsure. It reflected on the rest of the squad. They'd win some games, lose some games, never establishing any momentum.

Halfway through the 1971 season, they were only mediocre. They had won four games and lost three. Championships are not won on that percentage. What's more, they had fallen behind the Washington Redskins by two games in the Eastern Division race. Something had to be done. And fast. The coach, Tom Landry, had to make a big decision. One that would determine whether the Dallas Cowboys would make another trip to the Super Bowl. He needed a leader once and for all. He decided it would be Roger Staubach.

The situation at Dallas was a dilemma. Landry had operated with a two-quarterback system for the last three years. Strangely, it had met with success. During those three years, the Cowboys had had winning seasons. That is, if one looked at records alone. But the fact of the matter is that the Cowboys had never won a championship. That was the bottom line. They had come close the year before, losing to the Colts in Super Bowl VI, 16–13. It made the club an also-

ran. That's not what professional football is all about. Nobody settles for second best. Not the Cowboys or anyone else. Winning the Super Bowl is big casino. That's where it's at.

Staubach was in his third season with the Cowboys. In his first two years, he had seen only limited duty. Now he was expected to steady the team and take them all the way to the Super Bowl. It was a lot to ask. But Staubach had always had fierce competitiveness. He had had it when he played at Navy, and he had maintained it when he spent four years in the service as an officer. That was what Landry was depending on.

"The prospects didn't look too good to me, sitting on the bench," reasoned Staubach. "I was just turning 29, and I knew I must get on with it. I knew I could play. All I wanted was a chance to play. I wanted to be a starter, have a full career. I didn't want to sit on the bench half my career and play the other half.

"I mentioned my feelings to Coach Landry. I said if he didn't have any confidence in me this season, the best thing to do was to trade me. He said for me, entering my third season, my age was somewhat of a factor. He said I'd get a chance."

Landry finally gave it to him. It was a tough assignment. But Landry also gave him a strong vote of confidence. He told Staubach that, no matter what happened, he would be the number one quarterback the rest of the season. It was what Staubach needed to hear. He wouldn't have to worry that somebody was looking over his shoulder. The job was presented to him, and he had to earn it. He could only do that with his performance under pressure.

His first game as a regular was against the St. Louis Cardinals. Ironically, two years before against the Cardinals, Staubach had been benched. It had really hurt him. He had started the game and had been lifted in the second quarter. Staubach didn't forget it.

"I knew Coach Landry wasn't ready for me," disclosed Staubach. "We were 2–0 at the time. I was playing, and he took me out midway in the second period. I had thrown two interceptions, and we were losing by only 3–0.

"I was very disappointed. I was defeated. That was the first time in my life that I ever felt close to that. I just couldn't do anything about it. I was defeated by circumstances rather than actions. I could have defeated myself if I had played the rest of the way and we lost

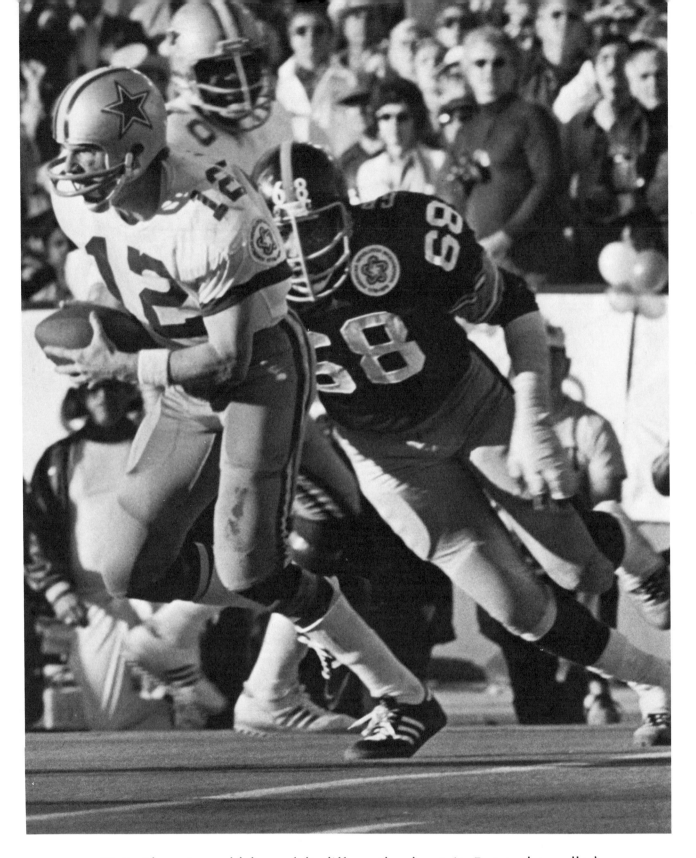

21–0. Then I would have felt differently about it. But to be pulled right in the middle of it really hurt.''

That was the memory Staubach carried into the game. At the half, the Cowboys were behind, 10–3. Yet Staubach didn't panic. He knew he had another half to turn it around. It was a much better feeling than worrying about being lifted. In the second half, Staubach made it happen. He led the Cowboys to a 16–13 victory. The come-from-behind win meant a lot.

Staubach gained greater confidence every week. And the rest of the team began to gain confidence in Staubach. So much so that they won all their remaining games. When the regular season ended, the Cowboys had won seven straight games and were ready for the playoffs. It was somewhat of a familiar setting. The Cowboys would make the playoffs, only to fall short of the championship.

But Staubach was determined. More than ever. He was in a winning groove. He wasn't about to stop. In the opening playoff game, Dallas defeated the Minnesota Vikings, 20–12. That was the first step. In the NFC championship game, the Cowboys edged the San Francisco 49ers, 14–3. That was the second step. Staubach had led the Cowboys into the Super Bowl. But it was different this time. Last year he had sat and watched and never played. This year he was the starting quarterback. What a difference.

The Cowboys had to prove they could win the big one. The stigma of not having done so had haunted them down through the years. In Super Bowl VI, they had to beat the Miami Dolphins. The Dolphins had captured a great amount of sentiment by beating the Kansas City Chiefs, 27–24, in a dramatic sudden death overtime victory for the AFC championship. It was the longest game ever played.

Dallas' game plan was to establish a running attack against the Dolphins. They were confident that they could do so by running away from the Dolphins' star middle linebacker, Nick Buoniconti. They were aware of Buoniconti's quick pursuit. So they planned to start running wide and then cut back against the flow once Buoniconti made his move.

Staubach's passing game would consist of short, play-action passes. In passing situations, Miami's linebackers dropped deep to get into zone coverage; and it was determined that Staubach could hit his backs short. It was all up to Staubach to execute.

He did. He had complete control of the game. The running game worked, and Staubach passed effectively. He hit on 12 of 16 passes for 119 yards, threw two touchdown passes, and was voted the game's most valuable player.

"It was a magnetic experience," remarked Staubach. "The guys were saying, 'See, we proved it. We're the best.' It was great seeing Bob Lilly trot across the field and suddenly jump high in the air. It was beautiful. I remembered a year earlier when he threw his helmet across the field after the Colts kicked that last-second field goal."

Staubach had clearly established himself as the Cowboys' number one quarterback. He was anxiously looking forward to the 1972 season. He was the quarterback coming off a championship season. Everything looked fine. But in the pre-season, the Cowboys didn't look too good. They didn't seem sharp. Staubach started to

press a little, taking it upon himself to get the team clicking. He began to run with the ball more, hoping to ignite the club. It cost him. He paid a heavy price, one that almost ended his career before it really peaked.

The Cowboys were playing the Los Angeles Rams in the middle of August. They appeared a bit sluggish in a game that was tied, 3–3. Staubach tried to get his team moving. He dropped back to pass.

Finding no one open, he decided to run for a touchdown on a third down play on the Rams' 12-yard line. As he neared the goal line, Marlin McKeever, the Rams' big linebacker, smashed into him. Staubach fell to the ground in pain. His shoulder was numb.

When he got up, he held his right arm close to his chest. He knew he was seriously hurt. He had hurt his left shoulder in the past, but this time it was the right one. The one he throws with. He was immediately taken to the dressing room. The doctor took one look and diagnosed a shoulder separation. He told Staubach that he was finished for the season. One play, and it was over. Staubach feared the worst, that his career had ended. He had a long time to wait to find out.

The hard part was recovering. After the pin was finally removed, Staubach began immediately to work out. His shoulder was weak, and he pushed himself to make it strong enough so he could throw. When he began to throw, his shoulder was stiff. There was pain. Finally, near the end of October, Staubach was reactivated. Remarkably, he got to play a little the following month. But he was far from ready.

Dallas finished the season with a 10–4 record. They had made the playoffs. But they didn't seem to have any momentum. They lost the final game of the season to a weak New York Giants team, 23–3. The Cowboys had to get it together before facing a tough San Francisco club in the opening round of the playoffs.

The Cowboys fell quickly behind as Staubach watched from the sidelines. He got his chance to play in the third quarter. There were less than two minutes to play, and the 49ers were ahead, 28–13, when Staubach went in. He got the Cowboys a field goal in the fourth quarter to cut the margin to 28–16. But it looked hopeless. There was only 1:53 left in the game when the Cowboys got the ball.

Despite a blitzing 49er defense, Staubach didn't panic. He connected on three straight passes. Then, after a time out, he threw a 20-yard touchdown pass to Billy Parks. The Cowboys now trailed, 28–23, but time was their enemy. Only 1:10 remained on the clock. The odds appeared too great. Incredibly, Dallas recovered the onside kick at midfield. There was now 1:03 left. They had a chance!

On the first play, Staubach ran straight up the middle and got inside the 49ers' 30-yard line. Then he quickly hit Parks with a sideline pass on the 10. He stepped out of bounds to stop the clock. The 49ers were ready for an all-out blitz. Staubach set up quickly and fired a touchdown pass over the middle to Ron Sellers. Miraculously, he had pulled out a 30–28 victory for Dallas. He had accounted for two touchdowns in a minute and a half against a strong 49er defense.

"It was the greatest comeback we ever had," exclaimed Landry.

In a sense, it was a long comeback for Staubach. He was drafted as a future player by the Cowboys in the 1964 college draft. Dallas

was willing to wait for years for Staubach until he fulfilled his service requirements as a Navy officer. When Staubach finally reported to the Cowboys in 1969, he was a 27-year-old rookie. There weren't many of them around.

So he learned the professional way and waited for his chance to play. When he did, he brought the Cowboys their first championship. In 1975, he almost brought them another. The season was supposed to be a rebuilding one for Dallas; but Staubach led them to the Super Bowl before losing to the Pittsburgh Steelers, 21–17.

"There will be a next year," philosophized Staubach. "We'll come back. We're still young and looking for better things."

There aren't many better than Staubach . . .

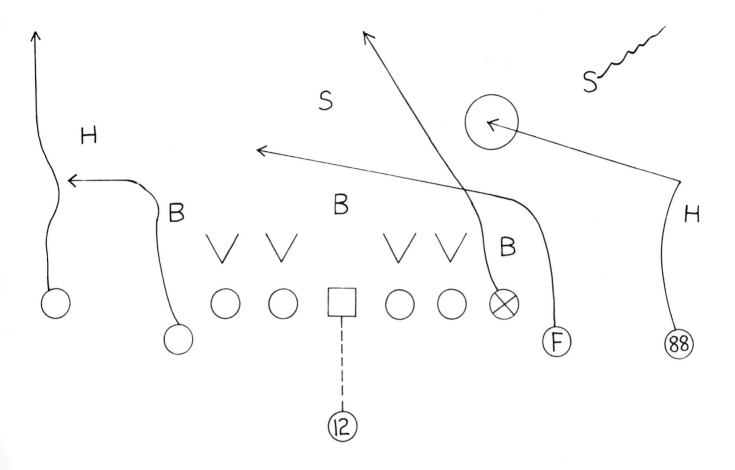

Diagrammed by Coach Tom Landry

Fran Tarkenton

The scene was familiar. Too familiar. Painfully so. He just sat there trying to figure out why. Trying to answer questions that had a meaning. Wondering, just wondering. And all the time it hurt. Deep down inside, where no one could see. The first time it was Houston. Then New Orleans. And now, Pasadena. It didn't seem possible. No quarterback could experience three Super Bowl losses. No one else ever did.

Only Fran Tarkenton knows the feeling. It is not a very good one. Not when you lose. And the veteran Minnesota quarterback doesn't lose very often. Only in Super Bowl games, it seems. It is the only prize that has eluded him in his storybook career. One in which he has rewritten the record books. Records that may never be broken. At least not for a very long time. That's how long Tarkenton has played this game.

But this was the one game that mattered. The one that meant the most for him because he may never play in a Super Bowl game again. At the age of 37, he won't have many more chances at the brass ring. He has to be realistic about his chances. Perhaps this hurt more than the rest. Not so much in being soundly beaten by the Oakland Raiders, 32–14, but in the fact that it could well have been his last Super Bowl. He didn't have the answers.

"We just didn't play any football at all today," said Tarkenton. "I don't have any answers as to why we didn't. We felt we were well prepared, and I think we were ready to play and had sufficient emo-

tion to be ready to play. Yet, when you come right down to it, we didn't make a single big play all day long. Except for the blocked punt, and we didn't score after that play. It hurt."

It didn't hurt anyone more than Tarkenton. A Super Bowl victory would have silenced his critics. The ones who contend that Tarkenton can't win the big ones. It's an unfair assessment. The mere fact that Tarkenton has led the Vikings to four consecutive Central Division championships is an indication that he has won enough big games. Even to the point of leading the Vikings to the Super Bowl in three of those years.

But Tarkenton has always been a subject for controversy ever since he played his first professional game in 1961. Or so it seems. Tarkenton joined the Vikings as a third-round draft choice from the University of Georgia. It was the Vikings' first year in the league. They were an expansion club coached by a former pro quarterback, Norm Van Brocklin.

When he played, Van Brocklin was the classic drop-back pro passer. That's the way the game was played then. Tarkenton was something else. He was not considered the normal drop-back passer. Far from it. Tarkenton was an opportunistic type. Either by fear or design, Tarkenton would scramble around in the backfield. Sometimes he would end up passing the ball, and sometimes, finding no one open, he would run. He had the capacity to improvise. It was definitely not the way that Van Brocklin preached. And the Dutchman was known to be quite vocal.

Van Brocklin had his philosophy, and Tarkenton had his. Neither could convince the other of his philosophy's benefits. The two often argued. Somehow they lasted six years together. Tarkenton was popular with the Viking fans and was their most exciting player. But they reached a breaking point in 1967. Tarkenton asked to be traded, and Van Brocklin quit.

"I run away from contact," emphasized Tarkenton. "I'm not going to sit back there and get blasted. I could never see much sense in giving up on a play, or eating the ball if there is any chance to salvage it."

In 1967, Tarkenton was traded to the New York Giants for four draft choices, which was how highly the Giants thought of Tarkenton. They were a mediocre team at the time and were in a process of rebuilding. In the next five years with the Giants, the club gained respectability. But Tarkenton still hadn't won a championship. Finally, his romance with the Giants cooled. He reached a disagreement with owner Wellington Mara over contract terms, and it was certain that the Giants would trade him. Ironically, he was sent back to Minnesota. Tarkenton was delighted.

"I would have gone anywhere the Giants sent me," exclaimed Tarkenton. "When I was told about the trade, I felt ten years younger. I have a lot of sentimental ties in Minnesota. I was there at the start of it, and I remember sitting in on the first meeting any Vikings' team ever had.

"In fact, I kept in touch when I played in New York, and so did they. In the back of my mind, I envied what they were going through in the five years that I was away. They had just gone over the brink, past the stage of being an expansion team and into the level of contender; and I wasn't there with them. I remember going to the Super Bowl in New Orleans in 1970 when they played Kansas City. I spent a lot of time with them, and I felt right at home."

The one individual who brought Tarkenton back home was coach Bud Grant. He had replaced Van Brocklin in 1967 and the following year had begun building winning teams. But in 1972, a year in which the Vikings finished 7–7, Grant needed a strong quarterback. He had played three that season, Gary Cuozzo, Bob Lee, and Norm Snead; and none of them had provided the leadership that Grant needed.

Grant desired Tarkenton so much that he sent the Giants five players in exchange. It was the greatest trade he ever made, and one that he'll never regret throughout his coaching career.

"I don't think there is any question that he is going to go down as the greatest quarterback to ever play this game," said Grant. "He is going to own all the statistics when he's through. But his greatest single asset is his enthusiasm for every part of the game.

"He is interested in every other player and every other team. He

is not a doubter, he is a doer. He assumes responsibility not only for himself but for every other player on the team. When he calls a play, he has a vision of what every player, his and the other team's, will do. He is always following a plan. He doesn't grab-bag. You watch his selection of plays, and he's building toward something. He reacts well to the blitz. He's as good as you'll find at spotting the open receiver."

Tarkenton paid dividends his very first year back with the Vikings. In 1973, he led the Vikings to the Super Bowl. However, he couldn't lead them past the Miami Dolphins who won the championship for the second straight time, 24–7. The next year he brought them right back, but once again they were defeated, this time by the Pittsburgh Steelers, 16–6.

Still, despite the frustration of defeat, Tarkenton has remained philosophical. He just scoffs at critics who sneer at his championship losses.

"I don't think any individual wins the Super Bowl, and I don't think any individual loses the Super Bowl," reasons Tarkenton. "That's a team goal, that's a goal all of us here have, a goal every team has. A lot of things have to happen to make it happen. It's not an easy thing. You can have the best team and not win it. You can have a lesser team and win it.

"I've been in two of them, and we haven't won; but I don't look back and say what a terrible, terrible thing that we didn't win and how awful it is. I think we have a good chance to go back, and it would be a tremendously satisfying thing for me. It would be the highest satisfaction for me because team goals are much more meaningful than individual goals. If I could win one Super Bowl and not end up with the most touchdown passes or the most yards passing, I'd take that first from a team standpoint. It's much more reinforcing. Every quarterback worth his salt has been criticized during his career. It's the nature of the position; it's a love-hate position. Everybody has an opinion about the quarterback."

Otto Graham, one of the all-time quarterback greats, has his opinion of Tarkenton. He's been around long enough to judge the position he played, and he has nothing but praise for Tarkenton.

"First, Tarkenton is very clever; and he is quick, with a good sense of what is going on around him," remarked Graham. "There are four qualities a great quarterback must possess: leadership, passing ability, football knowledge, and good mechanics. Most important, I think, is leadership. Bart Starr was the best example of that kind of leadership, a person who commands respect from his teammates. Tarkenton has that quality."

In his four years with the Vikings, Tarkenton has demonstrated his leadership. The Vikings did win their division in 1975, and many felt that they would be appearing in the Super Bowl for the third consecutive time. However, in the opening playoff game against the Dallas Cowboys, they were beaten, 17–14, on a last-minute pass play.

Still, he brought them back in 1976, a season in which he shattered all the passing records in pro football annals. His statistics are mind boggling. After 16 seasons, Tarkenton has thrown more passes, 5,637; completed more passes, 3,186; thrown more touchdown passes, 306; and gained more yards by passing, 41,801. In addition, he has run for more yardage, 3,669, than any quarterback who ever played the game.

He has gotten better with age. His two most successful seasons were in 1975 and 1976. In 1975, he hit on 273 of 425 passes for a percentage of 64.2. And last year he connected on 255 of 412 for a percentage of 61.9. The assault on the record books is one thing the critics can't take away from Tarkenton.

"It took a long time for established pro football writers and pro football people to accept me because I wasn't the classic mold of what they thought a quarterback should be," snapped Tarkenton. "I

wasn't strong enough; I wasn't big enough; and, of all things, I actually ran out of the pocket. That was a dastardly thing to do, for a quarterback to scramble around. Of course, they said I'd get killed. They said I wouldn't get past the first few years because I did it.

"So, I find it very interesting as I get to this point in my career. I find it very rewarding because I think you have to look at the data of what people do and not what you think they can't do or what you think their limitations are from the standpoint of size and strength. And I think the data has come through quite well.

"It's true I don't have a strong passing arm. The longest pass I ever completed in the pros covered only 57 yards in the air. As a matter of fact, in all the years I've played, I never had a backup quarterback whose arm wasn't stronger than mine. The difference has been that I am a passer, not a thrower.

"I think the records I've established will mean a lot more to me when I'm retired and I look back at what I did. This is mostly a team sport, and the whole reinforcement is to play for the team to win. I'd be very pleased if I didn't have to throw a pass all year and we'd win our championship and go on and win the Super Bowl."

That's the only thing missing. Tarkenton would like nothing better than to fill in the blank line. No one can deny he's done everything else . . .

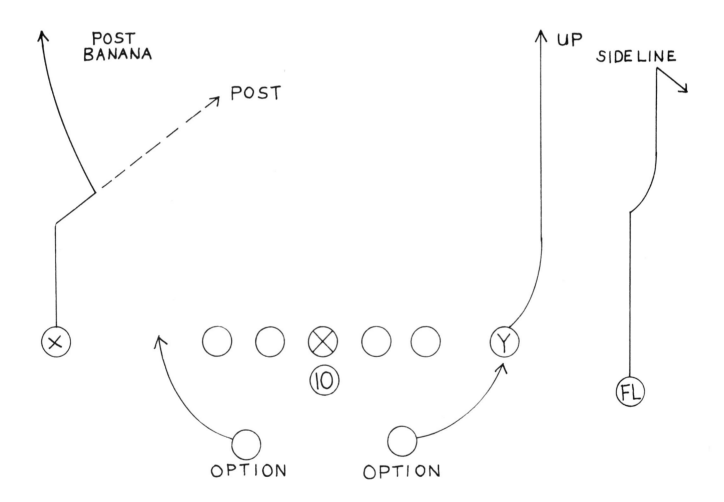

Diagrammed by Coach Bud Grant

The Receivers...

Fred Biletnikoff

He was an unlikely hero. His long hair hung down unruly. It was wet at the ends, almost in ringlets. The black charcoal underneath his eyes was smeared. He sat with a can of soda in one hand and a cigarette in the other. He leaned against the wall in a wet T-shirt. Every now and then he would lean forward to answer a question. The room was quite crowded and noisy, which made it difficult to hear. Yet he appeared relaxed. Which isn't something Fred Biletnikoff does very often during the course of a football season.

But today was something else. The Oakland Raiders had just won their first world championship. They easily handled the Minnesota Vikings, 32–14, in a game in which Biletnikoff was voted the most valuable player. It was a high honor because there were other outstanding players on the field. While the day belonged to the Raiders, it was special to Biletnikoff.

It was special because Biletnikoff didn't score any touchdowns. He didn't catch many passes, either. All he caught were four. Which doesn't seem like much. Not in relation to statistics. But three of the passes that Biletnikoff grabbed led directly to touchdowns. That's something statistics don't reveal. They also don't reveal the drama and importance of the plays.

Innocently enough, Biletnikoff's first reception yielded only nine yards. But the next three he caught ultimately proved to be the difference in the game. And the catches he made were just short of sensational. Two were on the acrobatic side, and the last one went for big yardage. That's what makes Biletnikoff so valuable.

Early in the second period, the Raiders were deep in Minnesota territory. They had a third down and three on the Vikings' six-yard line. They were ahead, 3–0, but needed a first down. They desperately wanted a touchdown to open up the game and put pressure on the Vikings. It was a clutch ball. Quarterback Ken Stabler called Biletnikoff's number in the huddle. He directed Biletnikoff on a quick turn in and fired a five-yard pass that his veteran wide receiver clutched as he was falling to the ground. On the next play, the Raiders scored their first touchdown.

Then, five minutes from the end of the period, Stabler and Biletnikoff connected again. With a first down on the Vikings' 18-yard line, Stabler sent Biletnikoff on an out pattern. Stabler threw, and Biletnikoff reached up high to snare the ball with cornerback Nate Wright all over him. He got the Raiders down to the one-yard line again. It took just one play to get their second touchdown and a 16–0 lead.

The Vikings didn't feel Biletnikoff's presence until the final quarter. In the meantime, they had reduced Oakland's margin to 19–7 and appeared to be picking up momentum for a game-winning rally. There were about nine minutes remaining to play, and the Raiders had a third and six at midfield. If the Vikings could hold and then come back and score, then Oakland would feel the pressure.

It was a passing situation. Stabler dropped back and looked over the middle for tight end Dave Casper, who was his primary receiver on the play. However, Casper was guarded closely. Stabler couldn't risk an interception at this point in the game. He quickly turned and looked for Biletnikoff. Stabler found him open on the 35-yard line and threw. Biletnikoff caught the ball without breaking stride and ran all the way down to the Vikings' two-yard line before he was finally stopped. The 48-yard play broke Minnesota's back. The Raiders went in on the very next play to increase their advantage to 26–7 and to kill the Vikings' chances for any comeback.

"I was surprised to hear that I was named the game's most valuable player," smiled Biletnikoff afterward. "I was so surprised I didn't know what to say at first. I would have liked to score all three times, but winning the game was the big thing. If I can get close for somebody else to score, it's all right with me. On that last one, I was looking for a gas station along the way.

"I really appreciate Stabler. He throws the ball where I can catch it, low and away from people. To me, Kenny Stabler is the best quarterback to play football. He doesn't pop off. We know what Kenny can do, and he knows what we can do."

Stabler looked over. He just shook his head and smiled. "I don't think there is any way that you can throw the ball that Fred can't catch it," he beamed. "As far as I'm concerned, he's the best receiver who's ever played the game. Like a great pianist, Fred is tops in his field. He's a master. I look at him sometimes and wonder how he does the things he does. He's always going to be where he's supposed to be, and no matter if it's a good or bad throw, he's going to come up with it.

"We've been together so long we know exactly what to expect from one another. I know where he's going to end up before he gets there, and he knows where I'm going to throw the ball almost before I do. Sometimes I'll let the ball go and start running upfield thinking of the next play before Fred even catches it. I see him coming off the break and the ball heading for him, and I just know that he's going to catch it."

There is nobody who can catch a football better than Biletnikoff. Simply no one. He has the surest pair of hands in the game. So sure, in fact, that if he drops the football, shock waves rumble through the stands. He is a perfectionist. He continually works in that direction when most players at his age of 34 might tend to take things easy. Not Biletnikoff. He practices long and hard, often when others have already left the field.

It's just that all his life Biletnikoff was a worrier. He worried about leaving the cold weather of Erie, Pennsylvania, to attend college. He worried about dropping passes and losing games. He even worried if he were good enough to become a professional player. By the time he was a senior at Florida State, Biletnikoff had worried himself into an ulcer. That's how much of a worrier he is.

There were a number of scouts who felt that Biletnikoff wasn't fast enough or tough enough to play pro ball. That didn't influence the Raiders in the least. They thought so highly of Biletnikoff's pass catching ability that they made him a second-round pick in 1965. And it was the Raiders who worried then.

It was a period before the merger between the older National Football League and the American Football League. It was actually war. The bidding for college talent had reached unprecedented heights. The Raiders were so fearful of losing Biletnikoff to the Detroit Lions that they hid him in a motel the night before the Gator Bowl. Then, when the game was over, Biletnikoff signed an Oakland contract underneath the goalposts on national television.

The Raiders' worries were over. But it didn't end for Biletnikoff. He worried through his entire rookie year. He was concerned about running pass patterns, about catching the ball, and about reading defenses. He was a big movie watcher. He would study game films for hours, stopping and rerunning the film in an effort to pick up habits of opposing cornerbacks. He was a bundle of nerves before and even after a game.

So intense was Biletnikoff that he would get an upset stomach before every game. It all started to build the night before. He couldn't even relax by watching television. He would sit and bite his fingernails. So much so that they would actually bleed. The next day in the locker room brought no relief. He would pace up and down

the floor, which didn't soothe his nerves any. Neither did a bottle of Maalox that he kept in his locker. Before he took the field, he often had to regurgitate. It was something his teammates got used to. They realized how much of a competitor Biletnikoff really was.

He displayed that at practice. The rookie would always be the last one off the field. He would endlessly run his patterns, catching one ball after another. He'd go after as many as 100 passes. If he dropped one, he would kick the ground in disgust.

Biletnikoff also did something else that others noticed. He would daily punch a light bag that boxers use in training. Not many players go around punching a bag. But Biletnikoff found that by doing so it sharpened his reflexes and at the same time helped his hand and eye coordination. That was the self-improvement he worked at.

"I didn't know what I was doing out there on the field my first year," confessed Biletnikoff. "I was really confused. Everything was just so much more complicated than in college. I was afraid of making a mistake, like running a wrong pattern or dropping the ball."

It was something that didn't happen. Besides being sure-handed, Biletnikoff ran picture book patterns and had an uncanny ability to get open. That's how good his moves were. The defense found it difficult to stop him, whether it was man-to-man or zone. Somehow, Biletnikoff would work himself free and catch a pass. He quickly became the team's clutch receiver.

"Everybody has it in his head, as soon as the defenses go into a zone, that you can't throw the ball," exclaimed Biletnikoff. "They all say that you can't get deep on a zone, but I've done it too often to buy that.

"Look, if your quarterback gets the protection he needs, and he's not going to get that big rush from linebackers when they're in a zone, and if your receivers read the defense, there are ways to beat it deep. That defensive back flying back to his deep spot, by the time a receiver gets to him, he's in man-to-man coverage.

"Sometimes, though, reading defenses can be a bit troublesome. You get a confusing look. Sometimes the cornerback is really playing a zone, but he'll bump you and run with you five or ten yards just like in man-to-man coverage. Then he'll release you and you'll suddenly realize that it's a zone and not a man-to-man after all. You have to develop a feel, kind of feel the whole thing in order to get the whole picture of what is taking place.

"If I don't read the defenses quick enough, I won't even get close to the ball. Against man-to-man coverage, you can play around a little bit on the defender. But against a zone, if you hesitate a little, you may be out of the play. They disguise it so well that sometimes you don't recognize the zone. You have to be ready to adapt. You run the same pattern whether it's man-to-man or zone, but you vary it to take what it gives you. The zone is supposed to eliminate the bomb, but they can't shut off everything."

One thing they can't do is shut off Biletnikoff. In his last ten seasons with the Raiders, he has caught 40 or more passes every year. He has averaged over 15 yards a catch, has 534 receptions, and 69 touchdowns in his entire 12-year career with the Raiders.

"I was lucky to be here," remarked Biletnikoff. "It took awhile for me to adjust. But I had a chance to grow with the team, learn the Raider system. With some other team I wouldn't have the time. They would have taken one look, and if I didn't fit, I would have been on my way."

It doesn't seem possible . . .

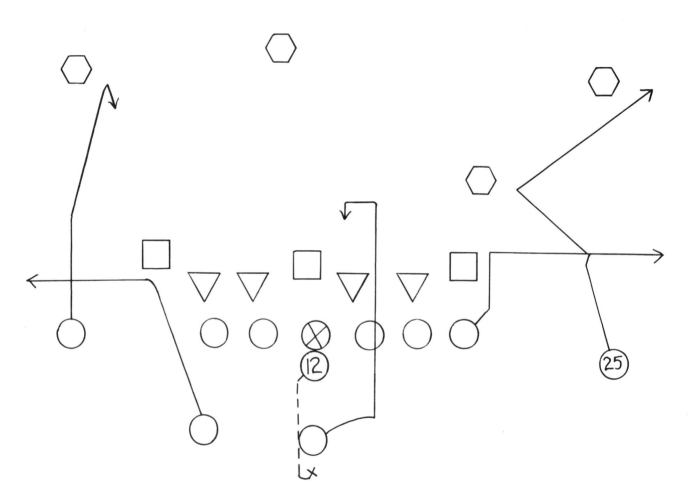

Diagrammed by Coach John Madden

Cliff Branch

He was an intruder. He had a big reputation for being a speed burner. Real smoke. Like running the 100 in 9.3. He had done that a couple of times. But that was in track. Professional football is another world. A whole different world. Track stars come and go. Like John Carlos and Jimmy Hines. Olympic stars, to say the least. Now there was another one. He had passed up an opportunity to run in the 1972 Olympics to play professional football with the Oakland Raiders. After all, he did play football in college. But Cliff Branch wasn't exactly an All-American candidate at the University of Colorado.

So, when Branch reported to the Raiders that summer of 1972, he was given a long look. He was selected on the fourth round of the college draft, so the Raiders thought fairly well of Branch. But the Raiders had such experienced receivers as Fred Biletnikoff and Mike Siani around, so just where would Branch fit in? Especially since he didn't distinguish himself as a pass receiver. When you have speed, you automatically run back kickoffs and punts in college. And that was exactly what Branch had done. Everyone felt that the Raiders grabbed Branch as a kick return man. What else?

In Branch, the Raiders envisioned a receiver who could go deep. A bomb threat. Biletnikoff and Siani were excellent receivers, but neither had the speed that Branch possessed. And in the preseason games, Branch did get deep often enough. When the regular 1972 season opened, Branch was in the starting lineup. Everything looked that good for Branch and the Raiders.

But in that first game, Branch dropped a long pass and immediately was exiled to the bench. That's where he remained practically all year. Then, late in the season, Branch caught a crucial third-down pass that clinched the Western Division title for the Raiders. It was the most significant catch of the three that Branch caught all year.

"I always had faith that I could do it," claimed Branch. "But nobody said anything to me when I wasn't playing, and it was hard to keep mentally prepared."

At first, Branch was regarded solely as a sprinter in a football world. In essence, he was an inexperienced receiver. He had caught only 13 passes his final year in college. The scouting reports on him said that he had outstanding speed but couldn't always catch a football. That was enough to downgrade him.

The Raiders felt that it wasn't a matter of ability. Rather, they were of the opinion that Branch didn't concentrate enough. And Branch shared the same view. He worked hard to correct it.

"I would walk around the house dropping a football and trying to catch it before it hit the ground again," recalled Branch. "I also worked in practice a great deal concentrating on making one-hand catches. My left hand was a problem because I was used to doing everything right-handed. Our receiver coach, Tom Flores, used to work with me a lot on catching the ball with just my left hand. I finally learned that and coordinated my left hand with my right hand when catching the football."

In 1973, Branch was still a reserve. But he was learning. He was also improving. His teammates were helping him to do so. Defensive backs Jack Tatum and George Atkinson worked with him. They would tell Branch what were his best moves, the ones most difficult for a defensive back to cover. And Biletnikoff would tell him about defenses, how to recognize them and what the other team might do in passing situations.

And Branch helped himself. Just about every night he took home films of Raider opponents and studied them intently. He would analyze what they would do and how he could beat them. During the 1973 season, he did manage to play a bit more. He finished the year with 19 catches and a better frame of mind.

Branch got his big break the following year. Siani got hurt and Branch replaced him. Coach John Madden told Branch that the Raiders were depending on him because there was no one else. It was a tough assignment. But Branch came through. He finished the season with 60 catches for 1,092 yards and 13 touchdowns. The Raiders had a long ball threat.

Perhaps his most significant catch occurred against the Miami Dolphins in the opening game of the 1974 AFC playoffs. Late in the game, the Dolphins were ahead, 19–14. Oakland had the ball on their own 28-yard line. On first down, quarterback Ken Stabler told Branch to go deep and come back, to be alert because the ball would be there.

Branch took off on a fly pattern down the sidelines. He was watched closely by cornerback Henry Stuckey. Stabler purposely threw the ball short. Branch stopped and came back for the ball. He dove and caught the ball on the Dolphins' 27-yard line. Stuckey, trying to follow Branch, slipped and fell. Branch immediately got up and easily ran the rest of the way for a touchdown. It was the biggest catch of Branch's young career.

"The biggest thing in my improvement was just playing," contends Branch. "I really started to get my confidence, and I could feel the team getting confidence in me, also. It was just a matter of learning and applying.

"I learned how to use my speed, when to go full out and when to glide. Like when I'm running a comeback. I go out full speed because I want the defensive back to think I'm running an up. But when I run a hook, I go into a glide and then accelerate after I catch the ball. I still have to learn how to cut at full speed like Warren Wells did or Paul Warfield does. I've studied movies on the way they did it."

What Branch did when he replaced Siani pleased Madden a great deal. He knew he had a dangerous deep receiver. And Siani knew that he had just about lost his job. Branch made everyone believers. They all forgot about his first two years.

"We have something now that we've lacked ever since Wells left a few years ago," pointed out Madden. "Wells was our deep threat. We have two receivers that we think are as good as anyone in Biletnikoff and Siani. But neither of these guys are bomb threats. So, we came up with a new bomb threat in Branch, and he's really been something. He has caught footballs all over the place, and he keeps those defenses honest."

The following season, the defenses began to watch Branch more closely. So much so that he often drew double coverage. Which didn't bother the Raiders at all. Stabler just looked toward Biletnikoff or his tight end or threw to his backs. Still, Branch managed to catch 51 passes for 893 yards and nine touchdowns.

Branch broke loose for his biggest season ever in 1976. He caught 46 passes for 1,111 yards and 12 touchdowns. He averaged a remarkable 24.2 yards a catch, second highest in the NFL. Only Roger Carr of the Baltimore Colts was better, with an average of 25.9.

Branch will tell anyone who will listen that he always wanted to become a pro football player. Even when he was a youngster growing up in Houston. He was the fastest kid on the block and would always run away from the others in a street race. Everyone figured he would end up being a track star.

"I was always fast on my feet," said Branch. "I could run away from anyone on the block. Even the big kids. It was a God-given grace, and I knew I had to do something with it."

The one person who helped Branch harness his speed was his junior high coach, Oliver Brown. He worked closely with Branch helping him to develop his running techniques. Then when Branch went to high school, Brown went along with him as track coach. Under Brown, Branch continued his improvement as a track star. He became the first Texas schoolboy to run the 100-yard dash in 9.3, accomplishing the extraordinary feat twice.

But Branch also played football. It's just that 155-pound receivers weren't in demand when it came to college. Still, Colorado offered Branch a football scholarship, figuring he could also run track. Which is what he did. His track accomplishments simply overshadowed anything he did on the football field. Colorado was a run-oriented team, and Branch didn't get much of an opportunity to play.

"What happens to guys with great speed in college is they run track in the spring," observed Madden. "So they miss spring football practice, and that's a time for working and preparing. Thus, they're farther behind than someone who does compete in spring practice.

"We drafted Branch mainly as a return man. But I've always had

the feeling that any player who can get open can be taught to catch a pass. Hands can be developed. But if a guy can't get open, it doesn't matter whether he can catch or not. He'll never have a pass thrown to him."

Branch realized that he needed more than speed to make it as a receiver. The rest was up to him. Running fly patterns straight downfield was one thing. That's something nobody could take away from him. But learning to be a receiver was another. He was willing to learn how to run patterns, play off a defender, all after first learning the proper way to catch and get hit. Preparing for a hit is very important for any receiver.

"I asked our cornerback George Atkinson about it," said Branch. "He's my roommate in camp and on the road. He's the kind of guy that hits people hard for a living. I asked him about footsteps once, and he told me, 'Clifford, you know that defensive man is going to hit you whether you catch the ball or not. He's going to hit you because you're there. But you're responsible for the ball, that's what they're paying you for. So you got to catch it.' That's the way it is, so I catch it."

Which he clearly demonstrated last year. It was no wonder that he constantly attracted double coverage. At one point during the season, he made one big catch after another. In five games during the middle of the year, he caught 19 passes for 632 yards, a phenomenal average of 33.3 yards a catch, and six touchdowns. Some of the touchdowns were the difference between winning and losing.

"When we first saw Branch, he was just a sprinter," remarked Denver cornerback Calvin Jones. "All you had to worry about was his speed. But people used to say he didn't have good hands. Now he's a totally different player. His feet are quick along the sidelines. He catches the ball with his hands. He looks for running room after he catches the ball, so you can't play way off him."

It's no secret now that Branch worked on his hands. But how he did it would make every kid a potential pass receiving star.

"My hands are not big, but they're strong," disclosed Branch. "I squeeze a lot of Silly Putty at home to get them strong. I also shoot a lot of pool and play ping pong to help my eye-hand coordination. Now I have begun to play tennis. It's good for the legs, gives you those quick breaks when you make your move on a pass route.

"I still watch Biletnikoff a lot. It's the best education a pass receiver can get anywhere. You can always learn something from him."

Defensive backs around the NFL are still trying to learn about Branch . . .

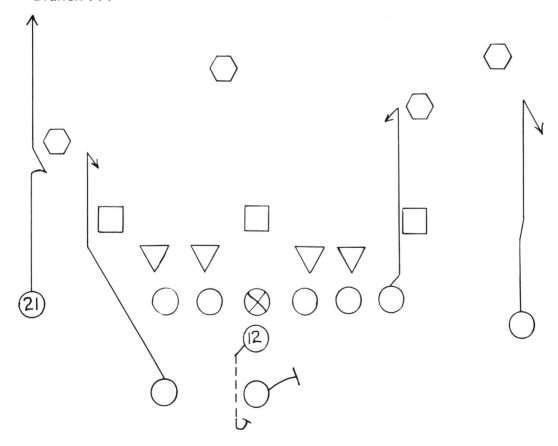

Diagrammed by Coach John Madden

Ken Burrough

They gave up on him. And quickly, too. He was the club's number one draft choice. He was tall, 6'4", fast, and he had caught a lot of passes at Texas Southern. But when the season was over, he was traded. It hurt. It hurt because the New Orleans Saints felt he wasn't that good. Neither were the Saints, for that matter. That's why it hurt all the more. The Saints had won only two games the entire season. Yet he wasn't considered good enough to be kept. Somehow the Saints had gotten the impression that he was scared. That he was afraid to get hit when a defender was close by. It's known as hearing footsteps. That's the worst thing that can happen to a receiver. That's the way the Saints' coaching staff felt about Ken Burrough.

Actually, Burrough's rookie season with the Saints in 1970 had started out very well. In an early pre-season game, he had shown the speed that he was known for. He had outraced the defensive secondary and had caught a bomb for a touchdown.

The Saints figured that they had a good one. Patient New Orleans fans felt that way, too. Especially once the regular season began. In the second home game of the year, Burrough caught a 15-yard touchdown pass and the Saints won their first game.

But the joy was short-lived. The following week, against the Kansas City Chiefs, Burrough got hurt. He reached high for a pass and was spun to the ground in a cartwheel. Burrough landed hard on the ground and broke his big toe. It didn't seem to be too bad an injury at first. But, for someone who utilizes speed, it was a troublesome one. Burrough didn't regain his early season form and wasn't the same the rest of the campaign.

"People don't realize what a broken toe means to a receiver," lamented Burrough. "It doesn't slow you down that much, but you can't cut. You can't run your patterns. You can't get open. It's very frustrating."

Also frustrating was the fact that Burrough began to hear talk. It was based on the fact that he had trouble concentrating on the ball. That he worried about getting hit too much. The Saints were so convinced that Burrough was uptight that they traded him to the Houston Oilers when the season came to an end.

Burrough had mixed emotions. He was disappointed at first. He had liked New Orleans. But he hadn't gotten the chance to prove what he could do about catching a football. On the other hand, Burrough was from Houston and was returning to his hometown. That was the best part. The Oilers themselves weren't much better than the Saints.

The "hometown boy makes good" drama didn't exactly unfold for Burrough. Although he did manage to see more action in 1971, it wasn't under normal conditions. The Oilers used Burrough a great deal in long yardage situations. That's sort of a handicap. It's certainly not the best way for a young receiver to develop. And Burrough was wondering if anything was going to change. He had just left a similar situation at New Orleans.

"My rookie year at New Orleans I was tall, fast, and a number one draft choice," pointed out Burrough. "But I had no pro experience. They sent me in on third-and-long and expected me to outrun somebody. I ran almost all short routes in college. For four years, I'd catch the ball short and try to turn it into a long play.

"You see a young receiver come into the league and make it big. When that happens, though, it usually means an old quarterback is throwing to that young receiver. The receiver might have speed, but the quarterback has to know where he can throw the ball against zone defenses. They always expected me to beat everybody deep. They must have figured, 'We've got Ken Burrough now. He'll score a touchdown or two every game.'

"Jim Bierne was having a great year in 1971. But when they wanted more speed, they'd send me in. It'd be third-and-20, and anybody with any common sense knew what to expect. I'd come off the line, and the defensive man would back up until he was nearly out of the park. If anybody could score deep touchdowns under those conditions, there wouldn't be a contract big enough for him. But when I failed to do it, people looked at my speed and size and thought something had to be wrong with me. I had plenty of critics.

"They'd start saying, 'He won't do this,' or, 'He won't do that.' You see, being good wouldn't have been enough to satisfy people. They expected me to be extraordinary."

For awhile, Burrough appeared just ordinary. But that wasn't his fault at all. The Oilers were a losing team, and they didn't have a good quarterback. When Burrough came to the Oilers in 1971, Dan Pastorini was a highly promising rookie quarterback. But he was only a rookie. And he needed time and patience to develop.

In 1971, Burrough caught 25 passes. In 1972, he caught one more. That may not seem like much improvement. But Burrough's receptions in 1972 averaged 20.0 yards, which was quite noticeable. And so was the fact that the Oilers won only one game that year.

It wasn't any better the next season. At least as far as the Oilers were concerned. They continued to wallow in futility, again producing only one victory. But Burrough improved, nevertheless. He grabbed 43 passes, averaging 13.4 yards a catch.

Significantly, the Oilers started to improve in 1974. And Burrough was headed for his finest season of his five-year career before he was injured. Three weeks before the season came to an end, Burrough suffered a dislocated elbow. Still, he finished with 36 catches for 492 yards, an average of 13.7 yards a reception.

"I have great confidence in myself and great confidence in Pastorini as a quarterback," reflected Burrough. "There were games in 1973 when I could have scored two or three touchdowns. I'd get open but Pastorini or Lynn Dickey would be sacked before they could throw the ball.

"Our receiver coach, Lew Carpenter, made a difference in me. He's the first coach I've had who played on a championship pro team. He knows how it has to be. He has a knack for pushing me and getting the best out of me without being on my back all the time.

"I've changed. People who don't have a lot of talent are lucky. They realize it and work hard. People have told me my talent is there. I started realizing after last season I needed to use more of it. Guys I went to the College All-Star game with in 1970 were making all-pro teams. I wasn't. I'm talking about guys whose tools were equal to mine. Maybe not even as good. I decided it was time to make my move."

Did he ever. In 1975, Burrough broke out. He had his best year ever, catching 53 passes and leading the entire NFL with 1,063 yards. He was the only receiver to reach that figure. He averaged 20.1 yards a reception and scored eight touchdowns as the Oilers finished with a 10–4 record.

His biggest day occurred against the Kansas City Chiefs midway through the season. It was an important game for the Oilers, in that they had put together a three-game winning streak. They had a 5–1 record and at the time were in first place in the Central Division. Since they were facing the Pittsburgh Steelers the following week, they needed a victory to stay in front.

Burrough was solely responsible for the Oilers' 17–13 win. He

caught seven passes that accounted for 177 yards. Even more important, he scored both Houston touchdowns on big plays. Both times he brought the Oilers from behind on their way to the victory.

As time elapsed in the opening quarter, Burrough scored his first touchdown. At the time, the Chiefs were ahead, 3–0, and the Oilers were in a difficult situation. They had a third and 16 on their own 23-yard line and time for only one more play. Pastorini decided to go all the way. He dispatched Burrough on a deep pattern down the sideline and hit him with a well thrown ball on the Chiefs' 32-yard line. Burrough took the ball in full stride and ran the rest of the way for the touchdown.

In the opening minutes of the third period, Burrough worked his magic again. The Oilers were behind, 13–7, and Burrough put them ahead to stay for the rest of the game. He took a short, two-yard screen pass from Pastorini on his own 45-yard line and darted his way down the sideline the remaining 55 yards for a touchdown. The 57-yard play put the Oilers in front to stay, 14–13.

"Kenny Burrough can fly," exclaimed Oiler coach Bum Phillips.

"He is great for the big play. He has an extra gear to shift into. If you give him enough time, he can fly past anyone. The defensive back will think the quarterback is being sacked, then Kenny will shift into overdrive and you are beat."

Phillips makes it sound so simple. Perhaps, with Burrough's speed, it is. But Burrough was learning how to beat the defensive backs with moves, too. He had to. He was now attracting double coverage. He was that good. The fact is, he was getting good at viewing game films. It helped him immensely. He made it a point to sit at home every Thursday night before a game and watch films for two to three hours. And, to make sure that he wasn't interrupted, he would take the phone off the hook. Now, that's a big sacrifice for a bachelor in his own digs, a four-bedroom house filled with plants in every room.

"I think watching films at home helps," conceded Burrough. "Particularly when we play a team outside our division. I look for how fast a linebacker gets outside to cover me, and how physical they are. If there's a cheap-shot artist, I want to know about him so I'll know how to change my patterns.

"If we're up against linebackers as fast as Ron Pritchard at Cincinnati, people who really zip outside to cover the wide receivers, I know I've got to move in a hurry. Some teams will put a linebacker right on me. We call that x-position. I need to prepare for that, too. I've never forgotten that to run well you've got to pump your arms with your legs. I used to buck. But that won't help you run relaxed, so I stopped bucking. A lot of people have to grunt to run fast. I'm not one of them.

"I enjoy those Thursday nights. It's near the end of the week and I'm tired. But I relax and concentrate. When we go on the field on Sunday, I feel I know the linebackers and backs I've never met personally. I didn't watch films my first five years in pro ball. I wish I had."

In 1976, Burrough wanted to become the first NFL receiver since the 1970 merger to gain more than 1,000 yards for two straight seasons. He just missed. But it wasn't for lack of trying. The Oilers had their problems as a team. They didn't have any running game and Pastorini had injury problems. It wasn't difficult to double- and sometimes triple-team Burrough. Still, Burrough managed to pull down 51 passes for 932 yards. He averaged 18.3 yards a catch and scored seven touchdowns as the Oilers slumped to a 4–10 record. Only the year before, they had been playoff contenders.

"Positive thinking helped me," explained Burrough. "A friend of mine helped me with it. He got me reading and thinking more. Now, thinking positively, I don't feel there's anything realistic that I can't do. I go into a game thinking I can't fail."

Not with his speed and hands . . .

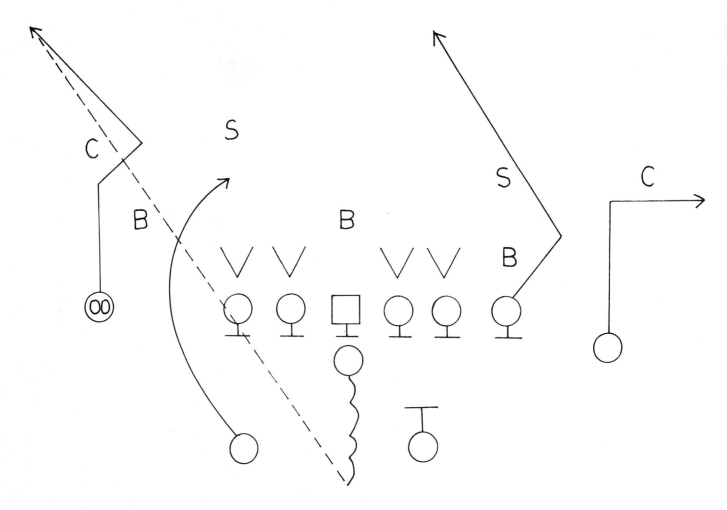

Diagrammed by Coach Bum Phillips

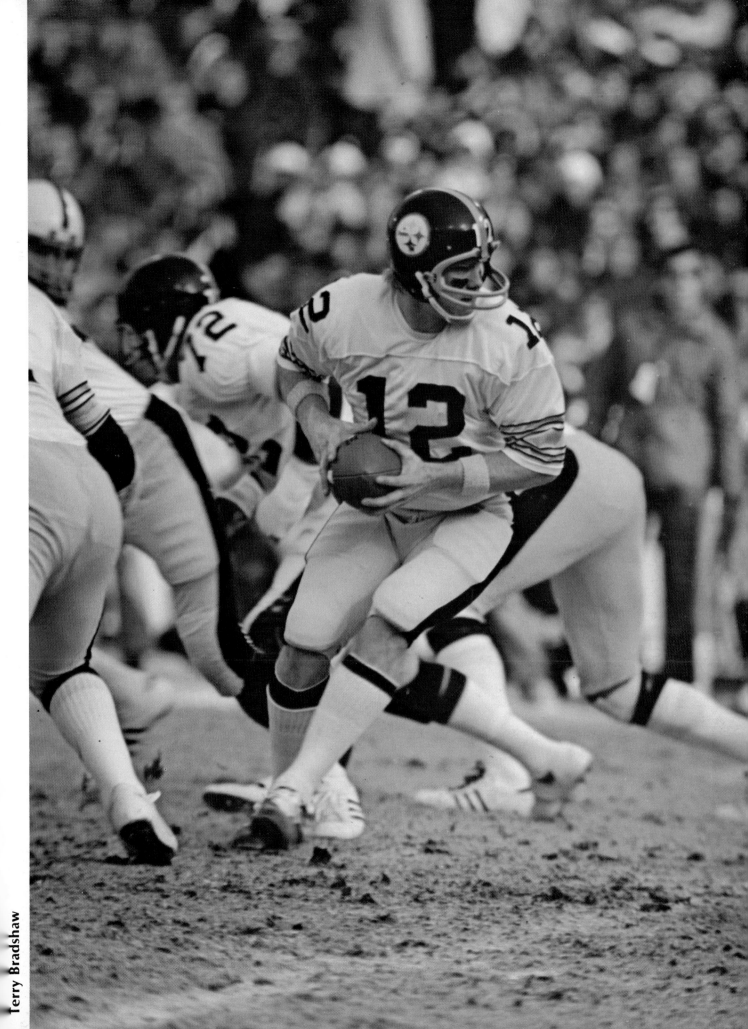

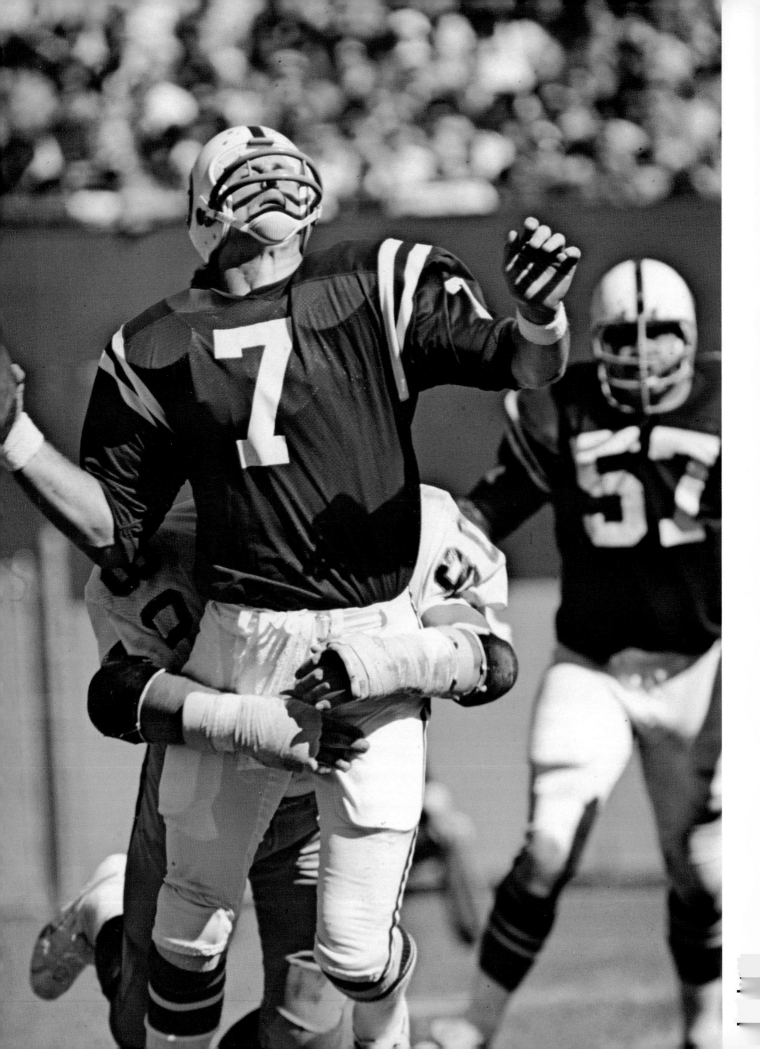

Franco Harris

Dan Pastorini

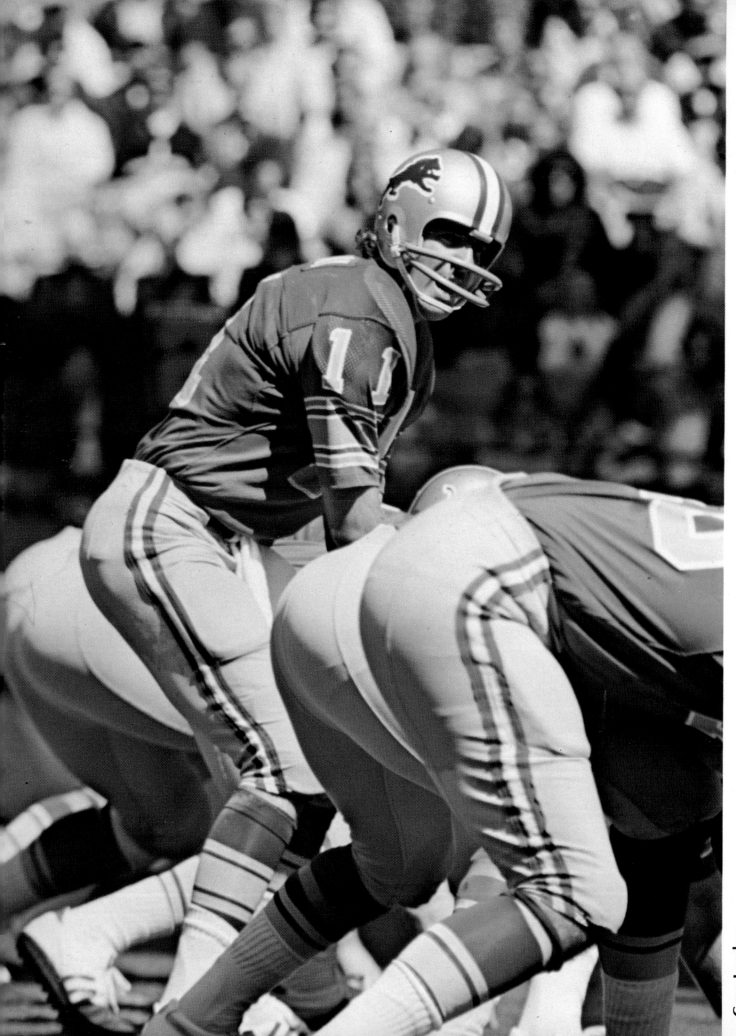

Greg Landry

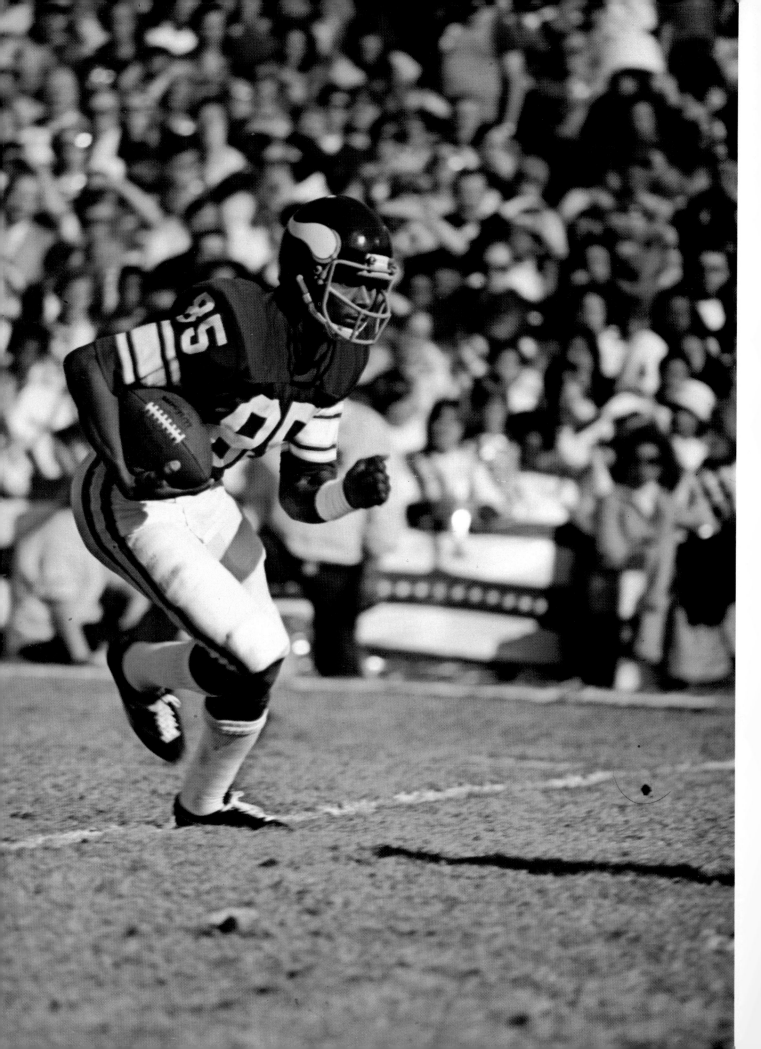

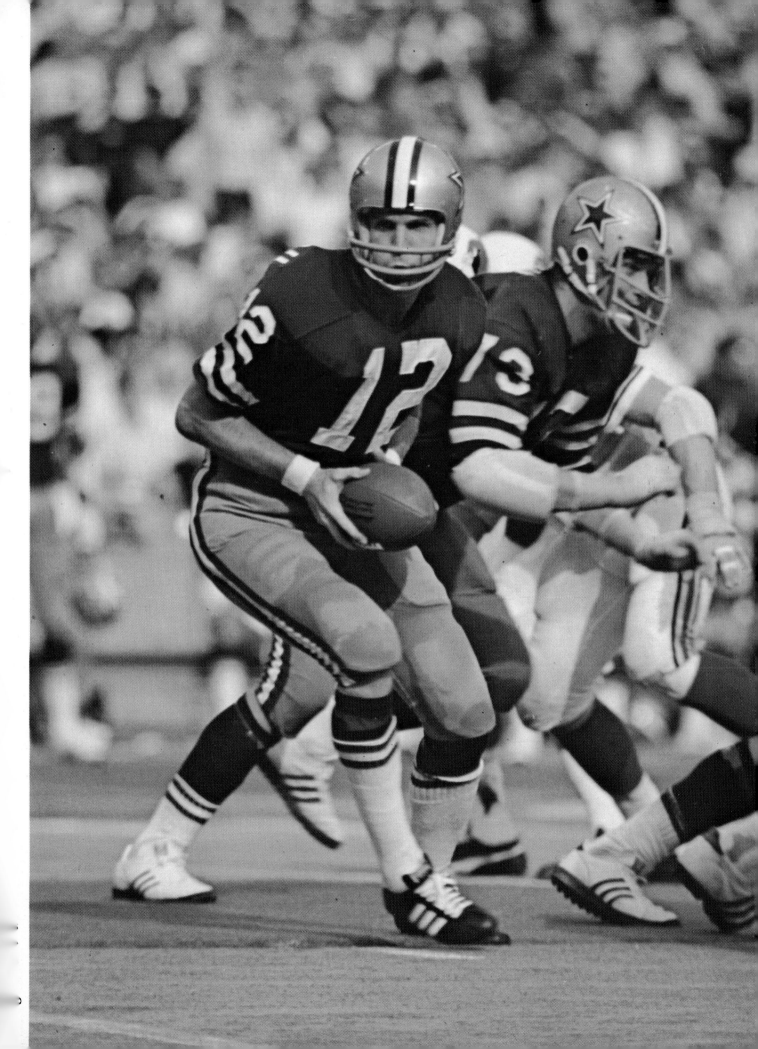

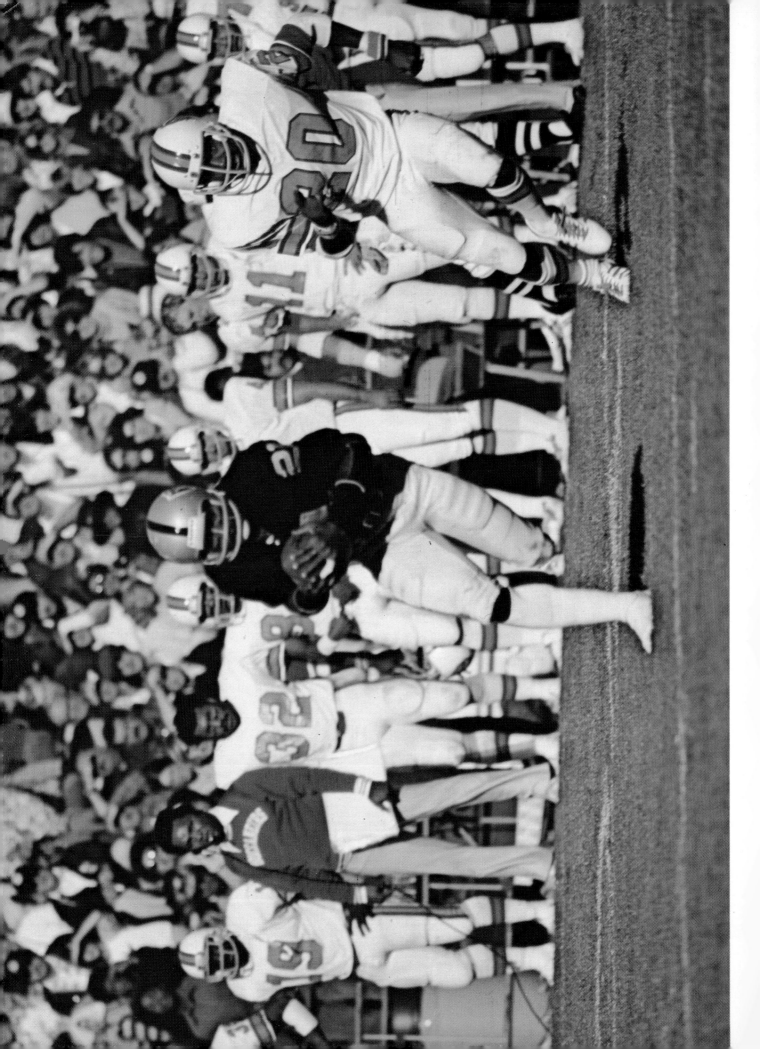

Roger Carr

He was like something out of Mark Twain. A real old country boy. He certainly didn't look like a first-round draft pick. They usually have flare. And a big reputation. But coming from a small school in Ruston, Louisiana, well, that's something else. All anybody ever knew about Louisiana Tech was that Terry Bradshaw went there. That's how it is with quarterbacks. Everybody knows about them. But a wide receiver like Roger Carr? They don't usually get the big build-up. And Carr was no exception, even though he was a number one draft selection in 1974.

The fact is, the Baltimore Colts didn't think they had anybody. Carr didn't show anything when he first began working out with the Colts his rookie season. One reason was that he had a painful number of pulled hamstring muscles. He hardly worked out. Carr was constantly examined by doctors. They only reported that the injury was not serious. But Carr insisted that it was too painful for him to play. He couldn't exert any pressure on his leg. And sadly, he couldn't run with the blinding speed that had made him attractive to the Colts in the first place. Coach Howard Schnellenberger wasn't convinced. He looked at Carr with a jaundiced eye. He was certain that Carr was dogging it. A private war developed.

One day Schnellenberger reached the breaking point. The regular season had just begun and the Colts weren't doing too well. Schnellenberger directed his frustration at Carr. He told a local writer, "I'm going to tell Carr to practice at full speed tomorrow. He

can either show me he can play or else tear the muscle completely and go home to Louisiana for the year.''

Schnellenberger never got the showdown. The next day he was fired. It was like an elixir for Carr. He immediately felt better. He couldn't wait to play. The Colts told him not to rush, but that weekend Carr got to play. By the eighth game of the season, Carr had worked his way into the starting lineup. Quietly, he finished the year with 21 receptions. The noticeable part was that he averaged 19.3 yards a catch. That was better than anyone on the club. He didn't score any touchdowns, but the Colts were pleased nevertheless. In his final game of the season against the New York Jets, Carr had his biggest day, catching six passes for 91 yards. Baltimore knew they had a good one.

In 1975, Carr started every game. He caught 23 passes, and his average climbed to 22.5 yards a catch. He again topped the club in that area. The only reason that he didn't catch more passes was that he often attracted double coverage. Then, too, he wasn't completely synchronized with quarterback Bert Jones. He, too, was playing his first year as the Colts' regular quarterback. Timing between a quarterback and a receiver is the most vital ingredient for success. That takes time. Still, Jones and Carr did manage to hook up on the longest pass in Baltimore's history. Carr scored on a 90-yard touchdown play against the Miami Dolphins. Only the week before, he and Jones tied the club record of 89 yards against the Buffalo Bills. Significantly, they were the first two touchdowns that Carr scored.

Defensive backs were becoming aware of Carr's speed. But what still confused them was his rate of acceleration. Carr doesn't go all out as soon as he breaks. Rather, he shifts gears from fast to faster. That's his secret of getting open. Defensive backs can't handle it.

"That's the whole secret to my ability to get open, deep,'' revealed Carr. "I break fast at the snap of the ball, and my speed is good enough so most defensive backs think I'm going all out. But actually I'm only going about 75 percent. If you let a defensive back stay with you for a couple of steps, he can get lulled into a feeling of confidence. Then you open it up into full speed and leave him.''

The Colts decided to open up their offense more in 1976. Basically, they wanted to get Carr open more. They figured they could accomplish this by sending tight end Raymond Chester on deep patterns up the middle. By such a maneuver, the defensive backs couldn't double up on Carr and risk leaving the dangerous Chester open. The post patterns that Chester would run would draw coverage away from Carr on the outside.

Baltimore's new approach delighted Carr. He admitted that he worried practically the entire 1975 season about not being able to catch more passes. He began to wonder if he was running bad patterns, if he wasn't getting open enough, or if Jones didn't have the confidence in him as he did in his other receivers. It was just a matter of making some adjustments.

"I knew it wasn't lack of speed or bad hands," remarked Carr. "As long as I can run, I know I can play. But nobody ever told me I was doing anything wrong. All coach Ted Marchibroda said was that I had to increase my receptions."

There was no question that Carr could catch a football. And there was no doubt that Jones could throw it. He has one of the strongest arms in the NFL. Jones quickly dispelled any doubts that Carr may have had about not having any confidence in him. In the second game of the season, Jones and Carr combined to lift the Colts from behind to beat the Cincinnati Bengals, 28–27, in a thrilling game in Baltimore.

The Colts scored first on a big second-down play. They had the ball on their 32-yard line, with a good opportunity to get a first down. But Jones took the Bengals by surprise. Instead of going for a first down, Jones went all the way for a touchdown. Carr grabbed the ball on the Bengals' 20-yard line and scampered the rest of the distance without any defender near him. His speed stunned the Bengals.

Cincinnati then took command of the game. Before the quarter ended, they tied the contest at 7–7. They then scored the next 10 points to take a 17–7 lead as the first half was coming to a close. However, Jones got the Colts on the move. He had a first down on the Bengals' 22-yard line. Then he suddenly appeared to bog down. He tried two passes to his other wide receiver, Glenn Doughty, and failed. He was now faced with a critical third-down play. With just under two minutes left, he looked to Carr. He again sent him streaking down the sidelines and hit him in the end zone for a 22-yard touchdown.

In the opening minutes of the third quarter, Jones and Carr struck again. And they did it quickly. Faced with a second and ten on their own 35-yard line, Jones called Carr's number. And the speedy Carr responded once more. Jones delivered the ball perfectly to Carr on the Bengals' 40-yard line. Without hesitation, Carr ran the rest of the way untouched for a touchdown that put the Colts in front, 21–20. It was his third touchdown of the game. When the struggle ended, Carr had caught six passes and gained 198 yards. He had come close to breaking Raymond Berry's one-game record of 224 yards set in 1957. What had stopped him was a penalty in the second period that nullified a 58-yard touchdown pass.

During the game, Baltimore fans saw a different Carr. One they had never seen before. After he caught the 68-yard bomb from Jones in the first period, Carr didn't pull up short in the end zone. Instead, he kept on running toward the goalpost. He then palmed the ball and spiked it over the ten-foot-high crossbar. It was definitely not a Carr mannerism.

"All I wanted was a little respect," explained Carr after the game about the spiking incident. "When they play me close, I feel I have

to beat them. It's a matter of pride. They're telling me I'm not quick. I really feel that I can run with anybody, white, black, or red. I want to hear them say, 'Hey, here's a white boy who can run.'"

Carr made believers out of three Bengal defensive backs, Ken Riley, Lemar Parrish, and Bernard Jackson. Riley was the one who played him close on the first touchdown. He positioned himself only five yards in front of Carr. It cost him.

"I thought I had him," confessed Riley. "He started out quick. Then once he got going, he got even quicker. There was no catching him."

After Carr's first-half heroics, in which he caught five passes, the Bengals did some adjusting. When Carr burned them with a 65-yard touchdown just after the third quarter began, the Bengals changed their coverage in the secondary. They went mostly with a double zone and extra linebacker coverage in an attempt to stop Carr from beating them deep. Although Carr didn't catch any more passes, he wasn't at all disappointed.

"They showed me respect, right?" he smiled.

It seemed that even as a youngster Carr searched for respect. At the age of 13, his parents were divorced. He left Enid, Oklahoma, two years later and went to live with his grandparents in Cotton Valley, Louisiana. He couldn't play high school football that first year because he was a transfer student. He wasn't eligible the following year, because his grades were too low. By midterm, he picked up his grades.

However, all that was left at that time of the year was track. Unfortunately, Cotton Valley didn't have a track team. But that didn't stop Carr. He dug a long jump pit and began practicing on his own. That's how determined he was. He became so good that he won the district, regional, and state meets. In the state meet, he set a Class B record by jumping 23 feet, 11 inches. It earned him a track scholarship to Louisiana Tech.

Carr made the football team as a walk-on. He did it as a punter. But one day after practice, backfield coach Mickey Slaughter noticed that Carr was running better patterns and catching the ball better than most of his receivers. Carr became more than a punter.

"My grandparents gave me love, took me to church, had supper on the table for me every night," praised Carr. "My mother tried hard to raise me but my stepfather worked on an oil rig and wasn't home too often. So it seemed that being with my grandparents was best for me. I will never be able to repay them. I attribute my speed to my grandfather showing me how to exercise my legs with weights."

The 6'3", 195-pound Carr runs fast enough to cover the 100 in 9.3. That's really fast. And in 1976, he kept on running away from defensive backs. He finished the year with 43 catches for 1,112 yards, the most in the NFL. His receptions averaged a phenomenal 25.9

yards a catch, highest of any receiver. He scored 11 touchdowns, only one less than NFL leader Cliff Branch of Oakland.

"Carr has confidence and a better awareness of what's going on," explained Marchibroda. "He knows what to do against a defender. He may have known in 1975, but he didn't have the confidence to carry it off. We knew that if we were to improve on offense, a lot of it had to come from Roger. It has now, maybe even more than we expected."

The soft-spoken Carr just takes it in stride. He's not one to make with the big talk. He just takes things nice and easy until he starts to run.

"I'm just a country boy from Louisiana who believes if the good Lord is willing, I'll be a superstar someday," said Carr.

Amen . . .

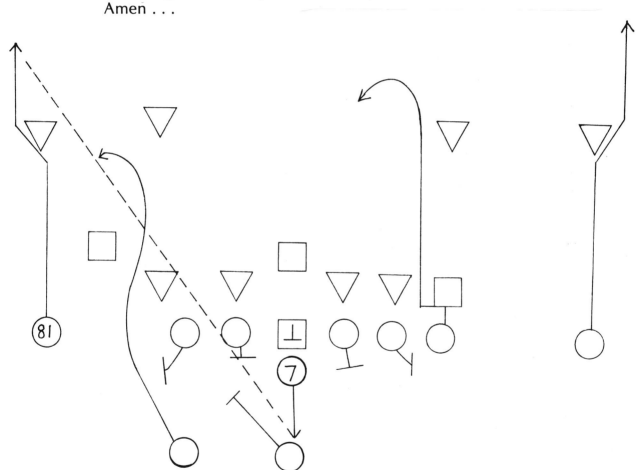

Diagrammed by Coach Ted Marchibroda

Richard Caster

The rap was always there. Right from the beginning. It was like a nightmare. He would wake up to it every Sunday. What hurt was that it occurred at home. In front of the New York Jet fans in Shea Stadium for everyone to hear. Every time he dropped a pass, the crowd would boo. It reverberated throughout the stadium. It hurt. It gnawed at him for five years. The criticism was that he had bad hands. That he dropped too many passes. But it was unfair. Even when he became an All-Pro in 1974, he still couldn't silence all of the critics.

Those were agonizing years for Richard Caster. The memory still haunts him. There were moments of deep depression. So deep that he thought about giving it all up. Innately quiet and sensitive, Caster didn't need the boos. What he needed was time. That was all that was necessary to overcome the pressure. He definitely had ability.

Caster was big, strong, and he could run. Oh, how he could run! He was 6'5" and weighed 228 pounds. What a target he would make for Joe Namath's long passes. Not too many people had heard of Caster. But the Jets had scouted him at little Jackson State, far away from the computers of big college football. They liked him so much that they drafted him on the second round of the 1970 draft. The selection surprised quite a few people.

The pressure on Caster was there from the start. After his rookie season, he was looked upon to replace the retired George Sauer. It was a lot to ask. In his short career with the Jets, Sauer had distin-

guished himself as one of the game's premier wide receivers. He was a precision moving receiver who was in consort with the passing artistry of Namath. Their timing was a thing of beauty. Both were young and the future was theirs. But Sauer walked away from it all. The challenge was given to Caster. It was a big one, too.

In his rookie year, Caster did display talent. Although he didn't play regularly, he nevertheless caught 19 passes. What made that figure impressive was that he averaged 20.7 yards a catch. That's what the Jets liked. They were certain that he could replace Sauer. And quickly, too. As fast as Namath could throw a football. That's what made the pressure so intense.

Naturally, comparisons were made as soon as the 1971 season began. It was inevitable. But Caster wasn't ready for it. He felt the pressure. He realized that he would be the prime target for Namath's passes. Just as Sauer had been before him. Perhaps Caster tried too hard. He appeared a bit tight. He wasn't as relaxed as he should have been. He dropped a few passes. Those were the ones the fans remembered. And they let Caster know about it. They booed every time. It got to him.

"I was really glad when the season was over," admitted Caster. "I had become pretty shaken by the whole thing. I think that I matured a lot during that time, though. I said to myself that it's not going to bother me. It was tough taking Sauer's place. George had such concentration that it was rare if he even dropped a ball in practice. It was something I had to work on. I knew I could catch. It was a matter of keeping my mind on the ball, forgetting about people in the stands and what's around me."

It was Namath more than anyone else who was a stabilizing factor for Caster. Namath knew the vast potential Caster possessed. Yet the two didn't really have enough time to work together during Caster's first two years with the Jets. And time is so vital to a young receiver's development. In 1970, Namath missed most of the season with a broken wrist. The following year, Namath tore up his knee in a pre-season game and didn't play until the final few games of the regular campaign. Then, when the 1972 season began, Caster was switched from wide receiver to tight end. Which meant more pressure Caster had to overcome. Far more pressure than Caster ever had before.

"I wasn't too happy at first," recalled Caster. "It's that much tougher to be a tight end. There are so many more things you have to learn and more people to come in contact with on every play. As a wide receiver, you just have to learn your pass routes and maybe a couple of blocking assignments. As a tight end, you have to do both. You're always in traffic."

Through it all, Namath never lost confidence in Caster. Which was important. Quarterbacks are known to turn away from receivers who fail to hold on to their passes. But not Namath. Time and again Namath would come right back to Caster after he had dropped a pass. It was great for Caster's morale. It showed everybody else that Namath had confidence in him. But the boos continued nevertheless.

"Joe is the kind of guy who would say it's his fault even when he's not at fault," disclosed Caster. "I had been tight and he helped me to relax. He makes you feel decent. I don't think I would have ever developed to my full potential if I hadn't played with Joe. He's the type who considers his receiver, who'll say, 'Forget it, we'll get it next time.' I've thoroughly enjoyed the experience of playing with him."

Namath knows all about the mental pressures. He realizes how important they are, how they're different for each individual. He recognized what could have been a big problem with Caster. He, more than anyone else, helped correct it.

"Richard is the quiet type," pointed out Namath. "When he drops a ball or runs a wrong pattern, which is rare, he gets dejected and feels badly. It's better to get a guy the hell out of that kind of feeling."

Caster was the first of a new breed of tight ends. Not only was

he big and strong, but he could go deep. It added a new dimension to the offensive phase of pro football. In 1972, the zone defense was becoming a predominant part of the game. The feeling was that a quarterback couldn't go deep on a zone. That he would have to shorten his passing game. Many of the teams did just that. But Caster and Namath showed how to beat the zone by going deep.

It was unheard of. A tight end running a deep pattern. He caught 39 passes, 10 of them for touchdowns. His average reception was 21.4 yards. That, too, was unheard of. Very few wide receivers average that. And now there was a tight end doing it. Suddenly, overnight, the position had a new look. It was a new weapon. Instead of the short passes to big, slow tight ends, the position required speed. Caster had established a revolutionary new trend. That's how much of an impact he made.

Like in one game against the Baltimore Colts. One in which Namath threw six touchdown passes in a 44–34 victory, in a classic duel against one of the game's all-time greats, Johnny Unitas. Namath and Caster collaborated on two long touchdown plays in the fourth

quarter that sealed the win. One went for 79 yards and the other for 80. The Colts were stunned to say the least. The plays left a couple of cornerbacks, Lonnie Hepburn and Rex Kern, talking to themselves. Caster had gotten behind both of them.

"The first one was a post pattern," disclosed Caster. "The strongside linebacker, Ted Hendricks, tried to stay with me for awhile, and then Hepburn was supposed to pick me up deep outside, but I sort of got behind him. When I got back to the bench, Namath said to me, 'Hey, I'm going right back to you again.' I thought to myself, 'Wow. I mean this is the Baltimore zone. You're not supposed to do that to them.'

"On the second one, Hendricks was blitzing. It was just me against Kern. He tried to bump me out of bounds, but I had a step on him and I turned for the ball at the last second and it was right there."

It was all beginning to come together for Caster. But Namath was hurt again in 1973 and Caster's production fell somewhat. He caught 35 passes, but for only 593 yards, a 16.9 average. He didn't have anyone to get him the ball deep. So, once more Caster had to adjust, this time to a different quarterback, one not in Namath's class.

The following two years Namath was healthy. And Caster benefited. In 1974, he caught 38 passes for 745 yards, an average of 19.6 yards a catch. In one game he shook loose for an 89-yard touchdown play against the Miami Dolphins. Then, in 1975, Caster led all tight ends in yardage with 820 yards. He also led the AFC at his position with 47 catches for an average of 17.4. And he set a club record when he caught a 91-yard touchdown pass against the Colts. Caster had overcome his early shortcomings. He could look back at it now.

"The first few years had been an education," revealed Caster. "They certainly didn't prepare you for boos in college. Weeb Ewbank, who was coaching the Jets then, used to tell me how another receiver, Don Maynard, went through the same thing, dropping balls. If you don't have the personality to deal with that pressure, you can't make it as a professional athlete.

"I realized that my play has to be predicated on concentration. I am always trying to score on every catch and running before I have the ball. I have to look the ball into my hands and forget where I'm going. Just catch it.

"I had problems. I'd take them out on the field with me. I'd drop the ball. The booing made everything worse. I'd be thinking, 'What's going to happen if I drop the next one?' I'd be so tied up that, when the ball would hit my hands, my fingers would tighten and I couldn't react. Well, I've gotten over that now."

The only problem was that the Jets couldn't get over losing. In 1976, they hired a new coach, Lou Holtz. He was supposed to lead the Jets into a new era. He was given a five-year contract to do it. It was the fourth coach that Caster had played for in the seven years he had been with the club. It was another period of adjustment. Holtz realized Caster's value from the very beginning.

"He's one of the premier players in the NFL," exclaimed Holtz. "He's an excellent receiver and one of the most highly respected players on the team for toughness and as a great competitor. He's one of the most sought-after players on the club. There are more inquiries about him about a trade than any other."

Still, it was a most difficult year for Caster. The team was young, Namath didn't have a good year, and the Jets experimented a great deal with a rookie quarterback, Richard Todd. Compounding the problems was the fact that the club's top wide receiver, Jerome Barkum, was injured and missed the entire campaign. Opposing teams immediately took advantage and began double-teaming Caster.

The season was a nightmare for Caster. In an effort to control the ball more, the Jets decided to run more than pass. That meant more blocking duties for Caster. And when they still couldn't win,

Holtz decided to put Caster at a wide receiver spot again. The Jets only won three games, and Caster caught only 31 passes for 391 yards, his lowest season total ever.

"I think I have had more success as a tight end," confessed Caster. "There has been more individual achievement playing there."

Nobody will disagree with him . . .

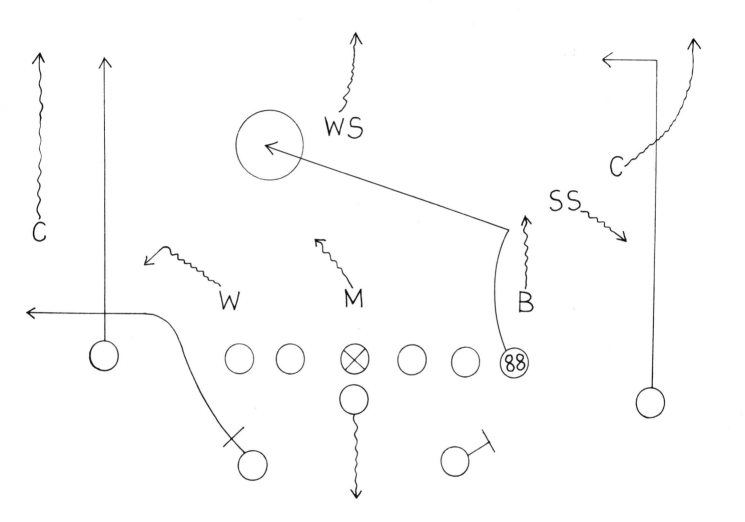

Diagrammed by Coach Walt Michaels

Isaac Curtis

The game was big. It was one the Cincinnati Bengals had to win. They were in first place throughout most of the 1976 season. But the Pittsburgh Steelers were coming on. The defending world champions had started the season slowly. But now they were chasing the Bengals in an effort to try for a third successive championship. Nobody had ever done it before. The Bengals were playing the Houston Oilers in a late season game. They were in trouble. And when they are, they usually look to Isaac Curtis.

Cincinnati had trailed the Oilers throughout most of the game. But now they were running out of time. And almost out of hope. The Bengals had a fourth down on the Oilers' 47-yard line and needed four yards for a first down. What made the situation even more desperate was the fact that there were only 42 seconds left to play and the Bengals were trailing by three points. It was the Bengals' last chance to pull out a victory.

Quarterback Ken Anderson waited for the play to come in from the bench. That's the Bengals' way of doing things. They call all the plays. Their thinking is that it takes a lot of pressure off the quarterback. A lot of times, games are won or lost on one play. That was the situation now. What Anderson and his teammates had to do was to execute.

Houston's defense was in short yardage formation. They wanted to prevent the first down. That was the percentage play. They were challenging the Bengals to make it. If Cincinnati could make it, they

could go for another and then attempt a field goal that would tie the game at 27–27. That was the way the Oilers figured it. And their strategy was right.

But the Bengals were figuring another way. Although Curtis had been watched with double coverage throughout most of the struggle, they had designed a play especially for him. It was a short pass, one that would gain the necessary yards for the first down. But they added something else. They told Curtis to split the defenders and maybe, just maybe, he could break loose for a touchdown.

The play had to be executed quickly. Almost as soon as the ball was snapped, Anderson fired a quick pass to Curtis. The fleet receiver caught the ball in the middle and managed to split the defenders. With the secondary playing in tight, Curtis had nothing but an open field in front of him. He sped the rest of the way for the touchdown that provided the Bengals with a thrilling 31–27 victory.

Houston's cornerback, Zeke Moore, and safety Mike Reinfeldt were responsible for coverage of the play. Still, Oiler coach Bum

Phillips didn't blame either for the touchdown. It was just perfectly executed.

"We had double coverage on the right man," explained Phillips. "But Curtis is like a topwater bug. We just couldn't get hold of him. Sometimes you can fault yourself and say you didn't do this or do that. It was just a doggone good play by Curtis. We had a hard time hitting him. He just didn't want to be hit.

"We had to be in a man-for-man coverage there, to stop any short passes. That's why there wasn't much pursuit around the ball. Curtis has really improved in the three years I've been watching him. He was good when he came up, but not as good as he is now."

But it wasn't always that easy for Curtis. In fact, his whole world nearly collapsed while he was at the University of California. He was a track star who could run the 100 in 9.3. He also played football as a running back. However, the National Collegiate Athletic Association (NCAA) ruled that Curtis wasn't eligible to play football his senior year. They claimed that he hadn't taken a certain test required of incoming freshmen three years before. Curtis was shocked. So were the school authorities. They maintained that it wasn't Curtis's fault.

The fact is, Curtis did take a freshman test. Unfortunately, it wasn't the one required by the NCAA. So the NCAA put California on probation and banned the school from playing in the Rose Bowl. That hurt. Curtis was so depressed that he quit California. Fortunately, however, he transferred to San Diego State for his senior semester.

The experience at California haunted Curtis. He was constantly approached by writers hounding him about the irregularities that cost the school a trip to the Rose Bowl. He felt like a criminal. He became aloof and withdrawn. He was tired of the hassle. All he wanted was to be left alone and play his final year of football. He didn't want any more interviews.

The switch to San Diego State was the best thing that happened to Curtis. The coach at the time, Don Coryell, decided to make Curtis a wide receiver. Curtis couldn't be happier. The move pleased him.

"I felt real good about switching to a receiver," admitted Curtis. "I wanted to be a receiver ever since I went to college. However, California needed a running back, so that's where they used me."

In 11 games as a receiver, Curtis caught 44 passes for 832 yards and seven touchdowns. Even though he didn't establish any records, he drew attention. He was often the target of writers off the field, while on it he almost always had two defenders guarding him. He played with a great deal of pressure.

"They were really scared of Isaac," remarked Coryell. "We had a lot of outstanding receivers over the years, but none had been double-teamed all the time."

Although he played only one season as a wide receiver, Paul Brown, who was coaching the Bengals back then, kept a close eye on Curtis. He was impressed with Curtis not only for his speed but also for his great ability to catch the ball. And he realized, too, that he did so under a great emotional strain. An athlete performing under those circumstances rates high with Brown.

The former Cincinnati coach has a sharp eye for judging receivers. When he was coaching the Cleveland Browns in their glory days, he had one of the premier ones in Paul Warfield. In Curtis, he saw another Warfield. He detected the finer things in Curtis. He realized that Curtis displayed quickness in short bursts. That he was smooth and ran good pass patterns. He didn't hesitate to make Curtis his number one draft pick in the 1973 draft.

"Curtis was the top-rated athlete on our list," exclaimed Brown. "He was the first guy we drafted to fill a skill position. In the past, when we were building the Bengals, we went for the meat and potatoes guys, linemen. Now we had someone special.

"I'll tell you this, those defensive backs who try to bump-and-run had better be able to run if they can't bump. He's a super prospect with superstar potential. I'm impressed with his exceptional speed and agility, and his ability to catch the ball. He should give us a definite outside threat."

Unfortunately, Curtis started out slowly with the Bengals. He had tried too hard in his first workout and had incurred a hamstring pull. That limited his workouts.

Curtis was told that he couldn't get by with just speed alone. He had to run precise patterns, work on timing with the quarterback. He also had to learn to control his blinding speed, not to go all out. Instead, he was instructed to turn on his speed at the proper time, when the defensive back wouldn't be expecting it.

It wasn't until the fourth pre-season game that Curtis saw any action. He didn't catch a pass and ran the wrong pattern. The next week he drew raves when he leaped high in the air on a "go-pattern" and blew past his defender for a 32-yard touchdown. Still, Curtis wasn't looked upon as a starter.

But fate interceded. The team's regular wide receiver, Charlie Joiner, suffered a serious leg injury just before the opener. Curtis began the 1973 season as the Bengals' regular receiver. And he handled the pressure well. The first half he spent learning and getting the feel of things. The rest of the campaign he burst into stardom. That fast. He scored eight touchdowns in seven games, averaging an amazing 42 yards a touchdown. Overall, Curtis finished his rookie year with 45 receptions for 843 yards, an average of 18.7 yards a catch. He also scored nine touchdowns, the longest being 77 yards.

"Every week I had to adjust to a different style," explained Curtis about his rookie season. "Some backs are more physical than others. Some will hit you once and then run with you, while others just keep on hitting you all the way down the field. After a while that gets to be ridiculous.

"The bump-and-run sort of takes away the timing in plays where the quarterback throws the ball before you make your cut. The

quarterback just has to hold the ball and watch you until you can shake loose and make your move."

That was obvious during the 1974 season. Curtis caught fewer passes, 30, but gained 633 yards and scored 10 touchdowns. His average catch was 21.1 yards, second highest in the AFC. It wasn't his fault that he caught fewer passes. The Bengals were decimated by injuries toward the latter part of the season, and that had an effect on the club's passing attack. In the last three games of the season, Curtis caught only one pass and the Bengals significantly lost all three games.

"Anderson and I can solve any zone if he has the time," claimed Curtis. "That was something he wasn't getting toward the end of the season. By then we were missing two regular linemen and out two running backs who were sidelined with injuries."

In 1975, Curtis had his best season. He caught 44 passes for 934 yards, an average of 21.2 yards a catch, which was the best in the

AFC. It might have been the result of his first full training camp. In his rookie year he was hurt, and in 1974 the players' strike delayed camp a month. At least he had a full summer to work with Anderson.

But in 1976, Curtis's production dipped a bit. He caught 41 passes for 766 yards, an average of 18.7 a reception. He reached a low of scoring only six touchdowns. It emphasized a weakness in the Bengals' passing game. Curtis was constantly double-teamed, simply because Cincinnati did not have another deep threat receiver to pull the coverage away from him. Still, his presence alone enabled Anderson to work his short passing game.

"The greatest thing I've learned as a pro is patience," revealed Curtis. "I have to take my time and be ready, not get flustered. The other teams know I have the speed to go deep downfield. Even if I go only once, twice, or three times the whole game, the defense has to be ready all the time. Because, as far as they know, I could be going deep at any time.

"I don't model myself after any other receiver. When I watch another game, I study the defensive backs because they are the guys I have to play against. I was always able to catch a ball and run. I've had to learn how to adapt myself to the defenses."

Apparently he has . . .

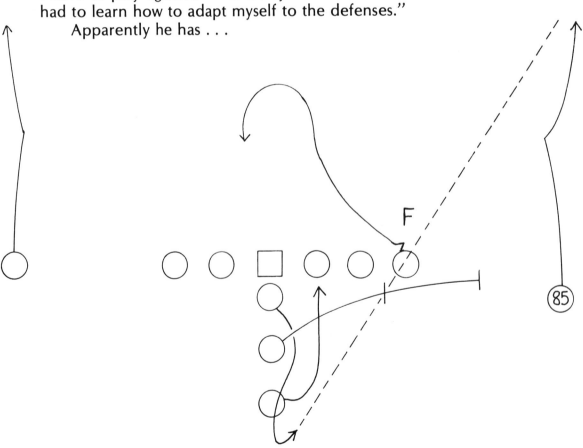

Diagrammed by Coach Bill Johnson

Russ Francis

It was unheard of. He didn't play any football his final year in college. There was some talk among the pro scouts that he was not easily motivated. Yet he was picked on the first round of the 1975 college draft. That had never happened before in the history of the National Football League. Nobody who had ever sat out a season was ever picked on the first round. That indicated how much of a prospect he was. He looked like all-world. He was tall, 6'6", weighed 240 pounds, and could do the 40 in 4.6. Though he was a free spirit who did anything he felt like doing, he was also a talented tight end. One that comes along once every seven years or so. Big, strong, fast, and fearless. The New England Patriots didn't hesitate in making Russ Francis their top choice in 1975.

Actually, the Patriots had been eyeing Francis for at least four years. Their scouts had been watching him ever since he enrolled at the University of Oregon. So were a lot of other teams after his junior year. But when he quit football his senior year, they lost interest. Except for the Patriots. They considered him a blue-chip prospect. And yet he was somewhat of a paradox. In his college career, Francis caught a total of 39 passes, didn't play his final year, and yet was coveted by the Patriots as a first-round draft choice.

Still, the previous spring, the Patriots had had a difficult time locating Francis. He had dropped out of school because football coach Ray Enright had been fired. Enright was the third coach he had played for at Oregon. He was tired of the changes, tired of start-

ing all over again; and besides, he felt that Enright had done a good job and shouldn't have been fired. That's what he believed, and all efforts to get him to return were futile.

What Francis did was to stay at his father's 320-acre ranch, which was located about 20 miles southeast of Eugene, Oregon. He had volunteered to look after the spread while his father conducted his business as a wrestling promoter in Hawaii and another brother was attending Arizona State University. It was Patriots' scout Dick Steinberg who finally succeeded in locating Francis.

"The hardest part was finding him," related Steinberg. "Once we found the farm, we were all right. I went out there in the spring with a guy from Atlanta. We weighed Francis, measured him, and tried to talk him into going back to school because we were worried about the World Football League or the Canadian League grabbing him.

"He came down to the school's track for us and ran a 40-yard dash. He only had bare feet and he wasn't in shape, but he ran 4.7. Twice! He was a phenomenal-looking guy. Size, speed. Physically he's everything you're looking for. In fact, he looks like a movie star."

The final report by Steinberg convinced the Patriots about Francis. He had been checked periodically by the team's local scouts. Which Francis didn't appreciate too much after awhile. He felt that it was just a lot of wasted time.

"You definitely feel like you're under a microscope," recalled Francis. "Guys grab you under your arms to see if you've got anything there. Then they talk to you to see if you've got anything there. If you talk to a national guy, like Dick Steinberg, it isn't bad. He doesn't make you feel so much like a product. It's the local guys who always are there with the same old stuff. I tried to avoid it as much as I could."

He did so by wrestling. Since his father had been a professional wrestler, Francis had an excellent background for the sport. He wrestled mostly in the Midwest, hitting such cities as Detroit, St. Louis, Chicago, Duluth, Winnipeg, and Minneapolis. At times he would participate in tag team matches with his brother or in a three-man tag team match when his father would join them.

"I was raised in Hawaii where my father wrestled quite a bit," disclosed Francis. "It was great. Every kid should grow up in Hawaii. The sun. The beach. We went swimming every day. But, it's a whole different world when you're a wrestler's son. You get into fights a lot. Kids are always challenging you, asking you about wrestling. You become a little introverted."

One day Francis had a scare. Not in the wrestling ring, but in an airplane. Francis, who flies his own plane, was going from Seattle to Portland to fulfill a wrestling engagement that night. Before he got there, he experienced the most frightening moment of his life.

"It was only a short trip, about 250 miles," explained Francis. "But there's mountains in between. I wasn't instrument-rated, and the weather wasn't good. The guy at the airport said, 'It's a marginal, but I think you can get through.'

"I got into the mountains and I hit clouds. Then I lost my directional wits. I felt like I was upside down; the plane was spinning, and I didn't know where I was. I was trying to read the map to find out where the mountains were. I was talking to Seattle, and I was trying to keep the plane straight all at the same time. I've never been so scared in my life.

"I made a 180-degree turn, and after that, I broke out into a small hole in the clouds to see a town down there. It was the greatest relief in my life. After landing, I looked at the map; and if I had gone straight ahead, I'd have run into the mountains in five or ten seconds. Any wider turn and I'd have run into the trees. I went home and really studied instrument flying after that."

There was even more to Francis. He was a surfer, skier, scuba diver, rodeo rider, and a good tennis and baseball player. He was such a good baseball prospect as a pitcher that he was drafted by the Kansas City Royals. But he was determined to play pro football.

"That's the reason I quit the rodeo bit," explained Francis. "I had some close calls. I was stepped on by bulls a couple of times, and it left me immobile awhile. I decided it wasn't worth it."

In another strange turn of events, Francis was selected to play in the 1975 College All-Star game against the Pittsburgh Steelers. He hadn't played football in a year. But he was such a great athlete that he was named to the squad. He showed why during the pre-game workouts by blocking everything in his way. He was so intense in the workouts that the coaches had to implore him to ease up because he was hurting too many defensive players. It was no wonder that he was voted one of the team captains.

"He's potentially the best prospect for a tight end that I have ever seen," exclaimed Patriot coach Chuck Fairbanks. "I'd have to say Francis has as much talent to play tight end as anybody to ever come along."

It wasn't long before Francis established himself as the Patriots' regular end. Three weeks into the season, Francis moved into the starting lineup. He replaced veteran Bob Windsor. Ironically, when Steve Grogan took over for the injured Jim Plunkett at quarterback, Francis became more of an offensive threat.

In a game against the Buffalo Bills, Grogan hit Francis with seven passes that accounted for 125 yards. Francis gave the Patriots another dimension in their passing game, a big tight end who could go deep. And the more he played, the more he was improving.

"His ability to get deep has made other teams get more concerned," pointed out Fairbanks. "We're seeing some different coverage directed at the tight end than we were seeing earlier. Francis has made some outstanding plays both as a receiver and as a blocker. He's still somewhat inconsistent in his overall play. But he's demonstrated his obvious physical talents right from the beginning, and he shows a continuing desire to excel."

Francis was learning a lot out on the field. Soon a great many linebackers began trying to intimidate him. Francis learned to live with it. However, he didn't expect it to be so violent at times.

"Frank Nunley of the 49ers was really something," disclosed Francis. "He swung at me all day long. He even tried to kick me. Then, after the game, he came over and said, 'I hope I didn't offend you. I just wanted to see how much you could take.'

"It was an aspect of the NFL I didn't expect to see. I saw some linebackers who would tackle a guy and hold only his leg and roll over hoping to screw up the guy's leg. I've seen people who twist an ankle in a pileup, punch you on the ground, spit at you.

"It doesn't seem like much, but football's such an emotional game. When a guy looking at you across the line spits in your face, it gets you kind of upset."

Francis didn't get that upset his rookie season. He caught 35 passes for 636 yards, an average of 18.2 yards a reception. Most wide receivers don't average that high. Francis also caught four touchdown passes. It was a good beginning.

Still, Francis wasn't totally pleased with his initial effort. Before the 1976 campaign began, Francis studied game films of his rookie season. He shook his head in disbelief at what he saw.

"I didn't get much chance last year to see what I had done on film," explained Francis. "From what I've seen, I can't believe how bad I was. I couldn't believe some of the things I did. Some guys said the Patriots made another mistake when they drafted me, and I guess because of that I wanted to do so well that I put pressure on myself."

Fairbanks admitted that Francis didn't play too well at the beginning. He felt that he made a lot of mistakes early in the season. But it was Francis's performance in the second half of the campaign that had Fairbanks thinking about 1976. He realized that both Grogan and Francis would benefit from a year's experience.

In a crucial early season game against the Pittsburgh Steelers, Francis made a dramatic clutch reception to help provide the Patriots with a 30–27 triumph. It was on a "Flow 136 Teddi," which is a tight end delay. It's a play in which everybody rolls in one direction and Francis cuts over the other way. It worked for a 38-yard touchdown. Francis finished the game with six receptions for 139 yards.

The only thing that slowed Francis the rest of the campaign was a pulled hamstring muscle. It caused him to miss quite a few games. As a result, his production dropped from the year before. He caught only 26 passes for 367 yards, averaging 14.1 yards a catch and only three touchdowns.

Still, the Patriots made it to the playoffs. In the opening round game against the Oakland Raiders, the Patriots expired in the final minute, 24–21. Francis was double-covered throughout the entire game. Yet he managed to catch four passes for 96 yards, one going for a touchdown. He took a physical beating, being mauled by the Raiders and suffering a bloody nose. He never wavered.

"I like running a pass route right and concentrating completely on the ball; then, when I catch it, switch my concentration completely on running because I like contact," disclosed Francis.

It's suicide to get in his way . . .

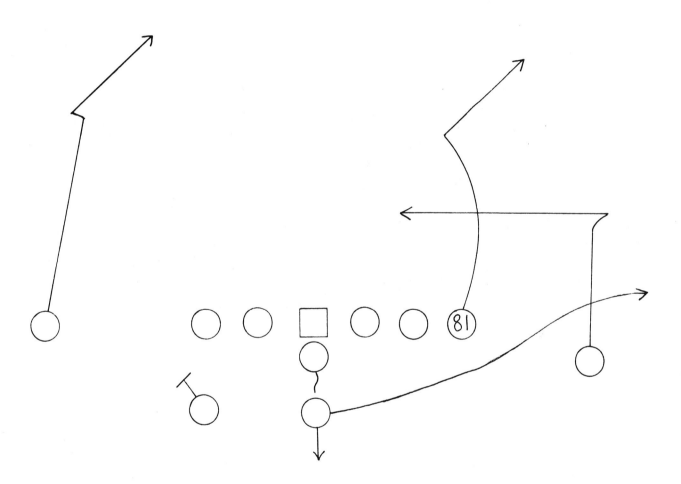

Diagrammed by Coach Chuck Fairbanks

Mel Gray

Time was running out. There were only 25 seconds left on the clock. The St. Louis Cardinals had the ball deep in Washington Redskins' territory. On the six-yard line. But it was fourth down. That's what made the next play so important. They were trailing in the game, 17-10. They needed a touchdown to tie the game and send it into overtime. The Redskins are a veteran team, one that usually doesn't give up a touchdown in such a situation. The Cardinals had to win to stay ahead of the Redskins in the close 1975 race for the Eastern Division lead in the NFC.

There was no question that quarterback Jim Hart was going to pass. He had a number of good receivers to throw to, like tight end Jackie Smith, wide receiver Earl Thomas, running back Terry Metcalf, or another wide receiver, little Mel Gray. At 5'9", 172 pounds, Gray was the smallest player on the field . . . almost. Washington corner-back Pat Fischer, who used to play with the Cardinals, was the same size. He and Gray had been going at each other all day.

Hart kneeled in the huddle and carefully went over the vital play. He looked up and saw that Gray was bleeding from a cut across the bridge of his nose. That was the result of a smash from Fischer. The feisty Redskin cornerback had snapped off Gray's face mask with such a jolt that he had cut the little receiver's nose.

It didn't matter now. What concerned the Cardinals was scoring a touchdown. And they had only one play to do it. Hart looked again at Gray after he had everyone's attention. He called Gray's number for the deciding play. Gray understood. Hart pleaded with his teammates to execute their assignments so he could deliver the ball to Gray in the end zone.

The Cardinals lined up for their last chance. Gray was flanked far to the right. Thomas was split on the other side. Hart called out the cadence clearly. Timing was so important now. At the snap of the ball, Gray darted straight down the sidelines. He gave a head fake toward the corner of the end zone and then cut sharply in the middle, right in front of the goalposts.

Hart's pass was a little high. But Gray leaped and clutched the ball in his midsection. He made a clutch catch between two defenders. Fischer immediately started grabbing Gray's arms to pull them away from the ball. As the two players fell to the ground, the ball popped loose.

Only a split second before, the Cardinal players had been excitedly leaping up and down with joy. Two officials had extended their arms straight overhead to indicate a touchdown. However, a third, noticing the ball rolling on the ground, ruled that the pass was incomplete. Was it a touchdown? Did the Cardinals tie the game? Or did they lose it on a controversial play?

Confusion took place. Both teams were arguing the play. Referee Fred Silva waved everyone away and conferred with all six members of his crew. They discussed it carefully. First one, then another. The outcome of the game rested on Silva's decision. A few seconds later, Silva held up his arms to signal a touchdown. The hometown Cardinal fans roared. The Redskins, led by Fischer, protested vehemently. It was to no avail. The Cardinals had tied the game at 17–17. The game went into overtime, and the Cardinals won it on a field goal, 20–17, to knock the Redskins out of the race. Yet, it wouldn't have been possible if Gray hadn't made his dramatic reception.

It was typical of Gray. He is one of the game's most feared receivers. He can make it happen on just one play. All because he can run like nobody else can. Gray has been known to run the 100 in 9.2. Nobody, but nobody, can do it faster.

Before his memorable catch, Gray was intimidated all day by Fischer. The Redskin cornerback tried to unnerve the speedy receiver. Fischer kept pulling at his jersey and giving him a lot of talk. Such nuances are intended to break a receiver's concentration. When they met earlier in the season, Fischer was a bit more physical. He belted Gray with a vicious forearm to the back of his helmet. Gray heard bells. Still, he hung tough waiting for his chance.

"I don't know why he does those things," remarked Gray. "He said I wasn't worth a damn and things like that. I didn't talk back to him. I don't like to talk to defensive backs during a game. But after the game was over, I told him that dirty players never win. He told me to get lost."

When the 1975 campaign ended, the Cardinals won the division title. Significantly, Gray experienced his finest season in his five years with the club. He caught 48 passes for 926 yards, an average of 19.3 yards a catch, while scoring 11 touchdowns. His yardage was tops in the NFC, and he tied Pittsburgh's Lynn Swann for most touchdowns in the NFL.

Still, when the Cardinals drafted Gray in 1971, nobody knew how good he would be. In fact, the Cardinals waited until the sixth round to select Gray, who played at the University of Missouri. The truth is, when you're only 5'9", there are not many pro teams who get excited. In fact, most of the NFL teams looked upon Gray as a brittle track star. He was known more for his exploits on the cinder track than on the gridiron. Gray had won all sorts of Big Eight meets in the 100, 220, and long jump events.

Gray, himself, wondered if he was pro material. He was aware that not many players of his size made it in the pros. He wasn't too certain if he would be drafted at all.

"When I was in college, playing pro ball was really up in the air," admitted Gray. "I knew my speed would help me out, but I still had doubts because of my size.

"I played running back in high school but I'd catch passes coming out of the backfield. Playing wide receiver at Missouri was a big change. At first, I would run as fast as I could, usually out of control. It took some time, but I learned how to run under control and concentrate on the ball."

In his first year with the Cardinals in 1971, Gray was used sparingly. When he did play, he displayed blinding speed. He was clocked at 4.3 in the 40, which is really moving. In the limited time he played, he caught 18 passes for 534 yards, a remarkable average of 29.7 yards a catch. The Cardinals also used Gray a great deal of the time on kickoff returns. He handled the ball more times there, 30, and averaged 24.7 yards a run. He showed enough to be named Rookie of the Year.

Gray's progress was hampered in 1972. He suffered a number of injuries that sidelined him for practically the entire season. He played so little that he caught only three passes and ran back only 17 kicks. It was a very frustrating year for Gray.

"I never thought I was at any kind of a crossroads, nor did I worry about whether or not I'd make it," disclosed Gray. "As a rookie, I was still learning, and we had people like John Gilliam and Dave Williams. There wasn't much a rookie could do then to break in. My biggest problem was nervousness when I did get to play. I was so nervous in one pre-season game my rookie year I blew a play. The quarterback had changed the play at the line of scrimmage, and I was so nervous I didn't hear it. I ran inside, and the quarterback was looking for me outside."

But the Cardinals remembered Gray's rookie season. When the 1973 campaign began, Gray had moved into the starting lineup. He grabbed 29 passes for 513 yards, an average of 17.7 yards a reception. He showed more speed when he broke loose on an 80-yard touchdown. It was the longest of the seven he scored.

By now, the Cardinals realized how valuable a weapon Gray was as a deep threat. In 1974, he was relieved of his kickoff duties. That was too risky. Instead, the Cardinals utilized Gray strictly as a wide receiver. Gray appreciated it. He pulled down 39 passes for 770 yards, an average of 19.3 yards a catch. He again accounted for an 80-yard bomb as he scored six touchdowns. Gray was named to several all-league and all-conference teams.

Naturally, Gray was getting accustomed to seeing double coverage. His catlike speed dictated it. But now that defenders aren't allowed to bump and run with him all the way until the ball is thrown, he is that much more dangerous. Now, the rules only allow one bump.

"With me being small and with my speed, they've got to get a good hit on me the first time because once I'm past the defender, I'm gone," exclaimed Gray. "Some of the teams are playing me looser, and some with double coverage. But mostly the defensive back is 10 to 15 yards off the line of scrimmage, so it takes me longer to get up on him and he has more time to watch me and the quarterback.

"I've learned to do more things now. I can read defenses better, so I react and make the defensive man try and come to me. I can work the sidelines on the short passes better, and I'll go over the middle on the post patterns more.

"Football is just like chess. There's always an opening somewhere in the secondary. There's always a move to counter anything they do. If I'm double-teamed, it feels good to split them both. If it's one-on-one, it feels good to beat him. It feels good every time I go downfield and I can get a good block.

"I make my speed work for me since I don't have the size to get into it with the bigger defensive backs. I'll vary my moves from play to play so as never to allow a back to get a good 'read' on me. I'll use different moves on the same play. There is more to running a pass pattern than just running it. It requires great concentration by a receiver to know what the defense will do in certain situations and to know the players who are working against you. It is also important for the quarterback and the receiver to always be thinking alike, to know each other so well that neither has to communicate verbally."

Before the 1976 season began, Gray was hoping he could gain 1,000 yards. He came close in 1975 when he gained 926. He might have made it then, but the coaches were thinking about the playoffs and didn't use Gray as much the final two games.

Although he didn't reach his goal in 1976, Gray nevertheless had another fine year. He again led the Cardinals in receptions with 36, and gained 686 yards. His catches averaged 19.1 yards, and he scored five touchdowns. He might have caught more, but he missed a lot of playing time with injuries.

"I think people are looking for me a little more now," reasoned Gray. "It's an intimidation kind of thing. I'm getting shots to the back of the head, forearms across the face, slaps on the helmet. If they just slap at me, I can duck a lot of times. But the thing you have to watch for is the forearm. Some defensive backs keep their forearms cocked back just to scare me away from blocking them on a running play.

"I used to have a complex. But now I don't look at my size anymore. I've proven I can play with the big guys and take the punishment."

He has indeed . . .

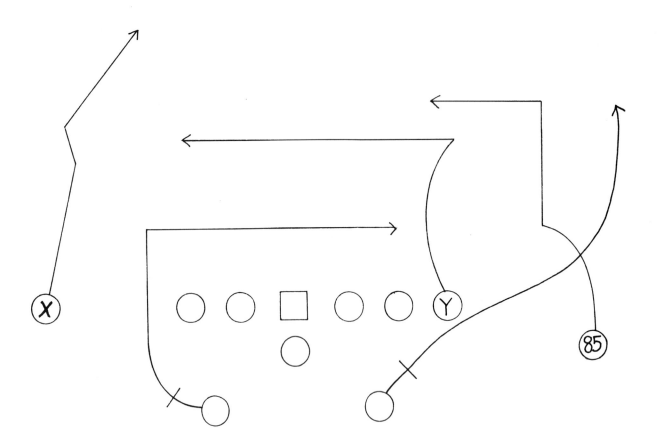

Diagrammed by Coach Don Coryell

Harold Jackson

It was one of those memorable performances. One that nobody forgets. Something that happens once in a lifetime. Like a command performance. It's something that takes endless hours of preparation. And then, boom! It happens. It is an entire lifetime taking place in a single performance. A cacophony of sound. And over 81,000 people cheering your every move. It's beautiful. It doesn't happen to many players. Only the great ones. Harold Jackson knows the feeling.

It happened in 1973. In early Autumn. On a warm October afternoon that Jackson will always remember. It was a game that had a little extra meaning. Any time you play the Dallas Cowboys, the adrenaline flows a little faster. Like Jackson's did that day. All week long he was filled with anxiety. He knew earlier that week that the game plan that the Los Angeles Rams had devised would revolve around him. Some guys get affected by the pressure. Jackson looked forward to it.

The Rams concurred that running against the Cowboys was a difficult task. They were practitioners of a flex defense, one that would bend but never give. Recognizing it was admirable. Not being stubborn enough to try to challenge it was intelligent. So the Rams' board of strategy advocated an aerial attack. In John Hadl, they had a veteran quarterback who could execute the plan.

Jackson was the prime target. They figured he could work himself free in the Dallas secondary. How open he could get before the game was over they never imagined. The Rams were merely looking

245

for a pass here and a pass there to make the Cowboys' defense snap. And they figured Jackson could do his number on Dallas cornerback Charlie Waters. Did he ever.

After a Dallas punt, the Rams took possession of the ball on their own 24-yard line. Hadl tried a short pass to running back Jim Bertelsen that picked up 12 yards. The other running back, Lawrence McCutcheon, attempted to run up the middle and gain only a yard. On second down, Hadl called a pass to Jackson. It was a long one. Jackson ran straight down the sideline and caught Hadl's pass on the Dallas 20-yard line and continued the rest of the way unmolested for a touchdown. The play covered 63 yards, and the Rams jumped in front, 7–0.

Within a minute, the Rams' offense was back on the field. The Cowboys had fumbled the kickoff, and the Rams had recovered on the 27-yard line. Then, on third down from the 21, Hadl hit Jackson with a short pass on the 14-yard line for a first down. At that point,

the Rams' attack sputtered. They were again faced with a third-down situation, this time needing 12 yards for a first down.

Looking over the Cowboys' defense, Hadl called a post pattern to Jackson. He was going deep. Jackson took off down the sideline and then cut up the middle of the field for another touchdown. Inside of five minutes, the Rams had moved into a 14–0 lead. However, before the first-period action subsided, the Cowboys scored on an interception to pull within 14–7.

It didn't take long for Jackson to shake loose again. In the opening minutes of the second quarter, the speedy little receiver got behind Waters and caught a 67-yard pass for his third touchdown. He left Waters shaking his head and the crowd cheering his exploits. It was enough to make a team quit.

But Dallas wouldn't yield. They came back with a touchdown to close the gap at 21–14. It was time for Jackson again. Los Angeles was in control on the Dallas 36-yard line staring at a second and nine situation. Hadl asked Jackson to go deep once more. Jackson took off and caught Hadl's pass on the 12-yard line and went in untouched for his fourth touchdown of the half! The Cowboys couldn't believe what was taking place and neither could the rabid Ram fans. Later they converted a 37-yard field goal for a comfortable 34–14 halftime advantage.

Jackson's adrenaline was really flowing. He wasn't even tired. He was looking to add to his impressive totals once the second half got underway. But the Rams didn't attack with any intensity. Instead, they were a citadel of conservation. Resorting to a ground offensive, they employed two tight ends and disdained the long pass. As a result, Hadl threw only six passes the rest of the game, one a 44-yard one to Jackson in the third quarter that positioned a 35-yard field goal. That was all the scoring the Rams did. They managed to withstand a Cowboy rally and walk off the field with a 37–31 victory.

The resourceful Jackson had experienced the biggest day of his career. He had finished the game with seven passes for 238 yards and four touchdowns. When the season was over, he had accumulated 40 passes for 874 yards. He had averaged 21.9 yards a catch and had scored 13 touchdowns to top the NFL in both categories. It was a gratifying year for Jackson.

It wasn't that way at the beginning of Jackson's career. The Rams drafted him on the 12th round from Jackson State in 1968. He was a low-round pick because of his size. At 5'10", 175 pounds, he was considered too small by many scouts to play in the NFL. He never played in a game that year and was traded to the Philadelphia Eagles at the end of the season. Jackson was somewhat relieved.

"I was on the Rams' taxi squad, and I was the receiver they worked on for each game," disclosed Jackson. "If we were playing the 49ers, I was Gene Washington all week. If we were playing another team, I was someone else.

"Actually, I don't remember much about my first year with the Rams, except that I got hit up the side of my head a lot. George Allen, who was coaching the team then, used to teach the linebackers and cornerbacks how to hold up the wide receivers at the line of scrimmage. So, I spent a great deal of time getting whacked around by Jack Pardee.

"I'll never forget the day Allen traded me, though. It was July 4th, Independence Day! That was a lucky break for me. I had a grudge against Allen, but I got it out of my system later on."

The trade was the best thing that could have happened for Jackson. Instead of being Gene Washington or anyone else, Jackson was himself. That's all he ever wanted. A chance to show what he could do. The Eagles immediately gave him the opportunity. In his first year with them, Jackson had a big year. He caught 65 passes and led the NFL in yards gained with 1,116. Overnight, everybody was talking about Jackson and the Rams were talking to themselves. He had quickly established himself in one year as one of the most explosive

receivers in the league. Suddenly, Harold Jackson wasn't small any-more.

It was because of speed merchants like Jackson that the zone defense was designed to curtail the effectiveness of the long pass. Jackson's receptions dropped to 41 and 47 the next two years, not so

much as a result of the zone as for the fact that the Eagles were weak offensively. Glaringly so.

Jackson broke open in 1972. He led the NFL in receptions with 62 and in yards gained with 1,048. The Rams had had enough. They wanted Jackson back. In one of pro football's biggest trades, the Eagles sent Jackson, running back Tony Baker, first-round draft choices in 1974 and 1975, and a third-round pick in 1976 for quarterback Roman Gabriel. That's how much the Eagles thought of Gabriel. Jackson was happy about returning to the Rams, who were a contender. He had developed as a blue-chip receiver with the lowly Eagles.

"I got zoned on almost every play my last year with the Eagles and still led the league in receptions," pointed out Jackson. "But I learned how to beat it. All you have to do is get between the defensive backs, and if you don't carry around too much height and weight, you can do that if you're quick enough.

"I love zone defenses because the defensive team has to run to get into the defense. In a zone, each of their players is responsible for an area on the field, but they disguise it when the ball is snapped and they run into it. All I do is get there before they do.

"What it boils down to is that I get there before the zone can work on me. I use my speed to beat the defense when they are dropping back, and when they see me, they know they just can't let me run free. Then I use my moves to fake them out. I try to get a defensive man away from where he should be, away from his zone. If my moves are good enough, I usually do, because he has to respect my speed. If you have the speed to run through the zones and the moves to fake the defense around, your quickness is bound to get you open."

Jackson showed how in his first season back with the Rams in 1973. Despite being double-covered most of the time, he caught 40 passes for 874 yards. His average of 21.9 yards a catch led the NFL, as did his 13 touchdowns.

While most coaches like big, fast receivers, Jackson showed them what a small, quick receiver can do. The fact that they also like them strong doesn't upset Jackson in the least. In fact, he feels he can beat any defense he faces and figures the little guy, if he's quick enough, can do it best.

"Little guys have the edge in pass offense today," claims Jackson. "People talk about big targets, but what the passer really wants is an open target, and I've learned how to get open. That's the important thing, getting open.

"Height isn't a problem. A 6'3" receiver in a crowd of 6'3" linebackers is harder to see than a 5'10" receiver like myself who is off by himself somewhere. The only trouble I've had is getting the confidence of the passers. If they'll stick with me another split second, I'm sure to get open.

"I read zones a lot better now. I'm smarter. In the beginning, I used to try and outrun everybody and just run into a crowd all the time. I read the free safety mostly now. If I'm supposed to run a post pattern and he is zoning that way, I'll bring it up short on a curl. But I like to suck up the cornerback with sideline routes. They got to play me tight. Then I can go deeper."

In 1976, Jackson led the Ram receivers for the fourth straight season. He grabbed 39 passes for 751 yards, an average of 19.3 yards a catch. It is quite an accomplishment when considering that the Rams' quarterback position hasn't been all that stable. During that span, Jackson has been teamed with at least four different quarterbacks. It's not an ideal situation. But Jackson has overcome it.

Just the way he did as a youngster. His mother didn't want him to play football. She was afraid that he would get hurt. So Jackson's first two years on a football field in high school were spent playing a trumpet in the band. He finally convinced his mother that he was fast enough to outrun anybody and that he'd never get caught.

Some of the defensive backs around the league know the feeling . . .

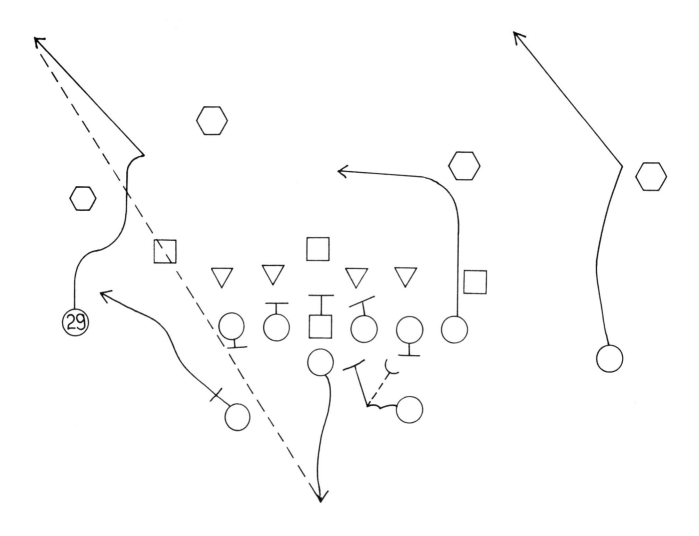

Diagrammed by Coach Chuck Knox

Charlie Joiner

It had taken him eight years. They were eight years without any sense of fulfillment. He had toiled quietly, almost in obscurity. Every time things looked good, something would go wrong. Like injuries. Nothing simple. But serious ones like broken arms and collarbones. Fate was unkind. It was really unfair. He was a quiet type who was liked by everyone. And just when it looked like he had found his place in the sun, someone else came along. It was enough to discourage most guys. And when you're not so big at 5'11" and 188 pounds, you can get discouraged easily. Especially when the breaks aren't going your way. That's how disheartening it can get. But Charlie Joiner never let it get to him.

Before the 1976 season began, Joiner was traded by the Cincinnati Bengals to the San Diego Chargers. He went from a championship contending team to a losing one. But Joiner never complained. Instead, he looked at it positively. It happened to be the biggest break in Joiner's somewhat checkered career. By the time the 1976 season concluded, Joiner had had a year he would never forget. One he was always capable of having but never did for one reason or another. Joiner finished as the American Football Conference's sixth best receiver. He had caught 50 passes for 1,056 yards, the third best total in the National Football League. It was also the second best figure in San Diego's history. Only the legendary Lance Alworth had produced five better seasons. Joiner had averaged a remarkable 21.1 yards a catch and had scored seven touchdowns. All for a team that won only six games.

It was a rewarding year for Joiner. He had been somewhat of a summer soldier. He first began his career with the Houston Oilers in 1969. At first, the Oilers planned to use Joiner as a cornerback. He was drafted by them on the fourth round from Grambling College. The Oilers brought Joiner and a few others into an early camp that spring to give the rookies a good look before regular training camp in July. Joiner was listed as a cornerback. But when he impressed the Oilers' staff with the way he caught passes, they quickly changed their minds. They adjusted their thinking and looked upon Joiner as a wide receiver. After all, besides his pass catching knack, he also had speed. He was clocked at 4.5 in the 40, which is a high rating on any team.

For three days Joiner caught passes. And for three days the fans who were allowed to attend the workouts cheered. They had taken a liking to the quiet youngster. The unassuming rookie didn't drop many either.

"Those people like Joiner so much that he could have fallen down and been cheered," exclaimed an Oiler official. "Joiner was the most impressive rookie in our camp and is one of the most exciting players to join the Oilers in years," added Don Klosterman, the club's general manager. "He has the speed, moves, and hands to become a truly great receiver."

Actually, Joiner was a natural athlete. As a youngster growing up in Lake Charles, Louisiana, Joiner played football, basketball, baseball, and softball. He really excelled in baseball. He didn't play high school football until his junior year. Even then he made all-state two straight years. At Grambling, he played both cornerback and receiver. When the regular split end was injured, Joiner took his place. He caught 30 passes, 10 of which he turned into touchdowns. He caught 35 passes his junior year and 42 his senior season and was named to the all-conference team in all three seasons.

When he reported to the Oilers' training camp, Joiner wasn't sure if he was going to be a wide receiver or a cornerback. He was willing to play either position. But the quick feet and good hands he displayed at rookie camp convinced the Oilers that Joiner would play on offense.

"Hard work is the only way you get anything," observed Joiner. "I'll do anything I can to help this team in any way. I expected a lot of cut-throating but there isn't any. Everybody's helpful.

"I have a tendency to make one long step on my inside and outside cuts, but I think I can correct that. What I really have to do is get all these patterns down. In college, the quarterback called the patterns and yardage in the huddle, considering the yardage that was needed. Here, everything is numbers."

Joiner continued to impress everyone with his pass catching. He was the club's third leading pass receiver during the pre-season campaign. But then he broke his arm and was sidelined for almost the

entire season. He did manage to recover soon enough to catch seven passes.

The following year, Joiner showed no bad effects from his injury. He was so improved that he was considered the best receiver in camp. But, once more, fate was unkind. He broke the same right arm a second time. And the potential superstar the Oilers envisioned was once again sidelined by a fluke practice injury. Joiner had stretched out his arm to catch a ball and had banged it hard on a teammate's helmet.

Three months later, Joiner had recovered. The season was halfway over when he was activated for a game against the San Diego Chargers. He made his debut a dramatic one. He caught five passes for 100 yards, one of them for a 46-yard touchdown. He was so open on the play that the Charger defensive backs didn't even bother to pursue him. Joiner finished the season with 28 receptions. He averaged 14.9 yards a catch, which was the highest on the team.

"I played six years of football prior to coming to the Oilers," revealed Joiner. "I had never been hurt. I think everybody who plays has to expect to get hurt. But I think my injuries were more accidents than anything else.

"I did two sets of 15 pushups each day during the off-season to strengthen my arms and shoulders. I didn't do the pushups on my fingers because I wasn't trying to build them up. I don't think I'll have any problems this time around."

Joiner was ready for the 1971 season. The Oilers felt that way, too. They traded wide receiver Jerry LeVias, their number two draft pick in 1968, to San Diego. That's how much they thought of Joiner. And Joiner didn't disappoint them. He topped the AFC receivers in pre-season with 27 catches. He didn't stop there. He kept on going during the regular season. When it ended, Joiner had 31 receptions for 681 yards. He had an eye-popping 22.0-yard average per catch and seven touchdowns.

It was the kind of season the Oilers had waited for, for three years. Yet, the laconic Joiner was unaffected by it all. He was just grateful that he had played a full season without any crippling injuries. He didn't even let opposing defensive backs bother him.

"A lot of them talk to you during a game, but I don't say anything back," confided Joiner. "They usually tell you how great they are, or how you can't possibly beat them, or how they are going to knock you on your backside. Some of them talk because they are cocky, but some of them talk because they're just plain scared."

In 1972, the Oilers added Ken Burrough to their receiving corps. He was a tall, swift flanker who could go deep. It was a move that Joiner welcomed. He was looking forward to an even bigger year, because opponents now had somebody else to worry about and couldn't concentrate entirely on him.

"Last season, almost every team we played defensed me the

same," pointed out Joiner. "They played a strong zone and rolled toward me. Burrough is a guy who can run a legitimate 9.4 100. There's just no way they can afford to double up on me now.

"I feel a lot more confident this year because I don't have to protect my arm. Now the only thing I have to worry about is catching the ball. It makes a big difference. Don't forget, I had two different quarterbacks throwing to me last year. Sometimes we'd switch at halftime. It might have given me a little trouble on timing. But, after catching both of them a full year, I don't mind."

So Joiner went out and caught 25 passes during the pre-season action to lead the AFC for the second straight year. Two went for touchdowns as he averaged 13.0 yards a catch.

Joiner never got to finish the season with the Oilers. At the end of October, he was traded to the Cincinnati Bengals. The honeymoon with Houston that had just begun was suddenly over.

"I was disappointed, I admit it," remarked Joiner. "I didn't think I'd be traded, because the Oilers didn't have any speed at the outside positions outside of myself and Burrough."

Now Joiner had to learn a new system. He had very little experience with the disciplined short and medium passing game that the Bengals utilize. He worked extra during the off-season with Bill Walsh, the Bengals' quarterback-receiver coach to master the system. His quickness was one thing the Bengals liked.

But fate surfaced again. Early during the 1973 season, Joiner broke his collarbone. Then, in 1974, Isaac Curtis, the club's number one draft choice of a year before, was the deep threat receiver the Bengals always wanted. Joiner saw less action, actually splitting playing time with Chip Myers. Still, in his last season with the Bengals in 1975, Joiner set a club record by catching seven passes for 200 yards against the Cleveland Browns, the most yards ever gained by a receiver in a single game.

Before the 1976 season, the Bengals traded Joiner to San Diego. Joiner welcomed the switch. He didn't like the cold weather and the artificial turf in Cincinnati. But, more importantly, he wanted to be reunited with Walsh, who was the new offensive coordinator for the Chargers. Walsh was probably the catalyst who initiated the trade.

"I would rank Joiner in the top ten of the AFC receivers," claimed Walsh. "The most significant measure of a receiver is his average per catch, and in that area Charlie was in the top five. He had a 19.6 average, which is only a yard and a half behind Curtis's 21.2, which led the league."

Joiner made his presence known early in the 1976 season. In the Chargers' first home game, against the St. Louis Cardinals, Joiner caught five passes for 134 yards and a touchdown in the 43–24 victory. His average yardage per catch that day was 26.8. Nobody averages better than that. He finished the year as the Chargers' best receiver and the fifth best in the AFC.

Nobody appreciated Joiner's efforts more than Walsh. He feels Joiner is the best technician in the league.

"When our other receiver, Gary Garrison, got hurt the second game of the season, Joiner had triple coverage and had been boxed in on nearly every play," stressed Walsh. "But Charlie is so smart he was able to get clear. He has been our best offensive weapon. Joiner is a real technician, the most technically competent receiver in the league. He's an expert in his business. Some are bigger and faster. But as far as being a technician, he's the best."

There is no way to improve on being the best . . .

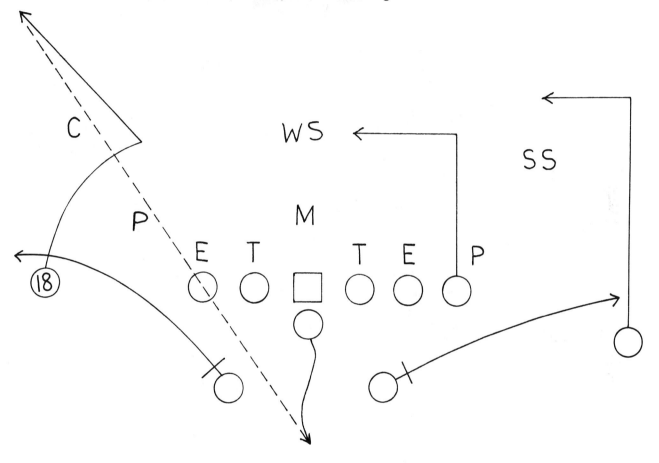

Diagrammed by Coach Tommy Prothro

Drew Pearson

He hadn't caught a pass all day. It was quite unusual. Only one had been thrown in his direction earlier in the game. It had been knocked away. The fact that he had never touched the ball was strange. After all, he was the team's leading pass receiver. And the year before, he was the best also. The only reason they didn't throw the ball to him this particular day was that he was double-teamed on practically every play. That's how much respect the opposing team had for him. And the strategy appeared to be effective. With only 1:51 left in the opening round of the 1975 playoff game, the Minnesota Vikings were leading the Dallas Cowboys, 14–10. And they had done it by stopping the Cowboys' star receiver, Drew Pearson, without a reception.

The situation looked hopeless for the Cowboys. They had the ball deep in their own territory on the 15-yard line. They had to go 85 yards for a touchdown. It seemed impossible. There just didn't seem to be enough time left to go so far a distance for a touchdown, not with the Viking defense looking for a pass on every play. That was what the Cowboys' Roger Staubach had to do—throw on every play he had remaining. And he had to call his plays from a shotgun formation to save precious seconds on every play.

On first down, Staubach threw a quick nine-yard pass to Pearson. It was his first catch of the game. Staubach tried another pass, but it failed. Then on third down, he went back to Pearson with another quick strike. Pearson clutched the ball on the 31-yard line for a first down.

The Cowboys got into trouble on the next play. Center John Fitzgerald snapped the ball low and Staubach recovered the ball on the 25-yard line for a six-yard loss. Staubach was upset. He attempted one pass and then another. Both were incomplete. Dallas was now in a desperate situation. They had a fourth down and 16 with only 44 seconds left on the clock.

The Cowboys were down to perhaps their last play of the game. Staubach gathered his players in the huddle. "I think I can beat Nate Wright on a corner pattern," said Pearson. "Okay," replied Staubach, "run it."

Staubach took the snap. Pearson broke upfield and turned. Staubach's pass was there. Pearson made the catch at midfield and came down out of bounds. The official, however, ruled the catch good, contending that Wright had shoved Pearson out of bounds.

Now there were only 37 seconds left in the game. In the huddle

Staubach looked at Pearson again. "Can you run the same pattern but go deep?" he asked. "No, man. I'm tired," answered Pearson. "Wait awhile."

So Staubach looped a short pass to his running back, Preston Pearson, who dropped the ball. The play took five seconds. Staubach turned once more to Drew Pearson. "Are you ready?" he inquired. "Yes, I'm ready," replied Pearson.

Staubach handled the snap cleanly. He looked for Pearson running down the right sideline. Then he threw the ball deep downfield. Pearson and Wright both leaped for the ball on the five-yard line. Wright fell to the ground. He tried to knock the ball out of Pearson's hands as he was falling down. Pearson secured the ball on his hip and walked in for the game-winning touchdown. It was a miraculous catch that stunned the Minnesota crowd.

"I came off the line, gave Wright a move about 15 yards out, and he started running with me," explained Pearson. "The ball was thrown inside, and I came back and got it. Wright pulled on my arm, and the ball slipped onto my hip and stuck there. It was still there when I went into the end zone.

"It is good to see the ball underthrown in that situation because it is easier for the receiver to find the ball. I was trying to get back to the ball. I knew there was some contact. I thought it might be a pass interference call, one way or the other. It could have gone either way. I thought I saw a flag whizzing by; but when it started rolling, I knew it was something else. It turned out to be an orange. It was a super-lucky catch. I thought I'd dropped it. I mean, my chances were slim and none. Someone must have been doing a lot of praying, and those prayers were answered.

"A lot of planning goes into these games. Everyone does his homework. But in this situation our plans couldn't help us. We had to improvise. Fortunately, Roger and I have good communication. I've made some big catches before, but this was the most thrilling catch of my career."

Staubach himself didn't see Pearson make the catch. There were too many players in front of him standing around and looking downfield.

"It was a Hail Mary pass," smiled Staubach. "We needed a miracle, and we got one. When I saw Wright turn to run with Drew, I felt we had a chance. I just threw the ball as far as I could and prayed.

"I never saw the catch. My accuracy isn't too good on those plays. If we did it again 100 times, we might make it work once. When I saw the official's arms go up for the touchdown, I was stunned. In a situation like we were in, you're just playing on instincts. Your thought is, 'What am I doing here?' Your instincts are doing the work. You're just throwing and hoping. You know there isn't much of a chance, but you're trying anyway."

Ever since he joined the Cowboys in 1973, Pearson had been

making big catches. He had surprised a lot of people. Nobody had thought much of Pearson when the 1973 draft took place. When the tedious process concluded after two days, 442 players were selected. Pearson was not one of them. He didn't impress anyone enough at the University of Tulsa to warrant a pick. It's hard to believe.

Pearson was considered too small by the pro scouts. He was six feet tall and weighed only 180 pounds. In his first two college seasons, he was a quarterback. In his final two years, Pearson was a wide receiver. But Tulsa was a run-oriented team that didn't throw the ball too much. So no one really had a good dossier on Pearson.

Three teams, Dallas, Pittsburgh, and Green Bay, contacted Pearson. All offered him a tryout. Pearson elected to try with Dallas first. He did so despite knowing that the Cowboys were well stocked with receivers, namely Bob Hayes, Lance Alworth, Ron Sellers, Mike Montgomery, and Billy Parks. His chances loomed no better than 1,000–1.

Pearson was among 41 free agents signed by the Cowboys. He attended the rookies' off-season practice sessions and was invited back to work with the veterans in June. He continued to make an impression and was asked to report to regular training camp in July. Pearson's eyebrows were raised when the Cowboys suggested that he move to Dallas.

Things happened fast in training camp. Alworth and Sellers were gone, and Parks was traded to Houston. Still, Pearson was listed behind Hayes, Montgomery, and Otto Stowe, who was acquired from Miami.

"Everybody was down on me because of my size," said Pearson. "But that's a lot of baloney. There are a couple of small guys in the league. It's not how big you are, but how much you want to play. I was disappointed when I wasn't drafted."

Pearson survived the cuts and made the team. He was used primarily on the special teams. After the ninth game of the season, the Cowboys suddenly found themselves short of receivers. Stowe was hurt and so was Montgomery. Coach Tom Landry gave Pearson an opportunity to start. He kept the job the rest of the season.

It was in the opening playoff game against the Los Angeles Rams that Pearson first drew raves. Early in the game, he caught a four-yard scoring pass from Staubach. The Cowboys were ahead, 17–0, when the Rams started to come back. They were gaining momentum as they cut Dallas' lead to 17–16. The Cowboys needed a big play, and they got it from Pearson. He grabbed a perfectly thrown pass from Staubach and turned it into an 83-yard touchdown that broke the Rams' back.

"It was on a play we call '72 Wide Bench,'" revealed Pearson. "The primary receiver was Hayes. When we think the defense is concentrating on the middle, we fake Hayes in that direction and

send him wide toward the bench. I was the secondary receiver, and Staubach told me to run a post pattern up the middle because I had been open on the same play earlier. That's always something I wanted to do, catch a touchdown pass when it really meant something. I never doubted my ability. I just worried about getting a chance."

By the beginning of the 1974 season, Pearson had firmly established himself as a regular. He had shown that he could be depended on for an entire season. And in 1974 Staubach gained even more confidence in Pearson. He went to him more often each game. When the campaign had ended, Pearson had caught 62 passes for

1,087 yards, an average of 17.5 yards a reception. He had done it all, despite playing with a slightly separated shoulder that he incurred early in the season.

Once again he came through with a dramatic catch that won a game. The Cowboys were trailing the Washington Redskins, 21–17, on Thanksgiving Day. They had the ball at midfield with only 15 seconds remaining in the game. Clint Longley was the quarterback at that point. Pearson told him that he was going to change his route on the next play. He did so successfully and caught a 50-yard pass for the game-winning touchdown.

"I don't really want to be known as a big-play man," confessed Pearson. "I'd rather be known as a consistent receiver. I like to contribute. And that doesn't mean I'm being an individual or trying to get my own thing built up. I feel I can contribute that way in a winning way. Do more things like taking a little pressure off the backs.

"The crucial part for receivers is to concentrate on the ball when it's coming, to watch it all the way, look it into your hands. Regardless of whether you have good hands or bad hands, if you concentrate so that you don't know or care about anything else, you'll catch it.

"I don't hear footsteps. I don't care about them. If you get a hard hit, you got to get up and try to put it out of your mind. The whole thing is intimidation. If the back hits you and you show him you're hurt and don't want to come over the middle again, he's accomplished his goal. That's the roughest area, the middle. That's where they can whack you. But if that's where you gotta go to catch the pass, you better be there."

He was there in 1975. Although he caught 46 passes, fewer than the year before, he gained 822 yards, which was an average of 17.9 yards a catch. He pulled down eight touchdown passes, which was six more than he grabbed in 1974. He does it all without great speed. He has the ability to get open, to shift gears and change directions as well as anyone else around the NFL.

Despite facing double coverage a good deal in 1976, Pearson managed to lead the NFC in receptions. He caught 58 passes for 806 yards, an average of 13.9 yards a reception. He got loose for six touchdowns as Dallas missed the playoffs for only the second time in seven years.

"Everywhere I go, people ask me about 'The Catch' against the Vikings," remarked Pearson. "The thing that bothers me is that the controversy has overshadowed the play. People don't say, 'That was some catch.' They ask me if I pushed off. I would like it to be recalled as a great play."

It most certainly was . . .

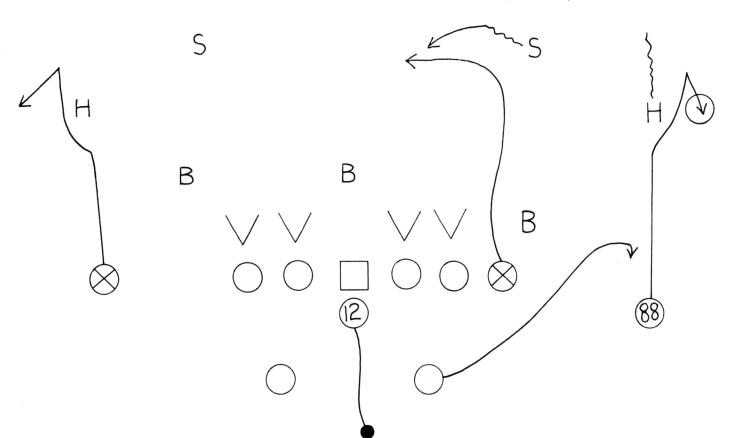

Diagrammed by Coach Tom Landry

Lynn Swann

His head ached. It was like a dull throb. The doctors told him he had suffered a concussion. That's a scary thing for a football player. All he could think about as he lay in the hospital bed was whether he would ever play again. That's what concussions do to players. He was constantly watched by doctors. They checked his eyes to see if his pupils were dilating. They checked his response to light. And to questions. There was nothing to do but wait. It's a helpless feeling. Just waiting. And wondering about the future. He had been in the game of football too short a time for it to end now. Only two years. Finally, Lynn Swann was told by the doctors that he could go home.

The two days that Swann spent in the hospital seemed like a lifetime. Just 48 hours before, he was playing for the Pittsburgh Steelers against the Oakland Raiders in the 1975 AFC championship game. Then, in one play, it was all over. He took a blow to the head that knocked him out. Just a second before, the swift wide receiver had caught a pass from quarterback Terry Bradshaw. He paid the price. He was hit by Raider defender George Atkinson with a forearm smash to the head. It was delivered with such force that Swann fumbled the ball after he caught it.

That didn't matter. What concerned the Steelers was how badly Swann was hurt. After he was revived, he was helped to the bench on rubbery legs. They kept working on him. And when he kept losing his equilibrium, almost falling off the bench a few times, they knew it was serious. He was taken to the dressing room and examined by the team doctor, who instructed the attendant to call for an ambulance because he feared that Swann had a concussion.

When he left the hospital two days later, Swann was told to rest. He was ordered to stay away from football. It didn't matter that the Steelers had defeated the Raiders and were preparing to play in the Super Bowl against the Dallas Cowboys in two weeks. The possibility strongly existed that Swann wouldn't be able to play. It's not easy to come back from a concussion.

As the Super Bowl approached, Swann still hadn't worked out with the team. He wasn't feeling that good. He was examined daily by a doctor. The worry now was that he had post-concussion syndrome. Like blurred vision, or dizziness, or even blackouts. That was the fear Swann had to live with. It was a frightful experience, to say the least.

Swann felt that the Raiders were head-hunting. He doesn't like to play the game that way. Offensive players really can't. They are not allowed to use their hands too liberally. Maybe to push off every now and then. Often the good ones, like Swann, are the victims. That's how the game is played.

"From watching their films, you could see that, all through the season, the method of tackling used by the defensive backs was to go for people's heads," detected Swann. "I don't know whether they feel they are too small to play it any other way, or they are trying to intimidate or hurt you.

"During the course of the game, I must have taken two, three, four shots to the head. Once I was so far away from the play when I got hit that it was ridiculous. I don't think there's any reason for that.

"I don't think Atkinson's hit was enough to have given me the concussion. It was a culmination of all those hits. I personally believe that anything you get away with in pro ball is okay. That's the way the game is played. Other than knowing which way he's running, a receiver hardly holds an edge. You're concentrating on running your pass route or catching the ball. If you think about getting hit, you might as well hand in your gear. You won't catch anything.

"A receiver can't go out there and pay somebody back. You have to be at an emotional high on offense, but it must be controlled. A defensive player can put more aggressiveness into his game. He can be vicious, if you want to use the word."

While the Steelers were waiting for the word from Swann, the two-year pro was quietly thinking to himself. The doctors had told him it was all right for him to play. But they also warned him about some built-in dangers. If he took another hard shot, it could easily cause other damage.

A few days before the game, Swann engaged in light workouts. No contact. He just ran some pass patterns and worked on his timing. He wasn't taking any chances. And the Steelers cautioned him

to take things easy. Yet something was wrong. Swann didn't seem confident.

"In the workouts I was worried," he admitted. "My timing was off. I didn't get dizzy, but I just didn't feel right. I dropped a lot of passes. I had to decide whether it would hurt the team or help the team if I played."

It was the biggest decision of Swann's life. And he pondered it over and over. He knew only he could make the choice. What helped him was a newspaper article he had read. It contained quotes by Dallas safety Cliff Harris, who was described as an agressive player. Harris felt that Swann might be intimidated. He claimed that Swann had to be thinking about his injury, and he'd be scared coming across the middle. That's where receivers take their lumps. It

is open season. It's an area that attracts a crowd of defenders, line-backers included.

"I read that stuff that Harris said," snapped Swann. "He was trying to intimidate me. He said that, because I had a concussion, I would be afraid out there. Well, he doesn't know Lynn Swann or the Pittsburgh Steelers. He can't scare me or this team.

"I said to myself, 'To hell with it. I'm going out there and play 100 percent.' Sure, I thought about being reinjured. But it's like being thrown by a horse. You've got to get up and ride again immediately or you may be scared the rest of your life. The doctors left it up to me whether I wanted to play or not. I decided to play."

The decision was a big one in regard to the Steelers' chances. The Dallas defense was geared to stop Pittsburgh's great fullback, Franco Harris. The power running Harris was the key to the Steelers' attack. He was such a potent force that he could dominate a game. If the Steelers could maintain ball control on Harris' running, they could wear down the opposition. Dallas knew this.

Amazingly, the Cowboys did contain Harris. They did such a good job of it that they led throughout most of the game. They scored first. And after the Steelers tied the game, they walked off the field with a 10–7 halftime edge. After a scoreless third quarter, Pittsburgh began to come back. They were ignited by a blocked punt and, with the benefit of a safety and a field goal, moved into a 15–10 lead.

With 3:02 left in the game, the outcome was still in doubt. The Steelers were faced with a third down and four on their 36-yard line. If they failed to produce a first down, they would be forced to punt. Dallas would then have sufficient time to generate a game-winning touchdown. In essence, the final outcome of Super Bowl X rested on that third down play.

Dallas contrived that Bradshaw would pass. The Steelers needed a first down to control the game. But the Cowboys were determined to exert enough pressure on Bradshaw to prevent it. As the Steelers huddled, Bradshaw emphasized the importance of the play. However, instead of going for a first down, Bradshaw ordered a "69 Maximum Flanker Post." That indicated he was letting it all out and going for a touchdown. It was Swann's play.

At the snap of the ball, Dallas' defense poured in. Linebacker D. D. Lewis blitzed from his outside position. Bradshaw saw him and ducked under his charge. He straightened up and looked for Swann, who was streaking down the right sideline. Bradshaw fired the ball a split second before he was leveled by Harris, who was also blitzing. The trajectory of Bradshaw's pass traveled 70 yards in the air. Swann cut up the middle of the field, reached up for the ball on the Dallas ten-yard line, and went the rest of the way for a touchdown. The dramatic reception was the difference in the game. The Cowboys scored when they got the ball, to reduce Pittsburgh's winning margin to 21–17.

Swann's catch was his fourth of the game. He had two other remarkable catches earlier in the game. One was a leaping 32-yard catch in the first quarter on the Dallas 16-yard line. The other was a 53-yard grab in which he out-jumped the Cowboys' Mark Washington on the Dallas 47-yard line. The other catch, too, was a beauty. He made a 12-yard reception when he dove for an underthrown pass on the Cowboys' five-yard line. Swann was the leading receiver of the game, catching four passes for 161 yards.

"I've never had a day when I felt so loose in all my life," exclaimed Swann in the crowded Steeler dressing room. "No one hit me hard enough to hurt me, just hard enough to want to get up and catch another one. One hundred and sixty-one yards and a touchdown in the Super Bowl is heavy.

"All week long they were checking my eyes for dilation and checking my stability with the same test used by a policeman pulling a guy off the road to see if he is intoxicated. I gave a little thought to not playing if it wasn't advantageous to my health.

"I would have felt bad emotionally and psychologically if I didn't play. But to get hurt and not play in the future would be worse. I was worried that my timing and concentration were off because I didn't have good practices during the week. But I told myself, 'Hey, this is it. Either play your best or not at all.' That first catch gave me a lot of confidence."

The Steelers had a lot of confidence when they made Swann their number one draft pick in 1974. Although he was only 5'11" and weighed 180 pounds, they liked his moves and the way he blocked at the University of Southern California. He had smarts.

In his rookie season, Swann ran back most of the Steelers' kickoffs. As a receiver, he was used sparingly. He caught 11 passes for 208 yards, an average of 18.9 yards a catch. The following season, as the regular receiver, Swann grabbed 49 passes for 781 yards, averaging 15.9 yards a reception while scoring 11 touchdowns.

His production dipped in 1976. He accounted for only 28 receptions for 516 yards. That averaged out to 18.4 yards a catch and three touchdowns. But it was no fault of Swann's. He incurred another concussion in the opening game of the season against the same Raiders. Again, Atkinson was the intimidator. Swann was paying too heavy a price for his talent. It sidelined him and even gave him thoughts about quitting the game.

"What happened only intensifies my feelings of football getting out of control," emphasized Swann. "When I'm home and I'm talking to friends, I'm wondering why I'm still going out there. Am I really in love with the game, do I enjoy it that much, or is the money that good that I want to keep exposing myself to these dangers when nothing significant has been done to protect people? Maybe I shouldn't be out there because another concussion could cause serious and permanent damage."

That would be the sad part . . .

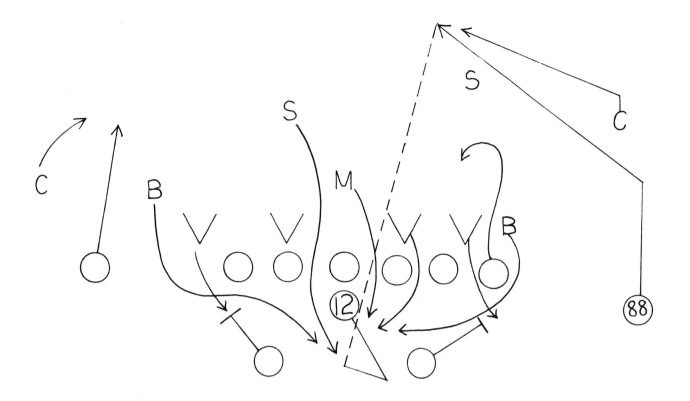

Diagrammed by Coach Chuck Noll

Sammy White

He loved to run. As a boy he would run all day. The bigger kids would tell him to run as fast as he could. And he would run up and down the streets of Monroe, Louisiana. He lived on Bryant Street, and one of the bigger kids who lived on the next block was James Harris. He lived on Dillon Street and was not only bigger but older. And he could throw a football farther than anyone else in Monroe. He had such a strong arm that he would challenge anyone to run as far as they could. He knew he could throw a ball farther than anybody could run. There wasn't anyone who could outrun his ball. "Run, run as far as you can down the street, Sammy; because there ain't a receiver alive who gets out of my range," boasted Harris. And the little guy would try. He would run until he was too tired to run anymore. And all the while Sammy White would dream about becoming a professional football player.

It's that much tougher when you're small. You have to dream big. And White kept running and trying to outrun Harris's passes on Dillon Street. The challenge remained in his mind all during the long hot days and nights. When he was in the sixth grade, he became hooked on football. One day his mother had given him enough money to see a local high school game. He was impressed with it all, the cheering, the glory, and everything else surrounding the game that a youngster gets wild-eyed about. By the time he reached high school, White was intent on becoming a football player. He didn't have any size, but he had desire.

He made the football team. By the time he finished high school, White was all over the field. He first played as a linebacker. Then he was a running back. Finally, he played as a receiver. He was so good that he attracted a good number of college scouts his senior year at Richmond High School. They had learned about his speed and his pass catching ability, and there were scholarships waiting for him. White was standing tall.

"I was a slow learner in football," admitted White. "I played linebacker but couldn't adjust to it. My sophomore year I was a running back; but they were looking for a receiver, and I raised my hand. It got so tough for a while that I wanted to quit. My mother said, 'Sammy, you made the decision, now you go back to it.'

"In my junior year I caught 51 passes and scored 13 touchdowns. The scouts called. I caught 63 passes and scored 21 times my senior year. The scouts ate dinner with us. I had so many good games my last two years. One game I caught four touchdowns and returned an interception 101 yards. People put money in my hand after that game."

The Minnesota Vikings put real big money in White's hands. They selected him from Grambling College on the second round of the 1976 college draft. The Vikings were looking for a wide receiver to replace John Gilliam, who had played out his option and expressed his desire to play elsewhere. No one, especially the Vikings, expected the 5'11", 189-pound White to make the starting lineup. Few rookies, if any, ever become a regular with the Vikings. Coach Bud Grant prefers to go with veteran players.

Soon after reporting to the Vikings, White began to play in the pre-season games. And he began to make some big catches. One in particular, against the Cincinnati Bengals, gave the Vikings a last-minute 23–17 triumph. Those are the kind of catches that impress coaches. And veteran quarterbacks like Fran Tarkenton, too. It was the type of play that Tarkenton had been looking for in the first three pre-season games.

"I was going to throw the ball away because everyone was covered," explained Tarkenton. "I didn't want to get sacked and get out of field goal range. Sammy kept running. This is a good indication of a good football player. He doesn't give up, keeps working, and finally makes the play. This is the type of thing we've been looking for at training camp."

Up until then, the Vikings had a bit of consternation about White. He didn't show too much at their early rookie camp that April. The weather had been cold and rainy, and White was clearly nervous. In the College All-Star game in July, White didn't catch a single pass. He was used as a decoy the entire game and never had a pass thrown to him. Then when he reported to training camp, all he heard was concern about who was going to replace Gilliam.

White at first felt he would be a backup receiver with the Vikings. He knew about their penchant for veteran players. But the more he saw action, the more confident he became of making the starting team. He was beginning to grasp the situation better and saw things a lot differently.

"It was like coming into a new environment," explained White. "I was trying too hard, and I was too tight at first. The attention of the press didn't really bother me. It was more the receivers who were in camp. But I was confident all along that I could be the big-play man and make the team.

"When I got to play, I started to relax. The coaches helped me, and Fran helped me. They helped me get the discipline I needed to run the pass routes. Young receivers have a tendency to break off their patterns too short, but Fran would tell me to go exactly 17 yards before cutting and no less."

By the opening game of the regular season, White had clearly established himself as a starter. The Vikings opened the season in New Orleans. It was somewhat of a homecoming for White. A great many of his relatives and friends had come from Monroe to see him play. He didn't disappoint them, either. As time was running out in the first half, White broke out on a pass pattern. Then he improvised and got free and caught a 47-yard touchdown pass from Tarkenton as the half ended. He kept working until he shook his defender.

"That catch was a big thrill," exclaimed White. "It was an indescribable feeling to catch a touchdown pass in my first game. Fran had talked to me earlier, and he told me to move around and look for the open spot when he starts scrambling. That's what I did, and he found me."

However, White's biggest catch of his young pro career occurred the following week against the Los Angeles Rams. It was an early season meeting of two teams who were picked to win their respective divisions. White had an outstanding day. He was the leading receiver of the game, finishing with nine receptions for 139 yards. One catch in particular established him as a big-play threat.

The game had been a defensive struggle between two strong defenses. Early in the fourth period, the Vikings were precariously clinging to a 3–0 lead. They had the ball on their 44-yard line. On third down and four, Tarkenton faced a passing situation. Determined to prevent the first down, the Rams blitzed. However, Tarkenton was prepared for it. He quickly got a pass off to White on the Rams' 30-yard line. The speedy rookie made a quick cut that cornerback Rod Perry couldn't handle. He fell, and White ran unmolested the rest of the way for a 56-yard touchdown. It was the Vikings' only touchdown of the day as the game ended in a 10–10 tie that went into overtime.

"The Rams had a safety blitz on," described White. "Fran called an audible that put me on an inside pattern against the cornerback. It was one-on-one coverage, and he tried to chuck me as I came off the line; but he slipped, and I was all alone."

Nevertheless, White experienced his biggest game of the year

against the Detroit Lions the first weekend in November. He grabbed seven passes for 210 yards to establish a new Viking record. He also scored two touchdowns in the 31–23 win. But it was a touchdown that he didn't score that everyone remembered, much to White's embarrassment.

The bizarre play occurred in the fourth period of a closely contested game. The Vikings were holding a thin one-point lead, 24–23. There were about nine minutes left in the struggle as Tarkenton faced a third and two situation on Minnesota's 45-yard line. Tarkenton sent White deep down the middle. Getting behind the secondary, White caught Tarkenton's pass on the Lions' 20-yard line. There was no one in front of him. As he was heading for the end zone, White slowed up near the three-yard line and held the ball high over his head in a moment of joy. However, Detroit safety Lem Barney caught up with White and tackled the unsuspecting rookie from behind. White fumbled the ball, and the Lions recovered. White's fumble cost the Vikings a seemingly easy touchdown.

The next time the Vikings got the ball, White made amends. It was on another third-down play. Minnesota had the ball on the Lions' 37-yard line, needing seven yards for a first down. Tarkenton gave White an opportunity to make up for his costly mistake. He sent the youngster on the same pass pattern down the middle. White slipped behind the defense, caught Tarkenton's pass on the ten-yard line, and scored an easy touchdown to clinch the victory.

"I learned my lesson on that fumble," confessed White. "That will never happen again. I'm still high-headed, and I'm so full of confidence now. When I first was drafted by the Vikings, I thought I'd be a back-up wide receiver. I was under the impression that the cornerbacks would be so tough in this league. I really didn't think I'd be able to catch this many balls."

When the regular season ended, White did indeed catch many passes. More than he anticipated. He finished his rookie season with 51 receptions, sixth best in the NFC. He gained 906 yards, the most of any receiver, as he averaged 17.8 yards a reception. His big play capabilities were reflected in the fact that he scored ten touchdowns to top the NFC. That's a lot of football for a rookie.

"We drafted White on the second round because he was a big-play man in college," related Jerry Reichow, the Vikings' director of scouting. "He has football instinct. He has the ability to catch the football, find the open spot, and run with it. A lot of scouts thought he'd be a running back in the pros. We looked at him as a wide receiver even though he could run the ball. We liked him even after he didn't do well with the College All-Stars. The only surprise is that he has made it a lot faster than we expected."

White continued to produce the big play in the post-season championships. In the opening game against Washington, White broke the Redskins' back in igniting a 35–20 victory. He did it with a play near the end of the first quarter. At the time, the game was closely fought. The Vikings were ahead, 7–3, and had the ball on the Redskins' 27-yard line. They faced a third and nine, and Tarkenton decided on a pass to White. As White broke down the middle, he was closely guarded by Ken Houston. The Washington safety adeptly deflected Tarkenton's pass. However, White, keeping his eye on the ball, caught it while he was lying on the ground. It was a legal catch on the one-yard line, and White merely rolled into the end zone to give the Vikings a 14–3 edge. He later caught another touchdown pass in the third quarter and finished the game as the leading Viking receiver with four catches for 64 yards.

"I'd like to sound like a prophet and say we expected White to play this well," remarked Grant. "His big thing is that he has continued to improve. He is intelligent, durable, has excellent hands, good speed, and good instincts. And he likes to play football."

That's all he ever wanted to do back on the streets of Monroe, Louisiana . . .

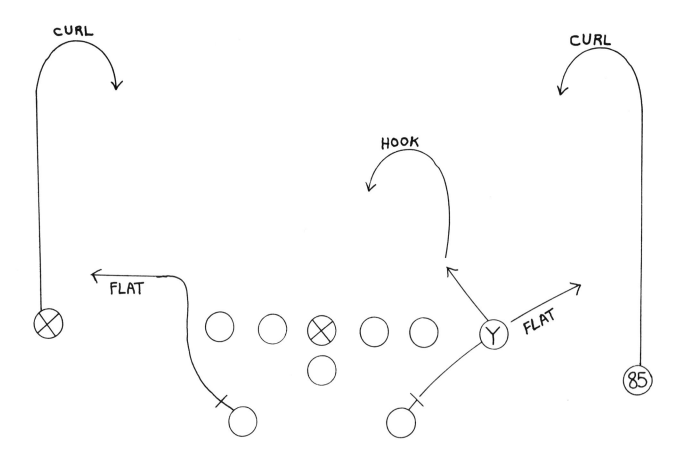

Diagrammed by Coach Bud Grant